THE BEST

OF

EAGLE

EDITED BY MARCUS MORRIS

MICHAEL JOSEPH
LONDON

Marcus Morris would like to
acknowledge the assistance of Denis
Gifford and Clifford Makins in
compiling this book.
He also wishes to thank the
International Publishing Corporation
for permission to reproduce the
illustrations.

First published in Great Britain by
Michael Joseph Limited
44 Bedford Square, London WC1
and
Ebury Press
National Magazine House
72 Broadwick Street
London W1V 2BP

AUGUST 1977
SECOND IMPRESSION SEPTEMBER 1982

IBSN 0 7181 1566 X (hardback)
ISBN 0 7181 2211 9 (trade paperback)

© text: Marcus Morris, 1977
© illustrations: International Publishing
Corporation, 1977

Printed and bound by
Fakenham Press Ltd,
Fakenham, Norfolk

Introduction by Marcus Morris

Eagle was the result of a glider accident and of my own strong interest in the problem of communicating with the general public. I had long felt that parish magazines (the parson's main written method of presenting himself to his followers) were dreary and ineffective. My appointment as vicar of St James's, Birkdale, Lancashire gave me my first chance to do something about it. I gradually converted a four-page leaflet into a magazine called *The Anvil*, in which 'issues' could be 'hammered out'. I had always been interested in journalism and had a great desire to 'edit' something. At Oxford I had read philosophy, ancient history and theology—not immediately identifiable with journalism—and *Anvil* liberated those pent-up editorial urges. I didn't see why a magazine aimed at conveying an intelligent view of Christianity should not try to be as professional as any other magazine. I based *Anvil* roughly on *Lilliput*, the pocket magazine created by that brilliant editor Stefan Lorant who also started *Picture Post*, and I managed to get some useful contributors—ranging from C. S. Lewis, C. E. M. Joad to Harold Macmillan.

I also got seriously into debt; the spirit was willing but the sales were weak. There was no money to promote the magazine, and though it spread from being a parish magazine to become a town, then a county, and finally a national magazine, it still lost money. My patient and loyal, if slightly incredulous, parishioners gave me immensely generous and practical as well as financial support, contributing funds and running bazaars to raise money. But I sank deeper into debt, though not into despair. *Anvil* had attracted attention and was described by one critic as 'a Christian magazine alongside the best secular publications'. And apart from the eminent contributors I had a special windfall: I discovered at the local art school a young artist, Frank Hampson, who became chief illustrator and cartoonist and designed the covers.

It was about this time that, with the help of a journalist Norman Price, I wrote an article for the *Sunday Dispatch*. It was headed 'Comics that bring Horror into the Nursery', caused quite a stir and earned me twenty guineas. *Anvil*'s debts were then about three thousand pounds. But at least it was a start.

The phenomenal rise and rule of the comic in America, plus a study of the papers and publications that children were reading in this country, seemed to point an obvious moral—and hence came the idea of *Eagle*. Many American comics were most skilfully and vividly drawn, but often their content was deplorable, nastily over-violent and obscene, often with undue emphasis on the supernatural and magical as a way of solving problems. But it was clear to me that the strip cartoon was capable of development in a way not yet seen in England except in one or two of the daily and Sunday newspapers—and that it was a new and important medium of communication with its own laws and limitations. Here, surely, was a form which could be used to convey to the child the right kind of standards, values and attitudes, combined with the necessary amount of excitement and adventure. And so to the problems of *Anvil* I added those of *Eagle*. There may have been fears for my sanity; certainly there were prophecies of doom.

Before starting on *Eagle* I had the idea of an exemplary character, Lex Christian, whose exploits

Frank Hampson

were to be told exclusively in strip-cartoon form. Hampson was most enthusiastic about this project. I thought we might sell the idea to a Sunday newspaper and very soon we had the interest of the editor of the *Sunday Empire News*, Terence Horsley. But not for long: he was tragically killed in a gliding accident.

This proved to be a turning point. I still recall a late-night visit to Hampson's house when I told him that we should pack up the idea of doing a single strip for any paper, and that we should be bold and resolute and concentrate our energies on producing an entirely new, original children's paper of our own. He agreed immediately.

This decision increased my hopes and determination to succeed. And naturally it increased the debts too. I found it absolutely essential to ensure some regular salary for Hampson and so I paid him £10 a week—later to go up to £14. There was a growing sense of urgency and it became clear that an addition to the team was imperative. Harold Johns was another gifted artist who came from the same art school as Hampson, and he went on to the pay roll. Before long I was paying out in total more than I was earning myself. Apart from the regular staff, there were contributors to be taken into account. In the *Anvil*/*Eagle* period, they included a vicar who was editing the Blackburn Diocesan Magazine for the Bishop of Blackburn. This was Chad Varah, who was to found the Samaritans. And there was Walkden Fisher, a designer for a local toy firm who did the first 'exploded' drawings for *Eagle*'s centre spread; Spencer Croft, who appeared as the scientist, 'Professor Brittain', and another promising young art student from Liverpool called Norman Thelwell.

CHICKO by thelwell

Eagle, like Dan Dare, its star attraction, was not born overnight. We were hard at it from the beginning of 1949 to April 1950. The title *Eagle* did not emerge for a considerable time. Then Lex Christian, who began life as a tough, fighting parson in the slums of the East End of London, became airborne, a flying padre, the Parson of the Fighting Seventh. Dan Dare was on the way. And throughout this time I tramped Fleet Street with the *Eagle* dummy tucked underneath my arm. I became a regular on the Sunday midnight train from Liverpool Lime Street to London Euston—after taking three ser-

vices, a baptism or two, maybe a wedding, and dealing with the general affairs of the parish. All the time I was trying to sell *Eagle*, back at Birkdale the work pressed on, days and nights of trial and error, chopping and changing in the search for perfection.

At one stage I had been in touch with Hulton Press (publishers of *Picture Post* and *Lilliput*) and a young man from that firm suggested that I should go to see John Myers, then Publicity Manager for J. Arthur Rank. Myers passed me on to Montague Haydon, director of the children's publications at Amalgamated Press (now IPC). Haydon's reaction was perhaps predictable. I had a feeling that he thought I was an impostor, even a mild kind of lunatic. Amalgamated Press did not want *Eagle*. But they got it in the end, about eleven years later.

Sir Neville Pearson of Newnes was next. I rang him from a phone box (my London office in those days). He asked me round and saw me with one of his chief executives. They were very courteous and expressed considerable interest. But in the end they said that *Eagle* was 'not an economic proposition'. I had a brief, fruitless meeting with Boardman's, American publishers of books and comics and then— for the life of me I can't think why—secured the interest of the editor of the *Sporting Record*. His name was Mike Wardell, he wore a black eye patch and he was a great Fleet Street character. But in the end he couldn't help me. I began climbing higher. I saw John Walter, General Manager of *The Times*, and Lord Camrose, proprietor of the *Daily Telegraph*. Beautiful manners again, but two more blanks. I never did see Lord Kemsley of the *Sunday Times*. I saw his very polite and handsome personal assistant, whose name was Denis Hamilton. He thought I was asking for a donation to some charity and pointed out that 'his lordship has many calls upon his purse'. Then back home in Birkdale, in the autumn of 1949, I had a telegram: 'Definitely interested do not approach any other publisher'.

It was Hulton Press, publishers of *Lilliput* and *Picture Post*, who finally took on *Eagle* and brought me and my family to London. Hampson came too, together with fellow artists Harold Johns, Eric Eden, Bruce Cornwell and Joan Porter. Also crucial in the development of *Eagle* was the eminent typographer, Ruari McLean, who became a close friend and worked intensively with me on the design and layout. The title *Eagle* came in the end from Frank Hampson's wife, and the lettering for it from Berthold Wolpe of Faber & Faber. The model for the *Eagle* symbol was the top of a large brass inkwell I bought at the White Elephant stall at the vicarage garden party.

Get your EAGLE diary NOW!

It's real *value*, with its Eagle-red cover, blocked with gold – 52 pictures of famous sportsmen, with full biographies – 48 pages of facts and pictures about sports records, railways, aircraft types, camping hints, services badges, breeds of dogs, star recognition, and many other subjects – 176 pages in all for only 2/6! It's an encyclopædia as well as a diary – one that every boy and girl should have!

For EAGLE Club Members there's the Club edition at the special price of 2/-, and for those who would like a presentation edition, for themselves or as a present to others, there is a limited number of copies in fine red leather, blocked in gold and with gilt-edged pages.

Ruari McLean has refreshed my memory (and his, no doubt) with the flavour of the period: 'I was on the payroll at £5 a week, as your typographic adviser. During the day I was working in Holden's advertising agency for George Rainbird and could only see you in the evenings. Shortly you asked me to find a flat that we could share during the week; my wife and family were in Essex, yours at Birkdale, so this sounded sensible. I found a flat in South Audley Street. You were unperturbed when we discovered that most of the other occupants of the building were tarts. It was the main activity in South Audley Street; doors banged and cars drove away at periodic intervals all through the night until breakfast time. Many evenings I was present in the flat when you briefed the artists who had been invited to work on this new project. Nearly always they had not done what you had asked them to do, but what they thought was *really* wanted. If, as quite frequently happened, they refused to be told how to draw their strips by a young parson who had never edited anything except a parish magazine before, and persisted in doing it how *they* wanted, they found themselves dropped.

'Often we were still at it at two or three or even four in the morning, at which time I was ready to agree with anything; but you *never* let anything go until you were completely satisfied, and would consult me about a comma or a hyphen, and argue about it endlessly, and curse me for being lazy if I said it didn't matter, and could I please go to bed? In retrospect, it seems to me that every word and every syllable in the early numbers of *Eagle* were chewed

over endlessly, until you were certain it was right. I cared about English too, but I didn't have your stamina.'

At that time in England the number of skilful strip-cartoon artists was limited, and the best of them were already in work. Eventually some of them came to work for *Eagle* (and later its sister papers) but meanwhile I had to find new 'untried' artists to do the job I wanted.

I am sure that the success of *Eagle* (a sell-out of 900,000 copies of its first issue) was due to the insistance on quality. Where *Eagle* was concerned, the quality of the paper, printing, artwork and writing set a new standard. There were bright colours, well-drawn pictures and exciting stories. Technically, the *Eagle* strips marked an advance on the standards of that time (standards that had stood still for years) when most strips were not true strips but merely pictures with captions underneath. We tried to tell the stories mainly through the dramatic sequence of the pictures, with the help of balloons— not too many—issuing from the characters' mouths and heads.

Eagle was to win the support of parents, schoolmasters, educationalists and clergy. Dr James Hemming, the well-known educationalist, writer and broadcaster, writes: 'I came in on *Eagle* originally because Johnny Metcalfe of Colman, Prentis & Varley rang me up to know if I was interested in the project. I was drawn in to taking the original dummy around to show the teacher and head teacher organisations. We met first around then. The launch complete, you asked me to stay linked as your consultant. So there we, very pleasantly, were. As for those early days, there was the sheer miracle of *Eagle* appearing regularly as, for months, perforce, we had no time in hand. Then there was the solid identification and teamwork that somehow got the work done week by week. I seem to recall that the dummy got lost on one occasion at least . . . And it

MUG OF THE MONTH

JOHN CHOWN

At the age of 16, as he went home from looking at the Christmas Tree in Trafalgar Square, at 9 o'clock on a dark windy night, a woman rushed out of a house in Paddington waving her slippers in her hand and shouting "Stop Thief!" Immediately ahead of him, in Craven Hill Gardens John Chown saw the figures of two men making off. He gave chase, caught up with the slower of the two men and tackled him. In a flash the man turned on him – with a knife. John Chown was stabbed in the chest and back. Both men made their escape, but John Chown was later able to give the police their description, and they were caught and tried at the Old Bailey. One got 8 years penal servitude, and the other 2 years imprisonment.

John Chown was awarded the British Empire Medal. As a result of his injuries he was in hospital for several days. He is still at school, a Boy Scout and Troup Leader; his ambition is to go into chemical research. The Scouts awarded him the Silver Cross. He is studying for the Higher Certificate, after which he is expecting to do his National Service.

always interested me the way the characters of *Eagle* were really alive for the readers. One one occasion, a boy asked me if Digby (in Dan Dare) would be willing to sign autographs. And there was that curious man who turned up and said he had an invention for Dan Dare to use.'

Chad Varah became one of the first—and best—scriptwriters for *Eagle* and a tower of strength in other activities associated with the paper. He writes: 'Even before I started the Samaritans I had a busy life, and had to do most of my writing between 10.00 p.m. and 3.00 a.m. Then there were the carol services, hugely successful and reflecting the spirit—and the circulation—of *Eagle* itself. The readers wanted to see you in the flesh (or failing you, me), so we did these marathon tours of cathedrals and had packed houses and writer's cramp through signing autographs.'

It was in November 1949 that Hulton Press accepted *Eagle* and I moved into their premises in Shoe Lane, EC4. I think they must have had some faith in me as an editor but, initially, not as a clergyman—after one of my early visits they rushed to check my credentials in Crockford's *Clerical Directory*. I have always been told that it was Tom Hopkinson, Editor of *Picture Post*, who was called down by management, shown the dummy and asked his opinion. Apparently he replied: 'You should publish this and take on whoever brought it here.' My first office in Shoe Lane was not very grand—in fact it was a kind of anteroom to the office of the chairman, Edward (later Sir Edward) Hulton. It was rather a comic situation. He did his best to take no notice of me on his way in and out. He could hardly have been unaware of my existence, but I had the feeling that he might be uncertain of my identity and none too sure of what I was doing there. In the end, I suppose, someone told him.

St. Paul's Cathedral. Marcus Morris conducts the Carol Service.

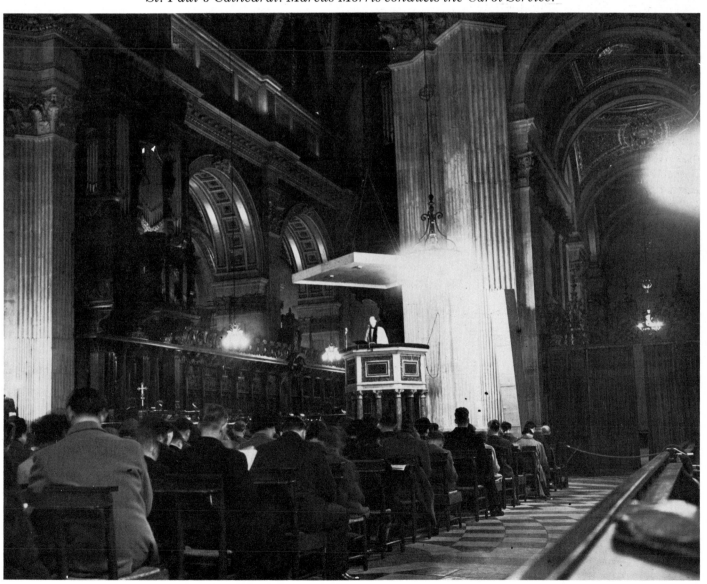

Right up to the publication of the first issue on 14 April 1950, the situation was chaotic. I was head cook and bottle-washer, and a man called Charles Green assisted Ruari McLean with the layout and typography. After the first issue, more than a month went by before *Eagle* acquired any staff: a sub, Derek Lord, who joined us from the defunct *Leader*, and an assistant editor, Ellen Vincent. She was to do this job admirably for eight years. Before she joined me from an advertising agency (the one that was to handle the promotion and launching of *Eagle*), Ellen Vincent's boss at Coleman, Prentis & Varley was most curious about the personality and physique of the editor of this new, still highly secretive paper for boys. The name of the paper had not yet been announced, but it was known by a code name. 'Try to see the vicar, duckie,' she was told. They wanted to know, she recalls, if the vicar was 'Fat, comfortable, tweedy and pipe smoking. I was curious too and not a little astonished to discover you to be youthful, slim, nervy, fashionably dressed and a cigarette chainsmoker. In addition, you were married to a beautiful actress, Jessica Dunning, and had four children to support. When you offered me the job on *Eagle* (it became known as assistant to the vicar), I played for big stakes. I told you I wanted £750 a year—double my CPV salary—and you agreed immediately.'

Before publication there was barely a trickle of staff but a huge and constant flood of writers and

Marcus Morris welcomes Dame Margot Fonteyn to the Boys and Girls Exhibition, Olympia

Ellen Vincent

artists and agents with a great variety of material— some good, some promising and some quite useless: in fact, the typical chaotic prelude to all new publications. There were many stages to negotiate before the germ of an idea attained its final form on the page. The frequent conferences with the scriptwriter before a final version was agreed were succeeded by even more lengthy (and more complicated) sessions with the artist who was often required to submit many 'rough' visuals before the finished artwork. This in turn required the work of a lettering artist to fill in the balloons, and the typesetting of any text matter (brief explanations, continuities, etc.) to make the strip-cartoon story fully comprehensive. Even material set entirely in type (fiction, non-fiction, the Editor's letter and news of various activities) almost always required illustration by way of drawings and photographs, in all shapes and sizes. Always the visual impact was vital in order to project a look of liveliness and enticement on every page. And naturally the pages did not fall haphazardly into place. The most careful attention had to be paid to the overall design and layout of each issue.

George Cansdale, Elizabeth Sellars, Sir John Hunt, Marcus Morris and friendly snake.

Small circle of concentration: the Editor plays tiddlywinks.

On Earth in Epsom. Frank Hampson, Marcus Morris and the late Alan Stranks (back to camera)

The eventual success of *Eagle* led to the acquisition of a fairly big staff. But we were a bit thin on the ground in the beginning and I was glad to appoint Rosemary Garland (editorial) and Michael Gibson (art department). A few years later, as the organisation grew, Rosemary Garland became Assistant Editor of *Robin* and Michael Gibson became responsible for books and annuals. In addition we had to appoint full-time assistants for lettering and the many illustrations and diagrams that could be done only in the office.

It was those artists and writers, examples of whose work appear in *The Best of Eagle*, who gave *Eagle* its distinctive style and stamp.

Best of all perhaps is the artist who is also the writer, and if not, is never a slave to the writer: he is always thinking visually, and it is here that Frank Hampson was supreme. Hampson, like his creation Dan Dare, was the corner-stone of *Eagle*. He shared my vision and had prodigious inventiveness and energy. In the beginning he drew Dan Dare, Pilot of the Future; the Great Adventurer (the story of St Paul); and Tommy Walls, our ice-cream advertising strip. In the end he drew The Road of Courage (a life of Christ). In between he was involved in working for the numerous annuals and books that came out of *Eagle*, and lending his name and ability to many of the toys and games produced by our merchandising department. He was a great stylist and a very demanding one.

Perhaps Hampson's heir, certainly his most notable successor, was Frank Bellamy, a most fastidious artist and scrupulous draftsman, and like Hampson at his best, often consumed with anxiety. Bellamy came fairly late to the *Eagle* scene and at one stage, somewhat reluctantly, took over Dan Dare. Some of his best work for *Eagle* may be seen in The Happy Warrior (Life of Winston Churchill), The Shepherd King (David), and later Montgomery of Alamein. Like Hampson, he excelled in colour work and was fascinated by machinery and technical devices. Bellamy died suddenly in July 1976.

The late Norman Williams was an old stager who hammered out his work in defiance of scriptwriters—even good ones. He did not need telling, did not even want to know about the techniques of the strip cartoon. Examples of his best work are Alfred the Great, The Baden Powell Story, and the Great Sailor (Life of Nelson), where he proved typically obstinate in the matter of the Battle of Trafalgar. His son Pat also did notable work for *Eagle*.

John Worsley, who excelled in black and white, was the most notable artist to draw P.C.49, based on the radio serial created by Alan Stranks, a highly gifted Australian who eventually took on the scripting of Dan Dare—and who astonished me by writing a lengthy underwater sequence. While still employed by the paper, Stranks died of a heart attack in Spain.

GREETINGS FROM EAGLE ARTISTS

CHICKO by thelwell

EAGLE ARTIST'S NIGHTMARE, drawn by GERALD SCARFE (*aged 16*), 160 Goldhurst Terrace, Hampstead, N.W.6.

Jack Daniel and then Frank Humphris drew Riders of the Range, based on another highly successful radio serial, this time by Charles Chilton, who is still a leading writer and producer with the BBC. One of the most successful early stunts was to send Charles Chilton to Tombstone, Arizona where he was made sheriff and where he met real cowboys and filed his impressions for *Eagle* readers. Martin Aitchison drew the exotic Luck of the Legion (a home-grown product) with script by Geoffrey Bond.

In the humourous vein three artists were outstanding. One was known long before *Eagle* and is still going strong. He is David Langdon, who created Professor Puff and his dog Wuff. Then John Ryan, the art master from Harrow who invented Captain Pugwash and Harris Tweed, Extra Special Agent. And finally, Norman Thelwell, who first created Chicko before he found his true comic niche with girls and ponies that refuse fences.

There were of course many more artists who contributed to *Eagle*, but I cannot mention them all; and those who contributed primarily to the other papers of the group (*Girl, Robin* and *Swift*) have, of course, no place in this anthology. As for the *Eagle* writers, their work, though invaluable, was of necessity overshadowed by the artists. This includes even Chad Varah, who was with me from the first and who brought his considerable powers of mind and invention to write not only the scripts for our Bible stories but also to take on the scripting of Dan Dare at a moment's notice. In a traditional form, the writing of school stories, Peter Ling deserves notice. And there was that distinguished journalist of his day (he is still distinguished) Macdonald Hastings, whose series Eagle Special Investigator may still be read as first-class documentaries of the period. Apart from the Editor's letter I wrote a great deal myself, in that fiddling, improving and revising way that most editors have. But again, like most editors, the bulk of my writing consisted of answering questions and making demands of management, accountants, printers etc. The letters from our readers were so numerous that after a few weeks' publication we were obliged to hire a staff to cope with the flood. The Eagle Club was another instant success, with applications from 60,000 readers after our first two issues. Two noble ladies were in charge of this department: Mrs Stark and Miss Mincher.

Hulton Press had achieved considerable success with *Picture Post, Lilliput, Housewife* and *Farmer's Weekly*. When

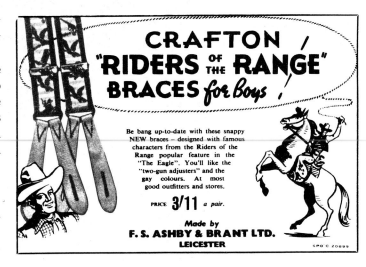

Letters to the Editor

5/- is paid for every letter published. Readers who want a reply should enclose a stamped, addressed envelope.

WEDDING BELLS FOR MR TWEED

I am a keen reader of EAGLE and my sister takes GIRL. We think that Miss Froth would make a lovely bride for Mr Harris Tweed — then they would be able to start a Co-ed School. *Leslie Coleman, Elloughton, East Yorkshire.*

* * * * *

TOBRUK AS IT IS TODAY

When I read *The Happy Warrior* in my copy of EAGLE dated 6th June, I thought you might like to know what Tobruk is like now.

After sixteen years, Tobruk still bears the marks of war. The bombed church, shattered buildings and shell holes still remain.

There are three war cemeteries, British, French and German. I have been to the British and German.

Since I have been here, a Minesweeper and Frigate (British) and two Destroyers (American) have been in this very pleasant harbour. Not long ago, an R.A.F. Sergeant came to school, and told us not to play with queer objects in case they were old bombs.

Omar Senussi, the King of Libya's nephew, is in my class at school. Some others and I went to the King's palace to celebrate Omar's ninth birthday.

I like Tobruk and its lovely beaches, and shall miss them when I return to England. – *Peter Spencer, Tobruk, Libya.*

OLD AND NEW

Recently I went to the British Railways Works at Derby, where, among old steam-engines being repaired, I saw many brand new Diesel trains in various stages of construction. It will make British Railways much better when these trains are put into regular service. This is a picture of me standing near a just-completed Diesel train. – *Andrew Stephen, Uppingham, Rutland.*

* * * * *

ARTISTIC VALUE

We are very interested in the pictures you print on the centre pages of EAGLE. We take them to school and draw them in our spare time. Then, when we have our art lesson, we take them with us and ask permission to paint them. When they are finished, our teacher hangs them on the wall with several others we have painted. Hoping to see some more interesting features in future issues of EAGLE. *Leslie, Michael and John Williams, Beaufort, Monmouthshire.*

*harles Chilton about
leave London, England,
or the Middle West,
.S.A.*

EAGLE GETS A WELCOME
FROM THE MIDDLE WEST

Here is a telegram of greeting to EAGLE readers from the tough cow-town of Tombstone, Arizona. As announced last week, Charles Chilton, author of the famous radio feature, *Riders of the Range*, is travelling to Tombstone for EAGLE to report on life among the cowboys and Red Indians of the Middle West, and to take part in the town's Heldorado (or rodeo).

The first of his articles, which is being telegraphed from Arizona, will appear in EAGLE soon.

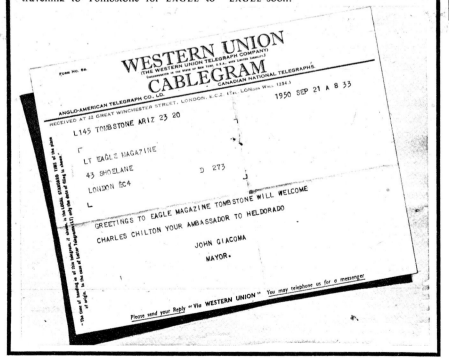

Cablegram from Tombstone, Arizona

Golden Eagle going for a ride

they took on *Eagle* the firm spared no expense to make it a winner from the start.

Gradually, while we amended, altered, revised and got together the first issue, the pattern emerged and launching plans were formulated. Copies were to be mailed direct, with a covering letter, to several hundred thousand people concerned with children and youth work—teachers, clergy, educationalists, club leaders, doctors and so on. The reaction was encouraging to a degree we had not dared to hope for.

The other important plan for the launch was the 'Hunt the Eagle' scheme. Huge golden eagles, 4ft 10in. high, 4ft 6in. from beak to tail, with a wing span of 4ft, were mounted on cars and driven round towns and villages up and down the country. Loudspeakers were fitted to the cars and Hulton Press representatives handed out 3d tokens that could be exchanged at a newsagent for a free copy of *Eagle*. Another hugely successful idea. There were other, wilder, notions, ranging from the Editor's descent by parachute into Hyde Park, and the release of 200,000 *Eagle* balloons throughout the country. These were abandoned, but a great amount of advertising space was booked in the national dailies and weeklies.

The two miracles that attended the first issue of *Eagle* were: getting the material to the printer in the first place; and his printing it the second. The printing of *Eagle* is a story in itself—a supreme example of craftsmanship and engineering skill overcoming apparently insuperable difficulties. The late Eric Bemrose of Eric Bemrose Limited of Aintree, faced with the problem of printing one million copies of *Eagle* for its first issue, designed,

The man who built the presses, the late Eric Bemrose (standing) with Vernon Holding, General Manager Hulton Press.

I know all about art and I know what I like

built and worked a new ten-unit photogravure rotary machine. With flair and improvisation he created the plant in twelve weeks from start to finish and trained a team to work it. On publication day there were long queues outside the newsagents. *Eagle* was a success and a sell-out, almost one million copies. We had tried to start a paper which would be the natural choice of the child, but, at the same time, would have the enthusiastic approval of the parent and the teacher; in this we succeeded.

It was a great moment at the end of the first day when the telegrams from our reps came pouring in with the good news. *Eagle* was off to a roaring start with Dan Dare, 'Cosmic Knight Errant'—a phrase of Maurice Richardson's—'racing to the rescue of Rocket Ship No. 1 trapped by the silicon mass on the fringe of the Flame Lands'. And waiting in the wings of an unknown, hostile universe was the Mekon.

Eagle had a fairly short life, from 1950 to 1970, by which time it had been merged with *Lion*. But its most successful life was even shorter, from 1950 to about 1962. In 1960 Hulton Press was taken over by Odhams and renamed Longacre Press. Soon after that I left to join the National Magazine Company. I was succeeded by my deputy, Clifford Makins. The following year Odhams was taken over by the Daily Mirror Group (now IPC) and then Makins left. *Eagle* died slowly and, it seemed to me, painfully, and so my choice of *The Best of Eagle* is confined to the years 1950 to 1962.

Those were exciting times—hard work but fun. And it is very pleasant to keep meeting 40-year-olds who say they were 'brought up' on *Eagle*.

While Dan and Digby are held prisoner on Venus, Rocket Ship No. 3 (manned by Hank and Pierre) dives towards the planet.

PHEW! THAT WAS A NARROW SHAVE!

— AND SINGE, MON AMI!

ROCKET SHIP № 1 (WITH SIR HUBERT & PROFESSOR PEABODY) FOLLOWS THEM IN.......

CUT THE ENGINES - SWITCH ON THE GYRO - STABILISER — START REACTOR JETS!

HAND ME THE HELM — I'M IN COMMAND HERE MISS PEABODY!

YOU'LL ANSWER FOR THIS LATER!

NOBODY WILL ANSWER FOR ANYTHING IF ONE OF US DOESN'T GET HOLD OF THOSE CONTROLS!

I CAN'T PULL HER OUT!

MEANWHILE - AT THE EARTH RESEARCH CENTRE ON VENUS

IF ITS NOT A RUDE ANSWER, WHAT DO YOU WANT US FOR?

FOR RESEARCH - WHAT OTHER PURPOSE IS THERE?

TAKE THEM AWAY AND GIVE THEM FOOD. WE ARE NOT READY FOR THEM YET

THIS WAY TO THE FOOD CHAMBER, GENTLEMEN

COO-ER LOOK!

LOOKS LIKE SOME SORT OF MUSEUM

YES, IT IS A MUSEUM THESE ARE REPLICAS, MADE FROM OUR STUDY OF YOUR FEEBLE EFFORTS ON THE EARTH!

SPACE FLEET UNIFORMS! YOU'VE CERTAINLY GOT US TAPED!

HM-M-M-M

THE FOOD BATH — THIRTY SECONDS IMMERSION WILL GIVE YOU ALL THE NUTRIMENT YOU NEED

HOW ARE YOU FOR PEPPER AND SALT, DIG?

GIVE ME A LANCASHIRE HOT POT EVERY TIME, SIR

WHAT DO YOU MAKE OF THESE GREEN HEADED HORRORS, SIR?

NOT MUCH. THEY'RE OBVIOUSLY QUITE INHUMAN —— BUT WE MUST REMEMBER WHY WE'RE HERE AND STRING ALONG WITH THEM AT THE MOMENT TO SEE IF THERE'S *ANY* HOPE THAT THEY'LL COME TO A PEACEFUL ARRANGEMENT TO SEND FOOD TO THE EARTH —— *IF* IT CAN BE GROWN HERE

WELL, I CERTAINLY FEEL A LOT BETTER FOR THAT! NOW HOW ABOUT THOSE MUSEUM UNIFORMS, SIR?

GOOD IDEA OF YOURS, DIG — I FEEL MORE LIKE AN ENVOY FROM THE UNITED WORLD GOVERNMENT IN THE OLD SUNDAY BEST

BRING THE EARTH-MEN NOW — I AM READY TO BEGIN MY EXPERIMENTS ON THEM!

The Treens prepare to experiment on the two spacemen.

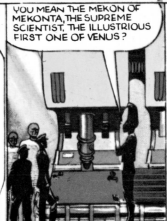

STOP!

WE'RE HERE AS OFFICIAL ENVOYS OF THE UNITED WORLD GOVERNMENT. I DEMAND THAT YOU TAKE US IMMEDIATELY TO THE CHIEF OFFICER OF YOUR STATE — YOUR PRESIDENT OR PRIME MINISTER OR WHO-EVER CORRESPONDS TO THAT..........

YOU MEAN THE MEKON OF MEKONTA, THE SUPREME SCIENTIST, THE ILLUSTRIOUS FIRST ONE OF VENUS?

THAT'S RIGHT — WE WANT TO SEE THE GAFFER

OBSCURE INSECTS FROM BACKWARD PLANETS — SUCH AS YOU, WOULD NOT EVEN BE ALLOWED TO ENTER THE SAME BUILDING AS THAT MAGNIFICENT BRAIN. YOUR ONLY INTEREST IS AS BIOLOGICAL SPECIMENS FOR MY EARTH RESEARCH— FASTEN THEM TO THE SLIDES

MASTER — THE THIRD ROCKET SHIP IS ABOUT TO LAND ON THE NORTHERN FRINGE OF THE FLAMELANDS!

WE HAVE TWO SPECIMENS— WE DO NOT NEED MORE

BUT ONE OF THESE IS A WOMAN O MASTER

RELEASE THE SPECIMENS— WE WILL STUDY THEIR BRAIN IMPULSES WHILE THEY WATCH THEIR FRIENDS CRASH

IT'S NO LAUGHING MATTER MISS PEABODY. — AT THE PRESENT RATE OF SINK-ING, WE'LL BE ENGULFED IN 48 HOURS. IF WE START THE JETS TO FREE THE SHIP SHE'LL BLOW UP!

AND IF WE TRY TO LEAVE THE OLD HULK WE'LL EITHER ROAST OR SUFFOCATE IN THE BOILING QUICKSAND.

LOOK, SIR HUBERT LOOK

WHAT?

THAT GLASS MOUNTAIN THING — *ITS MOVING!* — *TOWARDS US!*

CRUNCH

LOOK AT IT SWALLOWING THAT ROCK!

PON MY WORD, MISS PEABODY, THE CONFOUNDED THING'S *ALIVE*

AND HUNGRY!

MEANWHILE, IN MEKONTA, DAN & DIGBY ARE WATCHING THROUGH THE TELEVIEWER

WHAT ON EARTH'S THAT?

THE SILICON MASS THAT LIVES ON THE LAVA PLAIN. IT ENCLOSES AND CONSUMES SOLIDS - IT CAN EAT A MOUNTAIN

WE'VE GOT TO RESCUE THEM!

WHY, COLONEL DARE? THEIR DEATH WILL BE MORE INSTRUCTIVE THAN THEIR LIFE

WHY NOT LET THEM GO? ——WITH FOUR WE CAN SPARE TWO FOR DISSECTION!

H'M THAT IS SO. BUT HOW ARE THEY TO DO IT?

COLONEL DARE, I HAVE DECIDED TO LET YOU BRING IN YOUR COMRADES FROM THEIR PRESENT RATHER WARM SITUATION

O.K.! HOW DO WE GO?

UNFORTUNATELY OUR MAIN METHODS OF COMMUNICATION DO NOT EXTEND TO THE FLAME BELT—

SO?

SO WE ARE SENDING YOU BY TELESENDER TO THE MUSEUM OF MACHINES

YOU CAN TAKE YOUR PICK OF THE TRANSPORT AVAILABLE THERE

Rocket Ship No. 1 is slowly engulfed by the silicon mass

SLOWLY THE VENUSIAN HELIJET TAXIES THROUGH THE DOORS INTO THE MAIN AIR-LOCK

Dan decides to make friends with the Treen, though Digby thinks this will not work

WELL, I CAN BUT TRY

WE HAVEN'T BEEN PROPERLY INTRODUCED YET !

MY NAME IS SONDAR AND YOU WILL OBEY MY ORDERS COLONEL DARE

THE SHAKING OF HANDS IS AN EARTH CUSTOM THAT SEEMS ILLOGICAL TO US

AN ANCIENT GESTURE TO SHOW ONE DOES NOT CARRY ARMS — ALSO USED BEFORE BOXING MATCHES AND BY BUSINESS MEN ABOUT TO CHEAT ONE ANOTHER

ANY LUCK, SIR?

NO, DIG — HE'S ABOUT AS FRIENDLY AS A FRISKY STOAT !

WE ARE NOW APPROACHING THE SILICON MASS

LOOK! THERE'S THE SHIP SIR! BANG IN THE MIDDLE OF THAT OUTSIZE MINT HUMBUG

I WONDER IF THEY'RE STILL ALIVE ?

THAT IS OF MINOR IMPORTANCE. THE EFFECT OF THE FLUORINE SPRAY GUNS IS OUR MAIN INTEREST. WE SHALL DIVE NOW

MEANWHILE ON THE TRAPPED ROCKET

THE HULL WON'T STAND MUCH MORE OF THIS PRESSURE. IT CAN ONLY BE A MATTER OF MINUTES

LISTEN!

SHE'S BREAKING UP *NOW!*

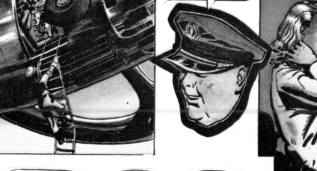

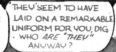

Dan and his companions see the tornado approaching

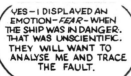

TREEN FORCES DEPART BY ELECTRO-SENDER . . . .

THEY ARE APPROACHING THE RIM OF THE CENTRAL SEA — WE WILL MEET THEM THERE.

AND IN MEKONTA . . . !

WE'VE GOT TO CLIMB THAT WATERFALL

BY GUM! WE'LL NEED THAT EXTRA 10% OFF GRAVITY.

STILL NO NEWS FROM VENUS

RADIO SILENCE BLANKETS DARE'S ROCKETS AS "RANGER" RETURNS TO EARTH

Space Station XI, Monday, 3 a.m.

SPACESHIP "Ranger" landed here an hour ago minus the three Rocket Ships which it carried to within 3,000 miles of Venus in the latest attempt to reach the mystery planet and find food to banish the threat of starvation from Earth.

Tired and worried-looking Captain Hunter, of the "Ranger", boarded a Helicar to the United Nations World Government Headquarters at New York. Thirty minutes later the following bulletin was issued from U.N.W.G.:–

COMMENT

DARE'S ROCKET THEORY JUSTIFIED?

There seem to be grounds for cautious optimism in the 'partial success' reported in the Government bulletin. The fact that the Rocket Ships built to Colonel Dare's specification did succeed in penetrating the mysterious Ray-screen which has taken such a terrible toll of previous attempts, is the first piece of good news which has come from the planet.

The sad fact that through a radio blunder this brave and brilliant officer and his equally courageous companions may have lost their lives must not be allowed to diminish the importance of their achievement for mankind.

"The Prime Minister regrets to announce that there is as yet no definite information of the success or otherwise of the Rocket Ship expedition to Venus.

In view of the partial success achieved in getting through the Ray-field, a further expedition will be fitted out with Rocket Ships.

The fate of the members of the present expedition is problematic.

The *Ranger* will return to orbit the planet in case any kind of signal is sent out by survivors.

Captain Hunter arriving in New York

TENSION MOUNTS IN FAMINE TROUBLE SPOTS

PEKIN, SUNDAY (*delayed*). Central and Southern China is in an explosive condition tonight according to messages reaching here from Canton, Hong Kong and Shanghai. The Teleview communications system has broken down, presumably owing to deliberate interference and messages are being transmitted by radio. Rioting is reported from many provinces as a result of the complete collapse of the food rationing arrangements. Ration cards have not been honoured for over two weeks in some cities.

SENATOR DEMANDS VITAMINEAT PROBE

World Senator Hartwell of North England has called for a U.N. Congressional enquiry into the activities of Vitamineats Inc., the giant International Company which makes and markets the well known Vitamineat Food Substitute Tablets. Charging the Company with using inferior ingredients and making excessive profits, the Senator also hinted that the sabotage of food supply arrangements may be charged against the combine.

Mr. Lucius K. Kettlewell, Chairman and Managing Director of the Company, commented last night, "the Senator had better be careful."

MRS. DIGBY SAYS "HE'S ALIVE ALL RIGHT"

Mrs. Digby and family at their Wigan home

OTHER NEWS

MASS CHANNEL SWIM BY EGYPTIANS

An entire company of the Egyptian Army entered the water at Cap Gris Nez yesterday evening to swim the Channel in formation.

SUCCESS IN EAST AFRICA— PEANUT ARRIVES IN LONDON

There was a touching ceremony at the Strachey Memorial in London yesterday when a whole unblemished peanut was handed to the Minister of Food by a delegation representing equally the native tribes in the groundnut area and the survivors of the Strachey scheme.

WIGAN, Monday
Interviewed in her Westbank St. home this afternoon, Mrs. Digby, wife of the only "Other Rank" member of the expedition, seemed very confident of her husband's safety. "He'll be all right," she said, when our reporter spoke to her in the parlour of this typically Lancashire home. "Albert's been in plenty of tight spots before with Colonel Dare."

continued on page 161

P.C. 49 in a New Adventure

FROM THE FAMOUS RADIO
series by ALAN STRANKS

THE CASE OF THE TERRIBLE TWINS
A NEW P.C. 49 ADVENTURE

I SEE P.C.49's BACK ON THE DUTY ROSTER, SERGEANT WRIGHT.

YES, HE DID A FINE JOB ON THAT "KILLER'S KEEP" CASE! I WONDER WHAT HIS NEXT JOB WILL BE?

WHAT THE DICKENS . . . !

GOT YOU!

AND I'VE GOT YOU!

COO! FORTYNINE.

LEMME GO!

HERE ARE THE CULPRITS, SIR. PAT AND MICK MULLIGAN—THOUGH WHICH IS WHICH I NEVER CAN TELL.

I NEVER DID ANYTHING.

ME EITHER

CONFOUND IT! THAT WAS MY FAVOURITE PIPE.

THE KIDS IN THIS DISTRICT ARE GETTING OUT OF HAND. CAN'T YOU DO SOMETHING ABOUT IT, CONSTABLE?

I'M SPENDING MY SPARE EVENINGS AT THE BOYS' CLUB. IF YOU'LL PASS THESE LADS OVER TO ME . . .

JUST GET THEM OUT OF MY SIGHT—THAT'S ALL!

YOU'RE PAROLED IN MY CUSTODY—AND I'M GOING TO TRY AND TEACH YOU DECENT MANNERS.

OYS' CLUB? BAH!

WASTE OF TIME!

WOTCHER, '49!

HELLO THERE, ARCHIE BOY.

I'VE JUST ROPED IN TWO NEW MEMBERS. WE'RE GOING TO SEE HOW TOUGH THEY ARE WITH THE GLOVES ON.

LUMME! THE MULLIGAN TWINS!

THAT MEANS TROUBLE!

. . . A FAIR BOUT. BREAK CLEAN. STAND BACK AFTER KNOCK DOWNS AND COME OUT FIGHTING.

HOW'S THAT?

HEY!

OUT FOR THE COUNT.

TRUST THE TERRIBLE TWINS TO FIGHT DIRTY.

THEY'LL SPOIL OUR CLUB!

LET'S CHUCK 'EM OUT!

The Adventures of P.C.49

FROM THE FAMOUS RADIO series by ALAN STRANKS

CONTINUING **THE CASE OF THE TERRIBLE TWINS**
AT THE BOYS' CLUB, PAT AND MICK, 'THE TERRIBLE TWINS', HAVE MADE A BAD START.

PAT AND MICK..!

...DO THE TRICK!

WOW! MY HEAD!

THEY'VE FLATTENED FORTYNINE!

WHAT A DIRTY TRICK.

LET'S TURF 'EM OUT!

WOW

LEGGO!

OUCH!!!

MEANWHILE OUTSIDE

WHAT'S GOING ON IN THERE, SLIM?

SOUNDS LIKE A RIOT, KNOCKER.

IT'S THE MULLIGAN TWINS CUTTING UP ROUGH AGAIN.

I RECKON WE COULD USE THOSE KIDS.

HEY, CUT OUT THE ROUGH STUFF!

THE MULLIGANS STARTED IT.

WE'VE CHUCKED THEM OUT

HOW WAS THAT, PAT?

SLICK, MICK.

IT'S A PITY YOU CHASED THEM OFF, BOYS. WE NEED THOSE TWINS ON OUR SIDE.

WISH WE HAD SOME CASH. I COULD EAT A TON OF FISH AND CHIPS.

HEY, YOU!

HELLO! WHO'S THIS?

I'M SLIM THIS IS MY PAL, KNOCKER. HOW WOULD YOU LIKE TO EARN TEN BOB?

The Adventures of P.C.49

FROM THE FAMOUS RADIO
series by ALAN STRANKS

THE CASE OF THE TERRIBLE TWINS

PAT & MICK, THE TERRIBLE TWINS, ARE THROWN OUT OF THE BOYS' CLUB FOR CREATING A RIOT. OUTSIDE THEY MEET SLIM AND KNOCKER, TWO BAD TYPES, WHO OFFER THEM MONEY TO DO A JOB.

WE WANT TO PLAY A LITTLE JOKE ON HIM, SEE.

KNOCKERS BROTHER IS NIGHT WATCHMAN AT MARLOW'S FACTORY.

MICK AND PAT...

WILL DO THAT!

WHAT DO WE DO?

SLIM AND ME WILL SHOW YOU.

COME WITH US.

OKAY.

MEANWHILE....

WELL, LADS.. TIME FOR ME TO START BEAT-BASHING AGAIN.

CHEERIO, FORTYNINE

SO LONG, ARCHIE-BOY.

SEE YOU TOMORROW NIGHT.

AND OUTSIDE MARLOW'S FACTORY...

WE WANT ONE OF YOU TO CLIMB THROUGH THAT WINDOW AND UNBOLT THE DOOR.

DON'T LET MY BROTHER HEAR YOU, OR YOU'LL SPOIL THE JOKE

I'LL GO, PAT. I'M THE BEST CLIMBER.

STAND FIRM, KNOCKER. I'M GOING TO JUMP

KEEP IT QUIET, KID.

I'M IN LUCK, HE'S ASLEEP!

ZZZZ

EASY AS SHELLING PEAS. STEP RIGHT IN.

NICE WORK, KIDS! HERE'S YOUR DOUGH!

NOW BUZZ OFF!

TEN BOB FOR OPENING AN OLD DOOR!

THEY MUST BE MILLIONAIRES!

The Adventures of P.C.49

FROM THE FAMOUS RADIO series by ALAN STRANKS

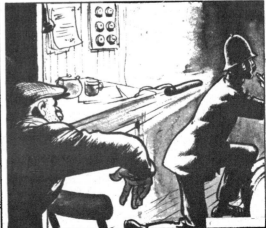

The Adventures of P.C.49

FROM THE FAMOUS RADIO series by ALAN STRANKS

CONTINUING

THE CASE OF THE TERRIBLE TWINS

WHILE INVESTIGATING THE OPEN DOOR AT MARLOW'S FACTORY, P.C.49 IS COSHED BY THE THUGS.

GOOD SHOT, KNOCKER-BOY.

HE NEVER KNEW WHAT HIT HIM. LET'S SCRAM.

THE TERRIBLE TWINS CAME IN HANDY. WE'LL USE THOSE KIDS AGAIN. COME ON!

WAIT 'TIL I KICK THIS COPPER "GOODNIGHT."

EVERYTHING LOOKS COCKEYED. WHAT FELL ON ME?

YES, INSPECTOR, MARLOW'S FACTORY. THE WATCHMAN'S BEEN COSHED AND THE SAFE'S EMPTY.

THAT WAS FORTYNINE! SOMEONE'S DONE MARLOW'S FACTORY. ORDER A SQUAD CAR AT ONCE, WRIGHT.

OKAY, INSPECTOR.

SOMETHING HIT ME — THEN EVERYTHING WENT BLACK.

SAME WITH ME.

THERE'S NO SIGN OF FORCIBLE ENTRY ON THE DOOR, GUV'NOR

THEN THE FIRST THING TO FIND OUT IS HOW THEY BROKE IN

LOOK AT THIS, INSPECTOR!

WHAT IS IT?

THIS LOOKS FAMILIAR TO ME.

AND ME, TOO!

I DON'T THINK THIS IS KID'S STUFF.

'COURSE NOT! I WAS COSHED — NOT CATAPULTED

IF YOU FIND THE OWNER OF THIS, WE'D LIKE TO TALK TO HIM.

I'M OKAY NOW.

BACK ON YOUR BEAT, FORTY-NINE — IF YOU FEEL UP TO IT.

IF THE TERRIBLE TWINS DO OWN THIS THING, THEY'RE IN TERRIBLE TROUBLE. I THINK I'LL PAY THEM A CALL.

I KNOW IT'S LATE, MRS. MULLIGAN, BUT I'D LIKE A WORD WITH THE TWINS.

DON'T TELL ME THEY'VE BEEN IN MISCHIEF AGAIN, '49. THEY'RE UPSTAIRS SLEEPING — I *HOPE!*

COO, MICK! IT'S P.C.49!

AND HE'S GOT MY 'CATTY'!

The Adventures of P.C.49

FROM THE FAMOUS RADIO series by ALAN STRANKS

CONTINUING
THE CASE OF THE TERRIBLE TWINS

P.C. 49, INVESTIGATING A ROBBERY AT MARLOW'S FACTORY, IS COSHED BY THUGS AND RECOVERS TO FIND A CATAPULT WHICH HE SUSPECTS BELONGS TO THE TERRIBLE TWINS.

DO EITHER OF YOU OWN THIS CATAPULT?

LET'S HAVE THE TRUTH, BOYS.

IT'S NOT MINE, FORTYNINE

N –NOT MINE EITHER.

I DON'T WANT TO DOUBT YOU BOYS BUT...

COME UP TO OUR ROOM AND WE'LL PROVE IT.

PAT AND MICK PROVE THINGS QUICK!

HERE'S MINE.

SORRY, BOYS—MY MISTAKE. NOW, BACK TO BED WITH YOU.

AND THIS ONE'S MINE, FORTYNINE.

GOOD JOB WE HAD A 'SPARE', MICK.

WE THREW OLD P.C.49 OFF THE SCENT PROPER, DIDN'T WE !

BUT WHEN THE LIGHT IS OUT, THE TERRIBLE TWINS BEGIN TO WORRY...

I WISH I HADN'T TOLD THAT COPPER A WHOPPER !

IF ONLY I'D OWNED UP.

...AND ALL THROUGH THE NIGHT THEY ARE HAUNTED WITH GUILTY DREAMS.

BUT NEXT EVENING ...

SHE'LL BE ALL RIGHT THERE WHILE WE GET A CUP O' CHAR.

I'M SO DRY I'M SPITTING SAWDUST.

IF EVER I SAW A LORRY ASKING TO BE KNOCKED OFF, THAT'S IT.

O.K., HE'S OUT OF SIGHT.

NOT EVEN LOCKED.

JUST WAIT TIL THAT COPPER IS OUT OF SIGHT

MEANWHILE ...

LET'S NIP INSIDE AND SNEAK A RIDE.

QUICK, MICK.

HOP IN, KNOCKER— WE'RE OFF.

O.K., SLIM — ALL CLEAR ! LET HER RIP!

HEY—COME BACK!

STOP THIEF !

HELLO, WHAT'S DOING?

The Adventures of P.C.49

FROM THE FAMOUS RADIO
series by ALAN STRANKS

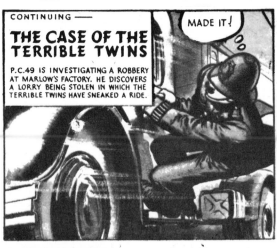

CONTINUING —

THE CASE OF THE TERRIBLE TWINS

P.C.49 IS INVESTIGATING A ROBBERY AT MARLOW'S FACTORY. HE DISCOVERS A LORRY BEING STOLEN IN WHICH THE TERRIBLE TWINS HAVE SNEAKED A RIDE.

The Adventures of P.C.49

FROM THE FAMOUS RADIO series by ALAN STRANKS

CONTINUING —

THE CASE OF THE TERRIBLE TWINS

THE TERRIBLE TWINS SNEAK A RIDE IN A STOLEN LORRY WHICH IS BEING TRACKED DOWN BY P.C.49. THE THIEVES REALISE THEY ARE CARRYING PASSENGERS....

HOLD IT, KNOCKER. IT'S THE TERRIBLE TWINS AGAIN!

TAKE YOUR PICK.—

PAT OR MICK!

WE DID? WE WEREN'T DRIVING WERE WE, KNOCKER?

YOU GAVE US A ROUGH RIDE ALL RIGHT.

NOT LIKELY! THIS LORRY BELONGS TO A PAL OF MINE. SOMEONE PINCHED IT.

WE STOOD IN THE ROAD AND FORCED THEM TO STOP.

BUT THEY BOLTED BEFORE WE COULD NAB 'EM.

JUST SIT TIGHT UP THERE AND GUARD THE LORRY TIL SOMEONE COMES ALONG. WE GOT BUSINESS.

MOST LIKELY MY FRIEND WILL GIVE YOU A REWARD FOR FINDING HIS LORRY.

MICK AND PAT —

WILL DO JUST THAT!

TOO BAD WE HAD TO DITCH THAT LORRY.

IF IT WASN'T FOR THOSE KIDS WE'D HAVE GOT AWAY WITH IT. BUT THE COPS'LL HAVE IT TAPED BY NOW.

MEANWHILE — AT POLICE HEADQUARTERS...

YOU'LL HAVE TO WAKE UP, CONSTABLE.

I'LL CERTAINLY KEEP MY EYES OPEN FOR THAT STOLEN LORRY, INSPECTOR.

YOU'RE HAVING A REGULAR CRIME WAVE ON YOUR BEAT LATELY, FORTYNINE.

ALL PATROLS HAVE BEEN ALERTED TO WATCH FOR THAT VEHICLE.

BUT IF *YOU* WANT TO FIND IT, YOU'D BETTER GET CRACKING.

IF ANYTHING ELSE GOES WRONG TONIGHT, BANG GOES MY CHANCE OF PROMOTION.

AS P.C.49 RETURNS TO HIS JOB OF 'BEAT BASHING', THE TERRIBLE TWINS ARE STARTING UP ANOTHER BUNDLE OF BOTHER FOR HIM.

LET'S HAVE A SHOT AT DRIVING HER, PAT.

RIGHTO, MICK!

HANG ON TO THAT WHEEL

YIPEE — WE'RE MOVING!

IF WE TURN DOWN THE HILL TO THE HIGH STREET, WE CAN DRIVE RIGHT BACK TO THE SPOT WHERE WE FOUND HER.

A FEW MINUTES — AND MILES — LATER.

LOOK, OUT!

HEY!

WHAT THE DICKENS!

LOOK OUT FOR THIS CAR!

I — CAN'T — STOP — HER!

THE STOLEN LORRY AND WHOEVER'S DRIVING MUST BE MAD — OR DRUNK!

COMPLETELY OUT OF CONTROL I'D BETTER NOT MISS *THIS* TIME.

The Adventures of P.C.49

FROM THE FAMOUS RADIO series by ALAN STRANKS

CONTINUING —

THE CASE OF THE TERRIBLE TWINS

THE TERRIBLE TWINS SNEAK A RIDE IN A STOLEN LORRY P.C.49 IS TRACING. THEY ARE DISCOVERED BY THE THIEVES WHO LEAVE THEM TO WATCH THE LORRY WHICH THE TWINS DECIDE TO DRIVE AWAY.

YOU TWO — MOVE OVER!

WE CAN'T STOP HER, COPPER!

DUCK QUICK, MICK!

LIE FLAT, PAT!

YOU YOUNG SCAMPS HAVE GONE TOO FAR THIS TIME.

HE STOPPED IT JUST IN TIME.

LUCKY NOBODY WAS KILLED.

NOW THEN YOU BOYS. YOU'RE COMING ALONG TO HEADQUARTERS TO ANSWER A FEW QUESTIONS.

HEY! — COME BACK!

STOP THOSE KIDS

WHERE ARE THEY?

THERE THEY GO!

AFTER THEM!

WHAT ARE WE GOING TO DO, MICK. I'M TOO SCARED TO GO HOME.

MAYBE WE KILLED SOME-ONE WITH THAT LORRY. I WISH WE HADN'T BEEN SUCH FOOLS.

GEE, I FEEL HUNGRY.

ME TOO. I WONDER WHAT MUM'S GOT FOR SUPPER.

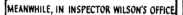

MEANWHILE, IN INSPECTOR WILSON'S OFFICE

THOSE BOYS AREN'T REALLY BAD, THEY'RE JUST MISCHIEVOUS.

YOU FOUND ONE OF THEIR CATAPULTS AT THE SCENE OF LAST NIGHTS WAREHOUSE ROBBERY.

AND TONIGHT THEY WERE DRIVING THAT STOLEN LORRY.

IT LOOKS AS IF THEY'VE BOLTED. THEY HAVEN'T BEEN HOME AND THEIR MOTHER'S REALLY WORRIED.

THERE'S MORE IN THIS THAN KID'S STUFF. SOMEBODYS PUT THEM UP TO THESE LARKS.

MAYBE YOU'RE RIGHT. ANYWAY, YOU'D BETTER PACK IT IN, FORTYNINE. YOU'VE DONE A GOOD JOB OF WORK TONIGHT.

IF YOU DON'T MIND I'LL STAY ON DUTY FOR A WHILE. I PROMISED MRS. MULLIGAN I'D FIND THE TWINS.

MIDNIGHT

THE MULLIGAN KIDS ARE SURE IN TROUBLE. I WONDER WHERE THEY'VE GOT TO?

WHO CARES? THEY'RE CARRYING THE BLAME FOR PINCHING THAT LORRY — THAT PUTS US IN THE CLEAR.

I TELL YOU WHAT, SLIM — LET'S DO THAT JOB ON THE CRACKERJACK FIREWORKS FACTORY TONIGHT.

WE COULD SURE USE THOSE KIDS TO HELP US IF ONLY WE COULD FIND THEM.

HERE COMES A FLATFOOT, WE'D BETTER BEAT IT, SLIM.

O.K. — LET'S GO!

I DON'T LIKE THE LOOK OF THAT PAIR. I WONDER WHAT THEY'RE UP TO.

DEAD QUIET, MICK! THAT SOUNDS LIKE FORTYNINE'S STEPS.

The Adventures of P.C.49

FROM THE FAMOUS RADIO series by ALAN STRANKS

CONTINUING —

THE CASE OF THE TERRIBLE TWINS

AFTER THE STOLEN LORRY CRASHES, THE TWINS ESCAPE FROM P.C.49. FROM THEIR HIDEOUT THEY HEAR THE THIEVES TALKING CLOSE BY. AS P.C.49 APPROACHES, THE THIEVES MOVE OFF—AND SO DO PAT AND MICK

HEY— I WANT YOU!

LEG IT, QUICK, MICK.

HERE I COME, CHUM.

THAT'S A DEAD-END THEY'RE HEADING FOR. I'LL NIP ROUND THE OTHER WAY AND CUT THEM OFF.

A FEW MOMENTS LATER . . . . .

HERE HE COMES!

OKAY, HOLD TIGHT!

THAT'S DONE THE TRICK, MICK.

LAID HIM FLAT, PAT.

COME ON PAT, AT THE DOUBLE.

LUMME, MICK, WE'RE IN TROUBLE.

I'M A PROPER COPPER, I AM! CAN'T EVEN NAB TWO NIPPERS.

AFRAID TO GO HOME AND FACE THE MUSIC, THE TERRIBLE TWINS ROAM THE STREETS UNTIL . . . . .

ONE O'CLOCK, SLIM. TIME FOR US TO GET CRACKING ON THIS JOB.

WAIT—HERE COME THOSE MULLIGAN 'DS AGAIN.

CRACKERJACK FIREWORK CO

I WISH I WAS HOME IN BED, PAT.

WE DAREN'T GO HOME 'TIL WE PROVE WE DIDN'T STEAL THAT LORRY. IF ONLY WE COULD FIND SLIM AND KNOCKER.

YOU'VE FOUND US, CHUMS.

SLIM! *YOU'LL* TELL FORTYNINE WE NEVER PINCHED THAT LORRY, WON'T YOU.

SURE, BUT FIRST WE NEED YOUR HELP ON ANOTHER LITTLE LARK.

YOU'RE A HOT SHOT WITH A CATAPULT, MICK. I'LL GIVE YOU TEN BOB IF YOU CAN SHOOT THE CUP OUT OF THAT MAN'S HAND.

DON'T DO IT, MICK. WE'RE IN ENOUGH TROUBLE ALREADY.

WHAT'S THE MATTER? SCARED?

ME SCARED? WATCH THIS.

WHAT THE DICKENS— —

COME ON—LET'S SCARPER.

KIDS, I'LL BET—AND IF I CATCH THEM . . .

STAY IN THE SHADOWS—HE CAN'T SEE US.

WE WON'T LET HIM HURT YOU.

The Adventures of P.C.49

FROM THE FAMOUS RADIO series by ALAN STRANKS

CONTINUING —

THE CASE OF THE TERRIBLE TWINS

TRICKED AGAIN INTO HELPING SLIM AND KNOCKER ON ANOTHER OF THEIR EVIL 'JOKES', THE TERRIBLE TWINS ARE NOW IN *REAL* TROUBLE

LOOK OUT!

GOOD WORK, KNOCKER!

DUCK, PAT!

STOP THAT KID!

A FEW STREETS AWAY, P.C.49, CONTINUING HIS SEARCH FOR THE TERRIBLE TWINS, HEARS THE SHOT.

THAT SOUNDED LIKE A SHOT!

MEANWHILE —

I'VE GOT TO GET HELP! I'VE JUST *GOT* TO!

AS PAT TRIES TO PULL HIMSELF TOGETHER, P.C.49 IS APPROACHING THE FACTORY FROM THE OPPOSITE DIRECTION.

THAT SHOT CAME FROM THIS DIRECTION. GOSH! WHAT'S THAT GATE DOING OPEN?

AT THE FACTORY —

OUCH!

SHUT UP-OR I'LL BREAK YOUR ARM!

QUIET! SOMEONE'S COMING!

IT'S THAT NOSEY COPPER AGAIN! TAKE THIS KID INSIDE, SLIM! I'LL DEAL WITH THIS LOT!

ONE PEEP OUT OF YOU AND I'LL LET YOU HAVE IT!

WATCH OUT FORTYNINE!

BUT MICK'S SHOUT COMES TOO LATE!

The Adventures of P.C.49

FROM THE FAMOUS RADIO
series by ALAN STRANKS

CONTINUING —
THE CASE OF THE TERRIBLE TWINS

HIS ATTENTION DISTRACTED BY MICK'S CRY FOR HELP, P.C.49 IS AN EASY VICTIM TO KNOCKER'S BRUTAL COSH ATTACK. INSIDE THE FACTORY DOOR, MICK'S SHOUTED WARNING HAS BROUGHT A GRIM REWARD. BUT AS HE GOES DOWN -- PAT, WOUNDED BY SLIM'S BULLET, HAS STAGGERED TO HIS FEET, AND------

I'LL TEACH YOU TO SHOUT 'COPPER'!

I'VE SIMPLY GOT TO FIND SOMEONE TO HELP!

NOT FAR AWAY AT THE BOYS' CLUB, DESPITE THE LATE HOUR, A COUNCIL OF WAR IS IN FULL SESSION.

I HEARD YOU GIVE THE EMERGENCY WHISTLE, SNORKY, AND CAME HERE AS FAST AS I COULD.

I HAD TO SNEAK OUT THE WINDOW

MY MUM WON'T HALF LEAD OFF IF SHE FINDS I'M NOT IN BED.

ME TOO!

PIPE DOWN WHILE I GIVE YOU THE GEN.

THE MULLIGAN TWINS ARE ON THE RUN. I HEARD MY MUM SAY THEIR MOTHER'S TERRIBLY WORRIED. WE'VE GOT TO FIND THEM AND BRING 'EM HOME, FELLERS.

MICK GAVE ME THIS SHINER!

PAT KNOCKED OUT MY TOOTH!

BUT FORTYNINE SAYS THERE'S SOME GOOD IN THEM.

OK — LET'S GET CRACKING.

CRUMBS — LOOK!

PAT MULLIGAN! -- WHAT?

I SAW THE LIGHT FROM OUTSIDE.

PAT — YOUR SHOULDER! — WHAT HAPPENED?

TWO CROOKS HAVE GOT MICK AT THE CRACKERJACK FIREWORKS FACTORY! ONE OF THEM SHOT ME AS I BROKE AWAY. YOU'VE GOT TO HELP ME RESCUE MICK, FELLERS! YOU'VE JUST GOT TO!

NOT 'TIL MICK'S SAFE.

YOU OUGHT TO GO HOME, PAT.

COME ON, CHAPS

WE'LL SAVE HIM, PAT, — DON'T WORRY.

AS SNORKY LEADS HIS SQUAD TO THE RESCUE, PLENTY IS HAPPENING AT THE FACTORY - - - - -

SLOW FUSE — THIS'LL TAKE ABOUT TEN MINUTES TO BURN.

POWDER ROOM
DANGER
NO SMOKING

JUST TIME FOR US TO CLEAN OUT THE SAFE AND MAKE OUR GETAWAY.

GUY FAWKES' DAY WON'T BE IN IT WHEN *THIS* LOT GOES UP!

I'VE MADE A PROPER MESS OF THINGS, HAVEN'T I, FORTYNINE? NOW PAT'S SHOT AND WE'RE GOING TO BE - - - - - -

CHEER UP CHUM! WE'RE NOT BEATEN YET. NOW, I'LL TELL YOU WHAT I WANT YOU TO DO - - - - - -

The Adventures of P.C.49

FROM THE FAMOUS RADIO series by ALAN STRANKS

CONTINUING

THE CASE OF THE TERRIBLE TWINS

AS SNORKY LEADS THE BOYS' CLUB TO THE RESCUE, SLIM AND KNOCKER ARE MAKING A FAST JOB OF ROBBING THE FACTORY SAFE. MEANWHILE, IN THE BASEMENT POWDER ROOM, MICK STRUGGLES DESPERATELY TO FREE FORTYNINE'S HANDS BEFORE THE BURNING FUSE REACHES THE CANISTER OF EXPLOSIVE POWDER.

The Adventures of P.C.49

FROM THE FAMOUS RADIO
series by ALAN STRANKS

The Adventures of P.C.49

FROM THE FAMOUS RADIO series by ALAN STRANKS

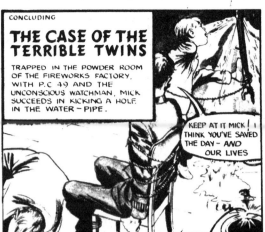

CONCLUDING

THE CASE OF THE TERRIBLE TWINS

TRAPPED IN THE POWDER ROOM OF THE FIREWORKS FACTORY, WITH P.C. 49 AND THE UNCONSCIOUS WATCHMAN, MICK SUCCEEDS IN KICKING A HOLE IN THE WATER-PIPE.

KEEP AT IT MICK! I THINK YOU'VE SAVED THE DAY – *AND* OUR LIVES

NICE WORK, MICK. IT'S OUT!

NOW ALL WE'VE GOT TO DO IS TO GET *OURSELVES* OUT!

AND THAT'LL BE ANY MINUTE NOW!

PAT!

LOOKS LIKE THE TERRIBLE TWINS HAVE TURNED UP TRUMPS AT LAST.

YOU'LL HAVE TO COME UPSTAIRS QUICK, FORTYNINE. WE'VE GOT SLIM AND KNOCKER CORNERED, BUT THEY'VE STILL GOT A GUN.

GOOD WORK, PAT! I'VE A SCORE TO SETTLE WITH THOSE TWO BEAUTIES!

COME ON, FORTYNINE – THIS WAY!

HURRY!

I'LL PUT THIS POOR BLOKE SOMEWHERE SAFE FIRST.

LUMME! IT'S "GUY FAWKES" DAY ALL OVER AGAIN!

OKAY, KIDS! HOLD IT – I'VE GOT A SPOT OF ARRESTING TO DO.

NOW THAT "BLITZ" IS OVER I CAN SEE AGAIN. I WON'T MISS *THIS* TIME.

ALL RIGHT, KNOCKER – THE GAME'S UP! YOU'D BETTER COME QUIETLY!

LOOK OUT FORTY-NINE!

COP *THIS*!

CAREFUL!

WATCH THAT GUN!

CLICK

!

IT'S A FAIR COP! I GIVE UP!

TRY AND TAKE ME COPPER!

OKAY, KNOCKER IF YOU WANT TO PLAY ROUGH YOU'VE COME TO THE RIGHT SHOP!

THERE'S TWO 'GUYS' WHO AREN'T WORTH A PENNY IF EVER I SAW THEM, MICK.

COME ON! DOWN TO THE STATION ALL OF YOU. I'LL HAVE TO SQUARE THESE MIDNIGHT CAPERS WITH YOUR PARENTS.

I SECOND THAT, PAT!

WELL, PAT AND MICK – I HOPE TONIGHT'S PROVED TO YOU THE *RIGHT* SIDE TO BE ON.

WHEN WE GROW UP, WE'LL TOE THE LINE –

– AND *BOTH* BE COPS LIKE FORTYNINE!

ANOTHER P C 49 ADVENTURE STARTS NEXT WEEK

PROFESSOR BRITTAIN EXPLAINS: RADAR

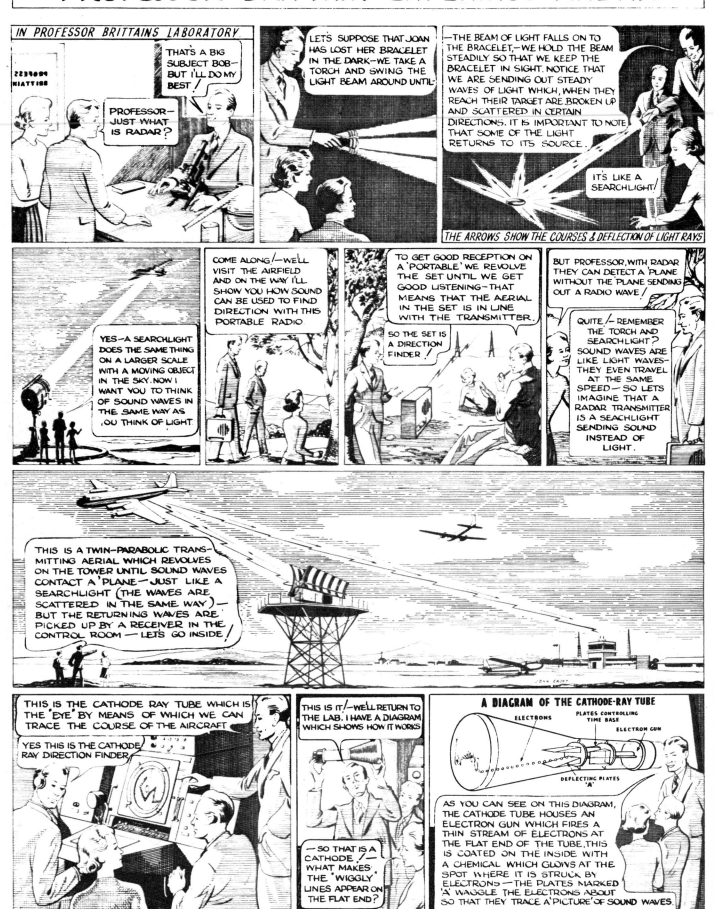

Any Questions?

Write to Professor Brittain, c/o E A G L E, if you have any questions or problems you would like him to deal with. He will be on this page every fortnight.

Join in the 6T6 Ranchers' New Adventure now!

JEFF ARNOLD IN *Riders of the Range*

BEGINNING TODAY —
THE ARIZONA KID

STORY BY CHARLES CHILTON
DRAWN BY FRANK HUMPHRIS

It is Christmas Eve and Jeff Arnold, Luke, Jim Forsythe and Rustler have just arrived in the small frontier town of Benson . . .

NO POINT IN GOING ANY FURTHER I GUESS WE CAN PUT UP HERE FOR THE NIGHT.

AREN'T WE GOIN' TO SPEND CHRISTMAS IN TEXAS WITH THE 6T6 OUTFIT?

WE'LL PRESS ON AS SOON AS DAY BREAKS. WE SHOULD MAKE THE 6T6 RANCH IN TIME FOR CHRISTMAS DINNER

GOLDARN IT, THE CHRISTMAS SHINDIGS HAVE STARTED ALREADY. THERE'S NOTHING I LIKE MORE THAN A BIT OF THAT OLD-TIME DANCING.

HOLD YOUR HORSES, LUKE—WE'VE HARDLY GOT INTO THE PLACE YET!

MERRY CHRISTMAS.

JUST A MINUTE, MISTER! CHECK YOUR GUNS OR YOU AREN'T ALLOWED IN.

PEACE AND GOODWILL PARK YOUR GUNS

BETTER DO AS HE SAYS, FELLERS — SEEMS IT APPLIES TO EVERYBODY.

THANKS, KID— TICKET NO. 17.

PEACE AND GOODWILL PARK YOUR GUNS HERE

GOLDARN IT, I ALWAYS FEEL UNDRESSED WITHOUT MY GUN.

HEY —WHOSE GUNS ARE THOSE?

THE KID'S! WHY— WHAT'S IT TO YOU?

THE KID'S? BUT THEY CAN'T BE! NEVER MIND. FORGET IT!

WHAT'S UP, JEFF? LOOKS AS IF YOU'VE SEEN A GHOST!

MAYBE I HAVE, LUKE. THAT KID — LET'S GET OVER TO HIM.

THERE HE IS, JEFF — OVER BY THE BAR.

EXCUSE ME A MINUTE. . .

FOR *PETE'S SAKE!*

49

JEFF ARNOLD IN *Riders of the Range*

CONTINUING —

THE ARIZONA KID

Jeff, Luke and Jim arrive at Benson on Christmas Eve and put up for the night at the 'Wagon Wheel'. While handing his guns to the doorman, Jeff's attention is drawn to a pair of Smith and Wesson revolvers deposited by a youth. Jeff's curiosity is aroused and he steps across to the bar to ask the young man a few questions . . .

STORY BY CHARLES CHILTON
DRAWN BY FRANK HUMPHRIS

. . . But the only answer Jeff gets is a crack on the head which lays him out . . .

OF ALL THE LOW DOWN TRICKS!

DON'T WORRY, LUKE — I'LL GET HIM!

OUTA MY WAY, D'YOU HEAR? OUTA MY WAY!

STOP THAT KID — STOP HIM!

GIVE ME MY GUNS — NO. 17 . . . AND QUICK!

YE-YESSIR — NO. 17? BUT YOU'VE ONLY JUST GOT HERE!

AND NOW I'M GETTIN' RIGHT OUT AGAIN!

BACK — BACK! UP NOW, MY BEAUTY — WE'VE GOTTA SPLIT THE BREEZES.

HEY — COME BACK! DO YOU HEAR ME? COME BACK!

WHE-E-E-E

I SAY — WHAT GHASTLY MANNERS!

A few moments later the boy has disappeared into the darkness. Jim returns quickly to the saloon of the 'Wagon Wheel' to find that Jeff has recovered from the nasty blow he has received, and the three friends retire to their room to dress Jeff's head and discuss the situation.

OUCH! STEADY, LUKE — THAT HURTS

AND THEN HE FIRED AT ME, EVEN THOUGH HE KNEW I HAD NO GUN . . . AND THE BULLET CAME SO CLOSE IT ALMOST PARTED MY HAIR!

WHAT MADE HIM SO ORNARY, JEFF? AND WHY DID YOU WANT TO TALK TO HIM ANYWAY?

I HAD A HUNCH, THAT'S ALL. TOMORROW MORNING I'M GOING ACROSS TO THE SHERIFF'S OFFICE TO FOLLOW IT UP. I'VE GOT A FEELING WE HAVEN'T SEEN THE LAST OF THAT KID!

Next morning, Jeff and Co. visit the Sheriff's office . . .

AH — THIS IS IT!

LET'S SEE IT JEFF.

WANTED
FOR TRAIN ROBBERY, BANK HOLD UP, AND MURDER.

WILLIAM B. DENNING
5000 REWARD

WILLIAM DENNING? BUT HE WAS CAUGHT YEARS AGO. WHAT'S HE GOT TO DO WITH A KID HITTING YOU OVER THE HEAD WITH A BOTTLE?

EVERYTHING! NOW COME ON. GET YOUR HORSES, WE'LL TRY TO PICK UP THAT KID'S TRAIL. IT'S MIGHTY IMPORTANT THAT WE DO!

JEFF ARNOLD IN *Riders of the Range*

STORY BY CHARLES CHILTON: DRAWN BY FRANK HUMPHRIS

CONTINUING —

THE ARIZONA KID

At the 'Wagon Wheel' in Benson, Jeff Arnold is hit over the head with a bottle by a youth who, when pursued, shoots at Jim Forsythe and then gallops away at top speed into the night. Next morning, after picking up an old 'wanted' notice from the Sheriff's office, Jeff, Luke and Jim set out from Benson to track the kid down.

FOR PETE'S SAKE, JEFF, WHAT GOES ON? WHY DO WE HAVE TO FIND THIS KID WHEN WE COULD BE HEADING FOR TEXAS AND HOME?

I THINK THAT KID WILL HELP US CLEAR UP A YEARS' OLD MYSTERY.

YOU REMEMBER BILL DENNING—ROAD AGENT AND TRAIN ROBBER?

AND BANK ROBBER. HE WENT TO JAIL YEARS AGO—YOU PUT HIM THERE.

..YEAH! WELL, YOU'LL REMEMBER DENNING ALWAYS HAD TWO ACCOMPLICES WITH HIM...

...THEY HELPED HIM PULL OFF EVERY CRIME HE EVER COMMITTED. THEY WERE INSEPARABLE. HE WAS ALSO KNOWN TO POSSESS TWO GUNS—THE FINEST PAIR OF SMITH AND WESSONS EVER SEEN IN THESE PARTS...

...BUT, AFTER DENNING'S CAPTURE, BOTH HIS GUNS AND HIS CONFEDERATES DISAPPEARED AND HE REFUSED TO GIVE THE WHEREABOUTS OF EITHER...

...FOR THAT, THE JUDGE GAVE HIM A STIFF SENTENCE AND, IN RETURN, DENNING THREATENED THE JUDGE.

YOU HAVE NOT HEARD THE LAST OF ME—MY GUNS WILL SPEAK AGAIN!

BUT, AFTER A COUPLE OF YEARS IN PRISON, DENNING DIED.

I FAIL TO SEE WHAT ALL THIS HAS TO DO WITH US CHASING HALF-WAY ACROSS ARIZONA AFTER A YOUNG BOY!

IT HAS A LOT TO DO WITH IT...THAT KID WAS WEARING *BILL DENNING'S* GUNS!

HERE HE COMES, PANHANDLE, AND ABOUT TIME, TOO!

ANYBODY WITH HIM?

Meanwhile, at a lonely derelict ranch-house in the hills . . . .

NO, HE'S ALONE!

GOOD! WOULD HAVE BEEN TOO BAD FOR HIM IF HE HADN'T BEEN.

HULLO, KID! 'BOUT TIME YOU SHOWED UP— WE'VE BEEN WAITING A LONG TIME.

WHERE DID YOU SPRING FROM?

JEFF ARNOLD IN *Riders of the Range*

CONTINUING —

THE ARIZONA KID

Jeff Arnold, Luke and Jim Forsythe are in pursuit of a youth who wears the guns of Bill Denning, a one-time notorious outlaw who was brought to justice by Jeff. The boy, after taking a roundabout route in the hope of throwing Jeff off the trail, arrives back at his hide-out to find two members of Bill Denning's old gang waiting for him.

STORY BY CHARLES CHILTON
DRAWN BY FRANK HUMPHRIS

JEFF ARNOLD IN *Riders of the Range*

CONTINUING —

THE ARIZONA KID

Jeff Arnold wants to question the youth who attacked him because the young man carries the guns of Bill Denning, who was jailed by Jeff. He trails the young man to a derelict ranch-house where, unknown to Jeff, the Kid has met Panhandle and Jake, two outlaws who used to ride with Denning. Jeff, Luke and Jim enter the house . . .

STORY BY CHARLES CHILTON
DRAWN BY FRANK HUMPHRIS

PUT UP YOUR HANDS! PUT 'EM UP AND KEEP 'EM UP!

WHAT THE..?

NOW TURN AROUND. FACE THE OTHER WAY. THE FIRST MAN TO TRY ANY FUNNY BUSINESS WILL GET A BULLET THROUGH HIM.

WHAT'S THE IDEA, KID? WHAT KIND OF A WELCOME IS THIS?

A few minutes later . . .

WHAT'S THE IDEA OF FOLLOWING ME? WHAT DO YOU WANT?

NOW TAKE IT EASY, KID! THE WAY YOU CARRIED ON BACK IN THAT SALOON IN BENSON AND THOSE GUNS YOU'RE CARRYING INTEREST ME. WHERE DID YOU GET 'EM?

I AIN' ANSWERING ANY QUESTIONS! STATE YOUR BUSINESS — OR GET OUT!

NOW, WAIT A MINUTE — EXCEPT THAT YOU HAVE NO MOUSTACHE, YOU MIGHT WELL BE A YOUNG EDITION OF BILL DENNING, THE OUTLAW...YOU MIGHT EVEN BE HIS SON!

WHAT IF I AM? I WANT NO TRUCK WITH YOU, ARNOLD — YOU ARRESTED MY FATHER AND HAD HIM SENT TO JAIL.

LOOK — WE WANT TO HELP YOU, AND WE WANT YOU TO HELP US. YOUR FATHER HAD TWO COMPANIONS — AND THEY WERE NEVER ARRESTED. HAVE YOU ANY IDEA WHERE THEY MIGHT BE?

I DON'T KNOW WHAT YOU'RE TALKING ABOUT. NOW GET — BEFORE MY TRIGGER FINGERS START TO ITCH.

ALL RIGHT, KID — IF THAT'S HOW YOU FEEL. WE WERE ON OUR WAY BACK TO TEXAS ANYWAY. GIVE US BACK OUR GUNS AND WE'LL GO.

I'LL GIVE THEM TO YOU OUTSIDE — GET OUT FIRST!

WE CAN'T MAKE YOU TALK IF YOU DON'T WANT TO WE AIN'T LIKELY TO BOTHER YOU AGAIN

JUST GIT — AND DON'T COME BACK!

WHY, THE PESKY-HIDED GALOOT — HE'S TAKEN THE SHELLS OUT!

NICE WORK, KID — YOU HANDLED THAT SITUATION JUST LIKE YOUR OLD MAN

I SHOULD HAVE KILLED HIM — WHILE I HAD THE CHANCE.

NO, KID — THAT WOULDN'T HAVE DONE ANY OF US ANY GOOD. NOW, DID YOU GET WHAT YOU WENT TO BENSON FOR?

YES, I DID — EVERY DETAIL.

IT SHOULD BE EASY — AND WORTH AT LEAST 50,000 DOLLARS.

NEVER MIND THE COMMENTS — JUST GIVE US THE FACTS.

The small town of Benson, in the early morning, three days later . . .

ALL RIGHT, KID — THIS IS IT! STAY PUT TILL WE COME OUT YOU KNOW WHAT TO DO THEN.

YES, PANHANDLE!

BANK

ALL RIGHT. DON'T MOVE, ANY OF YOU — THIS IS A HOLD-UP!

JEFF ARNOLD IN *Riders of the Range*

CONTINUING —

THE ARIZONA KID

Jeff, Luke and Jim, on the track of what is left of an outlaw gang once led by the late Bill Denning, track down Denning's son, the Arizona Kid. But the boy refuses to talk, so Jeff and Co. ride away, unaware that the Kid, with two of the old gang, Panhandle and Jake, intends to rob a bank in Benson.

STORY BY CHARLES CHILTON: DRAWN BY FRANK HUMPHRIS.

JUST STAY PUT—DO AS I TELL YOU AND NOBODY WILL GET HURT!

NOW, *YOU*—OPEN UP THAT TILL AND TIP THE MONEY INTO THIS!

LOOK OUT— HE'S GOT A GUN!

Meanwhile, in the 'Wagon Wheel' Hotel across the street . . .

FOR PETE'S SAKE! WHAT WAS THAT?

GUNFIRE—CAME —FROM ACROSS THE ROAD!

IT'S A BANK HOLD-UP!

AND ONE OF THEM IS THE KID! GET ME A GUN, LUKE...*QUICK*— THE RIFLE!

WHAT HAPPENED— WHAT WAS ALL THE SHOOTING FOR?

DARNED TELLER HAD A GUN. LET'S GET OUT OF HERE QUICK BEFORE THE WHOLE TOWN WAKES UP.

NICE SHOOTIN', JEFF —THAT'S ONE OF 'EM DOWN!

HELP— A HOLD-UP— STOP 'EM!

GET UP BEHIND ME QUICK!

THE MONEY... WHAT ABOUT THE MONEY?

NEVER MIND THAT NOW, WE'VE GOT TO GET OUT OF HERE—*RIDE FOR OUR LIVES!*

GOLDARN IT, THE KID'S TAKING THAT OTHER GALOOT UP BEHIND HIM. GET HIM, JEFF, QUICK.

NO, LUKE—RANGE IS TOO GREAT... I MIGHT KILL THE KID.

COME ON, GET YOUR CLOTHES ON—WE'LL GET A POSSE TOGETHER AND GO AFTER THEM!

THEY'LL HAVE A GOOD START ON US. WE'LL BE LUCKY TO CATCH UP WITH 'EM

 # JEFF ARNOLD IN *Riders of the Range*

CONTINUING —

THE ARIZONA KID

The Arizona Kid, with Panhandle and Jake, holds up the bank at Benson. But the sound of the gunfire during a fight with the bank teller, brings Jeff, Luke and Jim to the window of their hotel room. Jeff shoots down Jake's horse, but the crook climbs up behind the Kid and the robbers escape. Jeff and Co. prepare to give chase.

STORY BY CHARLES CHILTON. DRAWN BY FRANK HUMPHRIS.

HURRY UP, LUKE—WE HAVEN'T MUCH TIME!

JUST GIVE ME TIME TO PUT MY GUN BELT ON AND I'M RIGHT WITH YOU.

RIGHT— I'M SET! WE'LL HAVE THOSE BANK-ROBBIN' GALOOTS IN THE PEN IN NEXT TO NO TIME.

LUKE— YOU HAVEN'T FINISHED DRESSING!

HUH? GOLDARN IT, I THOUGHT IT WAS DRAUGHTY.

I RECKON THE SHERIFF HAS BEAT US TO IT.

GO ROUND TO THE STABLE, LUKE, AND GET THE HORSES —JIM AND I WILL SEE WHAT'S COOKING.

A few minutes later . . .

WELL, THEY DIDN'T GET AWAY WITH IT. THEY DROPPED THE LOOT WHEN JEFF'S SHOT BROUGHT ONE OF THE HORSES DOWN— BUT, IF WE CATCH THEM, WE CAN STILL ARREST THEM FOR ATTEMPTED ROBBERY.

IT'LL BE A BIGGER CHARGE THAN THAT, SHERIFF.

HOW DO YOU MEAN?

THE TELLER—THEY SHOT HIM—HE'S IN A BAD WAY!

WE'LL GET AFTER THEM. ANY OF YOU MEN WILLING TO JOIN IN THE POSSE, GET YOUR HORSES—ASSEMBLE OUTSIDE MY OFFICE AND I'LL SWEAR YOU IN AS DEPUTIES.

YOU CAN COUNT ME IN, SHERIFF!

AND ME!

AND ME!

Soon the posse is ready . . .

THEY HEADED NORTH ALONG THE MAIN TRAIL, BUT THEY'RE NOT LIKELY TO KEEP TO IT FOR LONG.

THEN LET'S GO—THEY'LL NOT GET FAR WITH ONE HORSE CARRYING A DOUBLE LOAD.

Meanwhile, out in the desert...

COME ON, YOU TWO—WE'LL NEVER GET AWAY AT THIS RATE.

TAKE IT EASY, JAKE, MY HORSE CAN'T TRAVEL FAST— NOT WITH A DOUBLE LOAD.

HEY, JAKE—WHAT'S THE IDEA? WHERE ARE YOU GOING?

FOLLOW ME! DON'T ASK SO MANY DURNED QUESTIONS.

THIS TWO MEN ON ONE HORSE BUSINESS IS NO GOOD— SOMETHING'S GOT TO BE DONE.

BUT WHAT? WE'VE ONLY GOT TWO HORSES BETWEEN THE THREE OF US.

JUST THIS . . . GET DOWN OFF THAT HORSE, KID— AND QUICK!

JEFF ARNOLD IN *Riders of the Range*

CONTINUING —

THE ARIZONA KID

After holding-up the bank at Benson and shooting a cashier, the Arizona Kid, Jake and Panhandle are being chased by a posse led by Jeff and Co. The Kid and Jake ride on one horse, but this slows the party up and Panhandle, determined to escape capture, deals with the situation.

STORY BY CHARLES CHILTON. DRAWN BY FRANK HUMPHRIS.

WHAT'S THE IDEA, PANHANDLE—WHAT DOES THIS MEAN?

I SAID GET OFF THAT HORSE—AND KEEP YOUR HANDS AWAY FROM YOUR GUNS!

GET HIS IRONWARE, JAKE.

YOU BET!

I GET IT NOW—YOU'RE GOIN' TO STEAL MY HORSE—LEAVE ME HERE, STRANDED AND UNMOUNTED!

IT AIN'T THAT BAD, KID. YOU'RE YOUNG— YOU'LL SURVIVE, BUT OLD-TIMERS LIKE US NEED FAST HORSES BETWEEN OUR KNEES IF WE'RE TO MAKE OUR GET-AWAY.

IS THIS HOW YOU SHOW YOUR GRATITUDE, JAKE, AFTER I STOPPED TO PICK YOU UP?

DON'T TAKE IT SO HARD— YOU'LL GET BY!

I NEVER DID HANKER AFTER THIS BUSINESS, ANYWAY. RECKON I'LL GO BACK TO BENSON AND MAKE A CLEAN BREAST OF IT—TELL THE SHERIFF HOW YOU ORGANIZED THE WHOLE THING AND TALKED ME INTO TAKING PART.

YOU WON'T DO THAT! THE CASHIER WAS SHOT, REMEMBER— MAYBE HE'S DEAD. AND YOU'RE JUST AS GUILTY AS WE ARE — THEY'D *HANG* YOU!

WELL, AT LEAST LEAVE ME MY GUNS SO THAT I CAN DEFEND MYSELF.

I'LL DROP THEM ALONG THE TRAIL—YOU CAN PICK THEM UP IN A FEW MINUTES!

THEIR TRAIL LEADS INTO THE BAD LANDS —WON'T BE EASY TO FIND THEM IN THERE!

THEY LEFT THE MAIN TRAIL HERE — WENT INTO THE ROCKS. THEY'VE PROBABLY SEPARATED, HOPING TO SHAKE US OFF.

THERE'S A CHANCE THEY'RE HIDING IN THERE, HOPING WE WON'T FIND THEM.

WE'D BETTER SPLIT UP—COMB THESE ROCKS UNTIL WE FIND THEM. BUT WE'D BETTER WATCH OUR STEP, FOR THEY'LL STOP AT NOTHING!

Meanwhile, back along the trail . . .

So the posse from Benson is split into three parts. One to continue along the main trail in case the fugitives have rejoined it further along. The second to ride to the far side of the bad lands in case they have ridden right through them. The third, led by Jeff, to comb the hills.

LOOKS AS IF A COUPLE OF THEM DISMOUNTED HERE. MAYBE THEY STOPPED TO TALK OVER THEIR POSITION AND DECIDE WHETHER TO PRESS ON, HIDE OR MAKE A STAND.

AND HOW DO WE KNOW WHICH?

WE DON'T! WE'LL KEEP LOOKING —FOLLOW THEIR TRACK. BUT WATCH OUT FOR AN AMBUSH!

NO SIGN OF 'EM! IF YOU ASK ME, THEY AIN'T HERE. BY NOW THEY'VE LEFT THESE HILLS AND ARE HIGH-TAILING IT FOR THE NORTH.

JEFF ARNOLD IN *Riders of the Range*

CONTINUING —

THE ARIZONA KID

The Arizona Kid, deserted by his companions, Panhandle and Jake, after the bank hold-up in Benson, during which the cashier was shot, is hiding in the hills. Jeff, Luke and Jim, part of the Sheriff's posse from Benson, comb the hills for the Kid and, unknowingly, come within a few yards of him.

STORY BY CHARLES CHILTON
DRAWN BY FRANK HUMPHRIS

HOLD IT A MINUTE!

WHAT'S UP, SON?

THERE THEY ARE!

IT'S PART OF THE SHERIFF'S POSSE.

WELL, YOU CAN GIVE UP SEARCHING THESE HILLS, JEFF—THEY AIN'T IN HERE, THAT'S FOR SURE!

HOW DO YOU KNOW?

BECAUSE WE'VE PICKED UP THEIR TRAIL. THEY MUST HAVE SKIRTED THESE HILLS TO PUT US OFF THE SCENT AND THEN JOINED THE NORTH TRAIL AGAIN ABOUT FIVE MILES FURTHER UP.

SHERIFF SAYS EVERYBODY IS TO JOIN THE MAIN PARTY AND TAKE UP THE CHASE.

PITY WE DIDN'T KEEP GOING ON THE MAIN TRAIL—BY NOW WE MIGHT HAVE CAUGHT UP WITH 'EM.

So Jeff, Luke and Jim join the Sheriff, and the rest of the posse from Benson, along the main trail and the pursuit is continued. But then, while they are examining the tracks left in a patch of soft ground, Jeff notices something that changes his mind about going on any further . . .

NEITHER OF THESE TRACKS ARE DEEP ENOUGH FOR ONE OF THE HORSES TO BE CARRYING A DOUBLE LOAD.

YOU MEAN WE'RE CHASING ONLY TWO OF 'EM—THAT ONE OF 'EM HAS BEEN LEFT BEHIND?

YES, I DO. MY HUNCH ABOUT THEIR BEING IN THE HILLS WAS RIGHT—AT LEAST ONE OF THEM MUST BE. IF YOU LIKE, SHERIFF, I'LL GO BACK AND HAVE ANOTHER LOOK... YOU KEEP GOING AFTER THE TWO WITH THE HORSES.

RIGHT! GIVE YOUR HORSES THEIR HEADS, MEN—LET'S SPLIT THE BREEZES.

Leaving the Sheriff to continue the chase, Jeff and Co. return to search the hills . . .

ONE OF THEM *MUST* BE IN HERE. WE'LL SPLIT UP—WE'LL HAVE A BETTER CHANCE OF FINDING HIM THEN. IF ANY OF US SIGHTS HIM, FIRE THREE SHOTS IN THE AIR AND THE OTHER TWO WILL COME A-RUNNING.

AS YOU SAY!

VERY WELL!

LONE RIDER—PLENTY GUNS—EASY FIGHT!

But, unknown to Jeff, Luke and Jim, other dangers lie in wait in the hills . . .

WHAT THE..?

COME ON, BETSY! IF YOU LOVE ME, HIT THE GRIT—AFORE THOSE HEATHENS TAKE MY SCALP!

The old-timer is in real trouble. How is he going to get out of it? Don't miss next week's exciting instalment!

JEFF ARNOLD IN *Riders of the Range*

CONTINUING —

THE ARIZONA KID

After the bank at Benson has been held-up by three bandits — the Arizona Kid, Panhandle and Jake — Jeff, Luke and Jim set out after them with the Sheriff's posse. Realizing that one of the crooks must be hiding in the hills, Jeff and Co. leave the posse and separate to make a search. Luke is attacked by four renegade Indians . . .

STORY BY CHARLES CHILTON. DRAWN BY FRANK HUMPHRIS.

As Luke attempts to escape, his horse puts her foot into a hole and brings the old-timer crashing to the ground . . .

It seems that nothing can possibly save Luke, then . . .

. . . the Arizona Kid, who has been hiding among the rocks, comes to Luke's aid . . .

LET GO! LET 'GO O' MY THROAT, YOU HALF BAKED, GOOD-FOR-NOTHIN' INDIAN!

THERE — THAT'LL TEACH YOU TO MONKEY WITH ME!

GREAT JUMPING RATTLESNAKES — TWO MORE OF 'EM! AND WITH MY BARE HANDS. I MUST BE A LOT TOUGHER THAN I THOUGHT.

OH NO YOU'RE NOT — I HAD A HAND IN THIS LITTLE SHINDIG! NOW, GET UP ON YOUR FEET AND KEEP YOUR HANDS IN THE AIR!

THE KID!

NOW WAIT A MINUTE — YOU CAN'T DO THIS TO ME. I'M SUPPOSED TO PUT *YOU* UNDER ARREST FOR ROBBING THE BENSON BANK!

JUST KEEP YOUR MOUTH SHUT, OLD-TIMER, AND YOU'LL COME TO NO HARM. ALL I WANT IS YOUR HORSE, TO MAKE MY GET-AWAY.

MY HORSE — YOU'RE NOT GOIN' TO TAKE BETSY, ARE YOU? SHE MEANS MORE TO ME THAN ANYTHING ELSE IN THE WORLD!

IT'S THE LEAST YOU CAN DO FOR ME AFTER I SAVED YOUR LIFE, AIN'T IT? MAYBE, WHEN I GET ME ANOTHER HORSE, I'LL SEND HER BACK. MEANWHILE, I'VE GOT TO GET OUT OF HERE AND I DON'T CARE WHOSE HORSE CARRIES ME.

OH NO YOU DON'T, KID — DROP THAT GUN AND PUT UP YOUR HANDS!

JEFF!

JEFF ARNOLD IN *Riders of the Range*

CONTINUING —

THE ARIZONA KID

Luke is attacked by four Apache Indians whilst searching the hills for the Arizona Kid, who took part in a bank hold-up at Benson with Panhandle and Jake. The Kid comes to Luke's rescue and saves his life. Then, to Luke's surprise, he holds up the old-timer and threatens to steal his horse. Suddenly, Jeff Arnold appears on the scene . . .

STORY BY CHARLES CHILTON. DRAWN BY FRANK HUMPHRIS.

THE GAME'S UP, KID—YOU'D BETTER COME QUIETLY! GET HIS GUNS, LUKE—BOTH OF 'EM.

YOU BET!

ALL RIGHT, ARNOLD— YOU'VE GOT THE DROP ON ME—*THIS TIME!*

NOW WAIT A MINUTE, JEFF— WHAT ARE YOU GOIN' TO DO WITH HIM?

HAND HIM OVER TO THE SHERIFF, ON A CHARGE OF BANK ROBBERY AND ATTEMPTED MURDER!

BUT I CAN'T LET YOU TAKE HIM IN LIKE THAT—HE JUST SAVED MY LIFE!

I'VE GOT NO CHOICE, LUKE. HE'S WANTED BY THE LAW—IT'S MY DUTY TO ARREST HIM.

BUT, JEFF, LET'S TALK THIS THING OVER. A KID THAT WILL RISK HIS LIFE FOR AN OLD-TIMER LIKE ME, CAN'T BE TOO BAD UNDERNEATH. AT LEAST LET HIM HAVE HIS SAY FIRST.

ALL RIGHT, KID, START TALKING— LET'S HEAR YOUR SIDE OF IT!

So the Arizona Kid explains to Jeff how he came to be mixed up with Panhandle and Jake, the notorious bank robbers, and how, by implanting in the Kid's mind that to join up with them was one way of avenging his father's death, they eventually persuaded him to help them rob the bank at Benson.

O.K., KID—YOU'VE TOLD ME YOUR STORY AND I BELIEVE IT! PANHANDLE AND JAKE TRIED TO MAKE A CRIMINAL OUT OF YOU AND NEARLY SUCCEEDED—BUT THE FACT REMAINS YOU WERE INVOLVED IN A BANK ROBBERY, AND YOU'RE AN OUTLAW.

BUT, GOLDARN IT, JEFF, IF YOU EXPLAIN THE FACTS TO THE SHERIFF AND HOW THE KID SAVED MY LIFE AT THE RISK OF HIS OWN...

ALL RIGHT, I'LL TALK TO HIM—BUT I DON'T PROMISE ANYTHING. MEANWHILE, YOU'D BETTER HIDE UP HERE FOR A FEW DAYS. I'LL LEAVE LUKE WITH YOU!

IF THEY GIVE ME A CHANCE, JEFF, I'LL GO STRAIGHT—I SWEAR I WILL!

Next day, in the Sheriff's office at Benson . . .

I TELL YOU, SHERIFF, THE KID'S BEEN MISLED—PANHANDLE AND JAKE ARE THE MEN WE WANT. THE KID WILL EVEN HELP US TO TRACK THEM DOWN.

BUT CAN WE DEPEND ON HIM?

I'LL GUARANTEE IT. ALL YOU HAVE TO DO IS BIND HIM OVER TO KEEP THE PEACE.

THEN I'LL GIVE IT A TRY! TELL HIM TO RIDE INTO TOWN AND REPORT HERE—ALONE AND *UNARMED!*

Two days later . . .

YOU GO IT ALONE FROM HERE, KID. SEE THE SHERIFF AND CLEAR YOUR NAME—AND GOOD LUCK!

THANKS, JEFF! TAKE MY GUNS WILL YOU, LUKE? UNARMED HE SAID—AND UNARMED I GO!

OH, HULLO, KID—COME ON IN, I'VE BEEN EXPECTING YOU!

PUT UP YOUR HANDS, KID— YOU'RE UNDER ARREST!

JEFF ARNOLD IN *Riders of the Range*

CONTINUING —

THE ARIZONA KID

The Arizona Kid, who took part in a bank hold-up at Benson, saves Luke from almost certain death at the hands of some Indians. Jeff arrives on the scene and arrests the young outlaw. Then Luke persuades Jeff to ask the Sheriff to give the Kid another chance. This the Sheriff promises to do, if the Kid gives himself up unarmed . . . .

STORY BY CHARLES CHILTON: DRAWN BY FRANK HUMPHRIS

WHAT GOES ON? I CAME HERE VOLUNTARILY — TO GIVE MYSELF UP!

SORRY, KID — WE COULDN'T TAKE ANY CHANCES.

WHAT CHANCES ARE *YOU* TAKING? I'M UNARMED JEFF ARNOLD TOLD ME THAT IF I CAME TO SEE YOU, YOU'D TALK THINGS OVER AND MAYBE GIVE *ME* A CHANCE!

AND YOU'LL GET IT — BEFORE A JUDGE AND JURY!

HOW DO YOU MEAN?

I MEAN YOU'LL BE STANDING TRIAL FOR ROBBING THE BENSON BANK AND WOUNDING THE CASHIER IN THE PROCESS!

SO THAT'S IT? THE WHOLE THING'S A TRICK — AND I BELIEVED ARNOLD WAS ON THE LEVEL.

MAYBE THIS'LL TEACH YOU TO TRUST *NOBODY* IN FUTURE! TAKE HIM TO THE JAIL-HOUSE, BOYS — AND SEE HE STAYS THERE.

WELL, I GUESS THE SHERIFF HAS HAD TIME ENOUGH TO TALK TO HIM NOW — LET'S RIDE DOWN TO THE OFFICE AND SEE WHAT'S GOIN' ON.

YEAH! I RECKON HE'LL BE WANTING US TO TAKE THE KID IN HAND, AND MAKE AN HONEST CITIZEN OUT OF HIM!

Meanwhile . . .

FOR PETE'S SAKE!

THERE MUST BE SOME MISTAKE — COME ON!

HEY — WHAT'S THE IDEA, SHERIFF?

I'VE PUT THE KID UNDER ARREST, THAT'S WHAT! AND I'LL THANK YOU TO KEEP YOUR NOSE OUT OF THIS!

But Luke has edged his horse close to the Kid...

THAT'S A LOW-DOWN TRICK, SHERIFF — YOU PROMISED TO TALK WITH HIM, NOT ARREST HIM!

WHAT THE...?

HEY — STOP HIM! HE'S GETTING AWAY!

STOP HIM — DO YOU HEAR?

SORRY, SHERIFF — YOU JUST TOLD ME TO KEEP MY NOSE OUT OF THIS!

STOP! STOP OR I SHOOT!

JEFF ARNOLD IN *Riders of the Range*

CONTINUING —

THE ARIZONA KID

The Arizona Kid, at Jeff's suggestion, gives himself up to the Sheriff. It has been agreed that the young outlaw will be pardoned and given a chance to prove himself a good citizen, but when the Kid arrives in town, the Sheriff arrests him. Then, while he is being taken to the jailhouse, Jeff and Co. give the Kid a chance to escape . . .

STORY BY CHARLES CHILTON : DRAWN BY FRANK HUMPHRIS.

STOP, DO YOU HEAR? STOP — OR I'LL LET YOU HAVE IT!

OH NO YOU DON'T, SHERIFF!

WHO FIRED THAT SHOT?

I DID! NOBODY SHOOTS ANYBODY IN THE BACK WHILE I'M AROUND.

DO YOU REALIZE I COULD ARREST YOU FOR OBSTRUCTING THE ENFORCEMENT OF THE LAW?

GO AHEAD AND TRY! THE KID SAVED MY LIFE —'T AIN'T FITTING THAT I SHOULDN'T EVEN THE SCORE IF I GET THE CHANCE.

ARREST HIM! ARREST THE OLD MAN AND PUT HIM IN THE JAILHOUSE.

SORRY, SHERIFF, BUT NOBODY'S ARRESTING ANYBODY. FIRST ONE TO LAY A HAND ON LUKE WILL GET WHAT'S COMING TO HIM! DROP YOUR GUNS — BOTH OF YOU! THROW THEM WELL AWAY FROM YOU.

IT WAS A ROTTEN TRICK YOU PLAYED ON THE KID, SHERIFF — FROM NOW ON, YOU CAN COUNT US OUT OF THIS BUSINESS ALTOGETHER!

YOU CAN'T DO THAT, ARNOLD! THAT KID IS AN OUTLAW — IT'S YOUR DUTY TO TRACK HIM DOWN.

AND I'LL DO IT, BUT IN MY OWN WAY — WITH NO HELP FROM YOU!

Meanwhile, the Arizona Kid gallops furiously across the desert away from Benson . . .

He plans to take his revenge for the trick played upon him . . .

Four days later, confident that his trail has not been followed, the Kid arrives at notorious Charleston – a town of 'wanted' men . . .

SALOON

The Kid rides at once to the town's only saloon, hitches his horse to the rail, mounts the steps, and goes inside . . .

DON'T MOVE — IF YOU SO MUCH AS FLICK AN EYELID, I'LL LET YOU HAVE IT!

THE KID — THE ARIZONA KID!

JEFF ARNOLD IN *Riders of the Range*

THE ARIZONA KID

Jeff and Co. appeal to the Sheriff of Benson on the Arizona Kid's behalf. The Sheriff promises to give the Kid another chance, so the young outlaw gives himself up. The Sheriff breaks his word and arrests the Kid, who escapes to Charleston, a hide-out of outlaws. The Kid finds Panhandle and Jake, and levels his guns at them . . .

STORY BY CHARLES CHILTON: DRAWN BY FRANK HUMPHRIS

HOW DID YOU GET HERE? WE THOUGHT...

YOU THOUGHT THAT I HAD DIED OUT IN THE DESERT, OR THAT WAS WHAT YOU HOPED

...YOU TOOK MY HORSE AND DIDN'T CARE WHAT HAPPENED TO ME, SO LONG AS YOU COULD SAVE YOUR OWN SKINS!

NO, KID — YOU GOT IT ALL WRONG. WE KNEW YOU'D BE OK. — WE KNEW YOU COULD LOOK AFTER YOURSELF!

NEVER MIND THAT — GET UP, BOTH OF YOU!

WHAT ARE YOU GOING TO DO TO US?

YOU'LL FIND OUT — KEEP YOUR HANDS UP AND START MOVING!

NOW TAKE IT EASY, KID — WE DIDN'T MEAN YOU ANY HARM!

WHERE ARE YOU TAKING US — WHAT ARE YOU GOING TO DO?

FIRST WE'LL FIND A PLACE TO TALK. YOU MADE A MONKEY OUT OF ME OVER THAT BANK HOLD-UP, BUT NOW YOU'VE GOT A NEW HORSE TO RIDE!

FROM NOW ON YOU WORK FOR ME — I GIVE THE ORDERS.

WORK FOR YOU — HOW DO YOU MEAN?

I'M OUTSIDE THE LAW NOW AND I INTEND TO STAY THERE. BUT FIRST I'VE GOT A LITTLE SCORE TO SETTLE WITH THAT RATTLESNAKE JEFF ARNOLD, AND YOU'RE GOING TO HELP ME DO IT.

In a nearby hotel room, the Kid outlines his plan of action. The Kid, believing that Jeff has tricked him, now makes up his mind to follow in his father's footsteps; to be an outlaw for good. Meanwhile, Jeff, anxious to overtake the Kid and explain that it was the Sheriff who had gone back on his word, is slowly following the Kid's trail, accompanied by Luke and Jim...

HE HEADED FOR CHARLESTON SURE ENOUGH.

WE CAN'T GO THERE, JEFF — THAT PLACE IS FULL OF OUTLAWS, AND MOST OF 'EM WOULD BE GLAD TO SHOOT YOU ON SIGHT!

BUT IF THE KID GETS MIXED UP WITH THE KIND OF COMPANY HE'LL FIND IN THAT TOWN, HE'LL GO WRONG FOR SURE — THEN THERE'LL BE NO SAVING HIM!

YOU MEAN YOU'LL RISK YOUR LIFE JUST TO TRY TO SAVE THE KID FROM GOING WRONG?

YES, LUKE, I DO. COME ON, AND KEEP YOUR EYES PEELED — THIS PLACE IS BOUND TO BE DYNAMITE!

JEFF ARNOLD IN *Riders of the Range*

CONTINUING —

THE ARIZONA KID

Jeff Arnold, who is determined to help the Arizona Kid, follows the young outlaw to Charleston, a town of 'wanted' men, in southern Arizona. Even though they realize that the place will be full of crooks, many of whom would be only too pleased to kill them, Jeff, Luke and Jim decide to ride into the town . . .

STORY BY CHARLES CHILTON. DRAWN BY FRANK HUMPHRIS

I DON'T LIKE THIS, JEFF — I FEEL AS IF THERE'S A GUN POINTING RIGHT AT MY BACK.

LAND SAKES — LOOK . . .

. . . AM I DREAMING, OR IS THAT JEFF ARNOLD?

IT'S HIM ALL RIGHT, OR I'M A RATTLESNAKE! HOW'S HE GOT THE NERVE TO COME HERE?

WE'D BETTER WARN THE BOYS!

HEY, FELLERS — LISTEN . . . JEFF ARNOLD'S IN TOWN!

HEY, WHERE ARE YOU GOING? THIS GAME HASN'T FINISHED YET!

DIDN'T YOU *HEAR*? JEFF ARNOLD'S IN TOWN — I'M GETTING OUT!

ME TOO!

WELL, JEFF ARNOLD DOESN'T SCARE *ME*. I AIN'T LEAVING TOWN ON HIS ACCOUNT — OR ANYBODY ELSE'S!

ALL RIGHT, LUKE, I'M HEADING TOWARDS THE BAR. KEEP YOUR EYES PEELED — IN CASE OF TROUBLE!

YOU BET, SON!

ME NEITHER . . . HEY, LOOK — THERE HE IS!

I'M LOOKING FOR A KID, A YOUNG KID, WHO RODE INTO THE TOWN A FEW HOURS AGO. HAVE YOU SEEN HIM?

WHY — NO — I'VE SEEN NO KID!

DON'T GIVE ME THAT OR IT'LL BE TOO BAD FOR YOU. *HAVE YOU SEEN THE KID OR HAVEN'T YOU?*

YEAH! I'LL TALK. LET ME GO AND I'LL TELL YOU ALL I KNOW.

HE WAS IN HERE ABOUT TWO HOURS AGO, PICKED UP PANHANDLE AND JAKE AND WENT OUT, BUT I DON'T KNOW WHERE HE WENT.

PANHANDLE AND JAKE — WHO ARE THEY?

ALL RIGHT, FELLERS — HE MUST STILL BE IN TOWN SOMEWHERE, AND IF HE IS — WE'LL FIND HIM. COME ON!

Meanwhile, the Kid is only a very few yards away . . .

YOU DON'T HAVE TO THREATEN US WITH A GUN, KID — WE'LL JOIN UP WITH YOU, YOU KNOW THAT. JUST TELL US WHAT YOU WANT US TO DO.

I AIN'T EXACTLY FIGURED WHAT I'LL DO YET. ALL I KNOW FOR SURE IS THAT I MEAN TO GET ARNOLD, SOME DAY!

YOU DON'T MEAN *SOME* DAY, KID — YOU MEAN *TODAY!*

THERE'S ARNOLD, DOWN IN THE STREET. IF YOU REALLY WANT TO GET HIM — *NOW'S YOUR CHANCE!*

JEFF ARNOLD IN *Riders of the Range*

CONTINUING —

THE ARIZONA KID

Jeff Arnold and Co. track the Arizona Kid to Charleston in an attempt to prevent him from becoming a permanent outlaw. They start to search the town, but fail to find the Kid who, with his two evil companions – Panhandle and Jake – plans to kill Jeff. Jake sees Jeff and Co. in the street below and calls the Kid over to the window . . .

STORY BY CHARLES CHILTON. DRAWN BY FRANK HUMPHRIS.

I'LL PICK HIM OFF FOR YOU RIGHT NOW— AND THAT'LL BE HIM OUT OF THE WAY FOR GOOD!

NO, WAIT— DON'T SHOOT!

DON'T SHOOT? BUT YOU JUST SAID . . .

NEVER MIND WHAT I SAID. FROM HERE, YOU MIGHT MISS ARNOLD AND HIT THE OLD-TIMER.

SO WHAT?

HE STOPPED THE SHERIFF OF BENSON SHOOTING ME IN THE BACK. GUESS IT DOESN'T HURT FOR ME TO RETURN THE FAVOUR.

GOLDARN IT, KID— YOU TALK LIKE A REGULAR SOFTIE, NOT A BIT LIKE YOUR OLD MAN!

THAT'S MY BUSINESS! THIS TIME, ON ACCOUNT OF THE OLD-TIMER, ARNOLD GOES FREE. BUT NEXT TIME WE MEET, HE'D BETTER LOOK OUT 'COS I'LL BE GUNNING FOR 'IM.

WELL, HE AIN'T HERE EITHER. THE ONLY PLACE LEFT TO LOOK IS THE HOTEL.

Meanwhile, Jeff and Co. continue their search . . .

BUT I TOLD YOU, MR ARNOLD, HE IS NOT HERE. I SWEAR IT! NOBODY'S CHECKED IN HERE FOR TWO DAYS.

THEN I GUESS HE MUST HAVE PULLED OUT OF TOWN BEFORE WE RODE IN. MAYBE WE'LL PICK UP HIS TRAIL.

WELL, THAT FOOLED 'EM, I RECKON— THEY'VE GONE NOW.

AND JUST AS WELL, OR IT WOULD HAVE BEEN TOO BAD FOR YOU!

Outside the town of Charleston an hour or so later . . .

WELL, JEFF OLD MAN, WHAT DO WE DO NOW?

WE GO UP INTO THOSE HILLS AND MAKE CAMP WHERE WE CAN OVERLOOK THE TOWN.

WHAT FOR? IF THE KID AIN'T THERE, WHY KEEP AN EYE ON THE PLACE?

BECAUSE I BELIEVE HE *IS* THERE. HE WAS JUST HIDING UP, WAITING FOR US TO LEAVE.

I GUESS THIS WILL DO. WE CAN WATCH FROM HERE WITHOUT BEING SEEN. WE'LL TAKE IT IN TURNS TO LOOK OUT.

Later that day . . .

HEY, JEFF— I'VE GOT SOMETHING!

IS IT THE KID?

YES, IT IS! AND TWO OTHER RUM-LOOKING CHARACTERS WITH HIM.

ALL RIGHT! SADDLE YOUR HORSES— THIS IS WHERE WE SEE SOME ACTION!

In the end Jeff captures the Kid who because of his youth and basic good nature is bound over to keep the peace.

THE EAGLE CLUB

AND EDITOR'S PAGE

14 *April* 1950

The Editor's Office
E A G L E
43 Shoe Lane, London, EC4

EAGLE, as you can see, is an entirely new kind of strip-cartoon paper – and it looks as if there is going to be a very big demand for it. So I suggest you ask your newsagent to order a copy for you each week. At the bottom corner of this page, you will find a form which you can cut out and hand to your newsagent. If you want to make sure of your copy fill it in straight away.

I'm sure you will agree that EAGLE is really good value for 3d. We are using only the best authors and the best artists.

The EAGLE CLUB is going to be one of the most important features in the paper and we've got a pile of ideas for making it a really good Club to join.

It has very definite aims and standards. To begin with, a member has to agree to the Club Rules. Here are the most important of them:—
Members of the EAGLE CLUB will:

(*a*) Enjoy life and help others to enjoy life. They will not enjoy themselves at the expense of others.

(*b*) Make the best of themselves. They will develop themselves in body, mind and spirit. They will tackle things for themselves and not wait for others to do things for them.

(*c*) Work with others for the good of all around them.

(*d*) Always lend a hand to those in need of help. They will not shirk difficult or dangerous jobs.

The other main aims are: *First*, to link together those who read and enjoy EAGLE. *Second*, to organise meetings, expeditions, holidays, camps, etc., for members. *Third*, to make special awards to members who achieve anything really worthwhile.

This is what you do to join the Club. Send to the Editor at the above address, (1) your name and address; (2) your age and date of birthday; (3) your school and club (if you belong to one) and (4) a postal order for one shilling. Especially don't forget to tell us your birthday.

In return we will send you: (1) THE EAGLE badge, made in gilt, like the one drawn here. (2) A Charter of Membership. (3) The Club Book of Rules.

The badge is really first-rate – and all those who join the Club *within the next four weeks,* i.e., before 14th May, will be able to get it as part of the 1/- membership fee. After four weeks, new members will have to send an extra 6d. to pay for the badge. So send in your application right away.

The first 100 members to join will get a special prize. They are to be divided into four groups of 25 according to where they live. Twenty-five living in the South of England will be taken free to Farnborough Air Display on July 8th. Twenty-five living in the Midlands will go to Silverstone Grand Prix Races on May 13th. Twenty-five from the North of England to a Test Match against the West Indians; and twenty-five from Scotland to the Highland Games. The younger members will be invited to bring one parent or guardian free of charge.

The winners will be those 100 members whose applications for membership are opened first, on Wednesday, April 19th.

Then there will be, from time to time, special expeditions for selected members – for example, a trip to the T.T. races in the Isle of Man, to the Edinburgh Festival, to the Monte Carlo Rally, to the 1951 Festival of Britain, and to interesting places abroad. There will be something to suit all tastes and interests.

But joining the Club is only the first step. There's a second special kind of membership.

This second step is to become a MUG. That may sound a rather strange thing to become. This shortly is what it's all about.

There are really only two kinds of people in the world. One kind are the MUGS. The opposite of the MUGS are the Spivs – also called wide boys, smart guys, hooligans, louts or racketeers.

The MUGS are the people who are some use in the world; the people who do some thing worth-while for others instead of just grabbing for themselves all the time.

Of course the spivs snigger at that. *They* use the word Mug as an insult. "Aren't they mugs?" they say about people who believe in living for something bigger than themselves.

That is why someone who gets called a MUG is likely to be a pretty good chap. For one thing, he's got to have guts because he doesn't mind being called a MUG. He *likes* it. He's the sort who will volunteer for a difficult or risky job and say cheerfully, "Alright, I'll be the Mug." That doesn't mean he is stupid. It means he's got the right ideas and doesn't think it is at all clever to be a spiv-type, like the gentleman we have drawn here.

So when you join the EAGLE CLUB the next step is to become a MUG. We shall then send you a special badge to attach to the ring at the bottom of the EAGLE badge. And there are many special privileges arranged for MUGS which we'll tell you about another time.

But you cannot become a MUG just by writing to us. You have got to do something to earn it and someone – not yourself – has got to tell us about it. If someone who knows you – say, a school teacher, Club leader, and so on – writes to us and suggests your name, we shall go into it carefully and, if you really qualify, award you a badge and special certificate.

One of the privileges that MUGS will have is to be invited to take a hand in running the EAGLE CLUB and EAGLE. At regular intervals, we shall be calling an editorial conference in London, to which we shall invite selected Mugs. They will be able to meet the Editor and his artists and writers and discuss the whole policy of the paper.

Of course, there are thousands of Mugs already – the great Mugs of history. People like Scott of the Antarctic, who gave his life to discover new lands; or Michael Faraday – people said he was talking nonsense when he said that electricity could be used to serve man; or the Curies – people said they were wasting their time when they were working to isolate radium.

Here, for example, is a picture of one famous Mug:— J. L. Baird.

People laughed at him when he started to suggest that there could be such a thing as television. They wanted him to give up trying – but fortunately for us he didn't.

Perhaps *your* picture may appear here one day. Each month we shall pick the MUG OF THE MONTH and publish his or her photograph. And at the end of the year, there'll be a special ' do ' laid on for the MUGS OF THE YEAR.

Don't forget to write and tell us what you think of EAGLE.

Yours sincerely
THE EDITOR.

CHICKO by thelwell

PLOT AGAINST THE WORLD

A gripping new Serial by Chad Varah

Chapter 1

The Ghost from the Sea

JIM suddenly felt himself falling.

He had been strolling home from the Club with his hands in his pockets, whistling a popular zither tune that was driving his family crazy, and gazing up at the sky trying to identify the Pole Star. Then he trod on nothing.

His feet shot sideways and downwards. Before he could get his hands out of his pockets, he had slid down a chute, giving his head a crack on the edge that made him see the Pleiades, and dropped several feet on to a rocky mountain. The avalanche he started took him with it and went on rumbling and pelting him even after he'd reached the bottom with his.

The taste of the grit in his mouth told him what had happened. Some fool had left a manhole-cover off, and Jim was now mixed up with somebody's coal ration.

Before he could pick himself up, he saw a shadow on the grimy whitewashed wall – evidently cast from a light in a connecting cellar. In spite of the grotesque distortion Jim saw what it was, and he could hardly believe his eyes. It was a man with a gun.

He stared as if paralysed at the sinister silhouette. The shadow began to creep towards him, and he recovered his wits in a hurry. He hadn't a chance in a million of being able to scramble out in time, so he got to his feet and picked up a huge lump of coal. He hurled it with all his strength, not at the approaching figure, which was still around the corner of the passage, but at the pile of coal behind him. As a fresh avalanche started, he yelled at the top of his lungs:

" Come on, chaps! And shoot to kill! "

The approaching shadow faltered. The man, it seemed, was not aware that his shadow could be seen. Encouraged, Jim hurled another lump (it felt like slate), and shouted:

" Wait for Tiger – then we'll rush them! "

A shot rang out, terrifying and deafening in that confined space. In the same moment Jim felt the pain sear into his knee. As he fell, he gasped:

"They got me, pals! Don't let 'em get away!"

Tenderly his hand explored the injured knee. He was astounded not to find it wet with blood. He waggled the kneecap. Nothing seemed to be broken. Then his hand touched a familiar object – a lump of slate with a shape he recognised. It had bounded back when he threw it, and clouted his knee.

He gave a whistle of relief. Then he looked hastily at the wall. The shadow had gone!

Had it ever been there? He could hardly believe it: and yet his ears still rang with the sound of the shot. Why wasn't a policeman

peering down the manhole by now, demanding to know "What's all this 'ere?"

Jim stood perfectly still, and listened. It was then that he heard it – a sort of scuffle in the next cellar, and a strange animal sound. There was something horrible and uncanny about it, and his skin crawled. He wasn't a coward, but he'd had plenty for one night. The gunman was bad enough, but this – this slithering, snuffling sound made him think of some hideous reptile – an alligator, perhaps.

"I'm getting out of this!" muttered Jim.

He scrambled up the coal, and managed to pull himself up on to the chute. But it was slippery, and he fell off. As he picked himself up again, he cast a glance at the wall that was faintly lit.

Cripes! It *was* an alligator! Lower down than the shadow he'd seen at first, crawling on the floor, was a monstrous shape.

Jim let out a yell and jumped for the chute, scrambling frantically against the side walls, and scraping his fingers raw. At last he got a grip on the edge of the manhole, and hauled himself up until his head and shoulders were out in the clean night air.

He was just going to heave himself out of the hole when he saw a burst of flame at the end of the street. The bullet whipped past his head with a "zwoo-EEP" just before he heard the crack of the shot. He ducked instinctively, lost his balance, and fell back into the cellar. This time he caught the point of his chin on the edge of the hole. Just before he lost consciousness he sobbed "O gosh – the *Thing!*"

WHEN he came to, he couldn't remember at first where he was. He was lying on something soft and warm – and sticky.

He opened his mouth to yell, and then thought better of it. For there was an unmistakable smell right against his nose and a familiar texture against his mouth.

The smell was boot-polish and the texture was wool. The contrast between these homely things and the horror his strained imagination had pictured was so great that he giggled.

His face was pressed against someone's shoes and socks, and so far as he knew, alligators didn't wear either.

Then he stopped giggling. He was lying on a man, and the man was badly hurt. The stickiness against his hand was not reptilian slime but human blood.

Was the man dead?

Jim carefully rolled off him, felt along his body to his face, and was reassured by the warm moisture of breathing.

Obviously this must be the victim of the man with the gun and his accomplices, if any. And he needed help badly.

But it was too dark in the coal cellar. Jim crept cautiously round the corner, down a very short passage and into another cellar, parallel to the first. It was lit by a hurricane lamp hanging from a hook in the ceiling.

He could see the marks on the dirty floor where the man had painfully dragged himself along. They started from a row of wine-bins along the passage wall. It looked as if the man had crawled from one of the bins.

In the wall opposite, an opening led to a short flight of steps curving upwards. At the top he could just see a door, battered but stout, with a rusty lock. Grumbling under his breath at the grit that crunched beneath his feet, Jim stole up the steps and gently tried the door. It was locked.

He stood uncertainly for a moment, eyeing the door. Then he noticed the bolt on the inside, near the top. It was coated with rust. A long struggle followed before the bolt gave way to Jim's frantic heaving and shot suddenly to. He hoped the corroded staple would hold if the gunman should return.

Swiftly he returned to the wounded man and again heard the snuffling noise that had

scared him before. The man had recovered consciousness and was trying to talk. He must be gagged! Jim felt for the man's mouth and his fingers solved the problem. There was a sorbo ball in his mouth! He got it between his finger and thumb and managed to pull it out.

For a few moments the man made inarticulate noises, then he whispered thickly, "m'han's, m'feet, tied." Jim fumbled with his sore fingers at the knots, glad that in his days with the Scouts he'd learnt to deal with knots blindfold. At last his companion was free. Jim helped him back into the lighted cellar, and made a rough bandage for the nasty wound in his shoulder.

He was relieved that it was no worse. But the man needed help, for he had lost a lot of blood, and his wrists and ankles had been tied cruelly tight.

Jim made him as comfortable as he could against a wall and the man smiled his thanks.

"You a miner?" he asked.

"Certainly," replied Jim. "I'm only sixteen."

"I said 'miner', not 'minor'. You look as black as a sweep."

"Oh, that," said Jim, looking down ruefully at his clothes and hands. "Yes, I don't know what Mum will say. If it comes to that, you're pretty filthy too. Did *you* fall through the manhole, as well? Some fool left the cover off."

"No – I was the fool. They chased me down into the cellar, and I tried to get out of the manhole, but they pulled me back. If you hadn't happened along, they'd have . . . Well, never mind about that now. Do you think you could get me out?"

"I've bolted the cellar door, so I think you should be safe while I get up through the manhole and fetch the police – unless that chap's still shooting. Can't think why they haven't turned up as it is."

"Not the police, if you don't mind," said the man, looking up at Jim enigmatically. "And they *are* on the job – I heard a police whistle just as you fell, after the second shot. I don't think there'll be anyone watching the manhole now."

For Jim, one thing stood out of all this.

"Why not the police?" he asked. " Are you a criminal?"

"No," said the man. He looked Jim straight in the eye, with such a frank gaze that the boy felt inclined to believe him. "I'll tell you part of the reason later. Can you get someone who won't talk to help me out and put me up for the night?"

Jim frowned. Then his face cleared.

"Yes," he said.

BEFORE climbing out of the manhole, Jim pushed out a large rounded lump of coal, half expecting it to be shattered like a bullet. When nothing happened, he dropped it and climbed out. He found the manhole-cover, replaced it, and carefully noted which of the row of bomb-damaged houses it belonged to before moving off.

He made his way along the street as fast as he could, limping a little from his bruised knee and aching from the cracks on his head and chin. His imagination conjured up shadowy figures lurking in doorways, and once from just behind him the long-drawn howl of a tom-cat sent shivers down his spine.

At the door of the house he was making for h.. paused uncertainly, then turned away and went round the back alley. There was no light in the window, and he wanted to get Ken without waking his mother. It must be very late – what on earth would Mum say when he got home? Especially when she saw the state he was in!

Thirty-nine, thirty-seven, thirty-five. No number on this back gate, but it must be thirty-three, the one he wanted. Bother, it was locked. He hoped there was no broken glass on the yard wall as he leapt and caught the top with his fingers.

He hauled himself up, one foot on the latch of the door. But the wall was too high for a jump down into the yard. Instead, he walked along the top, balancing precariously, and managed to climb on to the slate roof of the outhouse. As quietly as he could, he crawled up the roof over the scullery.

He had nearly reached the back bedroom

window when his injured knee gave way, and he slipped. He clutched wildly at the roof, breaking the rest of the nails on his sore fingers, and at last managed to get the side of his foot into the gutter to arrest his fall. As he thought of the result if he'd fallen flat on his stomach and nose on to the flags below, he shuddered, and blessed the honest workman who had fixed that gutter so securely.

He lay for a moment, recovering his senses and listening. There was no sound except that of his own laboured breathing. His slide had made surprisingly little noise.

Resisting the temptation to call it a day and get down and knock at the door, he crawled up the roof again. The window he was aiming for was still open a little at the top, so it couldn't be latched. He managed to get his long-suffering finger-tips under the bottom half of the window, trying to cling to the sloping roof by vacuum-suction, pressing his hollow stomach against it. The window squeaked slightly, but inch by inch he managed to raise it until the opening was big enough to get through.

There was no sound from the room. His eyes had got used to the darkness by now, and he could faintly make out a hump in the bed-clothes which told him that the occupant of the room was still sleeping soundly.

He put his arms and head through the window, and got his chest across the sill.

Suddenly the window slammed down on to him with such force that it knocked all the breath out of his body. A moment sooner and it would have guillotined him.

He shouted, "Ken, Ken! It's me, Jim!"

At least, he thought he shouted, but it was only a choked whisper from his crushed chest. Then he passed out for the second time that night – or was it morning, now?

WHEN he came to, he was lying flat on the floor, and someone was trying to pull his trousers off! Before he could open his eyes, he felt warm water on his face. When he was sure he wasn't going to get a soapy flannel in his eyes he opened them, and looked up. Ken's sister Pru was squatting by his head in her pyjamas, bathing his face.

He made a hasty grab at his trousers, and heard Ken's voice from somewhere near his feet.

"All right, Jim," it said. "Can't put you into Pru's bed in these filthy things."

"Bed?" squeaked Jim. "I can't go to bed – I've got an urgent job to do."

"Sh, not so loud," whispered Pru. "You *must* get to bed – you're all in."

"Pru nearly killed you!" murmured Ken. He had the cheek to sound slightly amused about it.

"What happened?" asked Jim, trying to sit up, and groaning as his bruised ribs decided otherwise.

Ken gave another pull at his trousers, but Jim kept a tight hold. He'd nothing else on by now except his shirt.

Pru answered demurely:

"I heard someone on the roof, and thought we had burglars. There wasn't time to get anyone – they all sleep like the dead . . ."

"Good thing, too!" interjected Ken. "Keep your voice down, for Heaven's sake!"

"And in any case," continued Pru more quietly, "I thought the man might be armed and it would be better to take him at a disadvantage."

"You certainly did!" complained Jim.

"So I crept out of bed, arranged the pillow to look like someone asleep, grabbed the cricket bat Ken had left here when we changed rooms, and flattened myself against the wall near the window."

"Some girl!" grunted Jim admiringly. "How is it you didn't knock my head off with the bat?"

"She didn't want to kill the chap," explained Ken. "If she'd knocked him silly he'd probably have fallen off the roof and killed himself."

"Besides," said Pru, "I've always wanted to guillotine someone with a window – nasty of me, I know."

"Look here," said Ken, "we're the ones that want some explanation. Who's been beating you up . . ."

"Apart from me," put in Pru slyly, transferring the soapy flannel from Jim's ears to his hands and arms to his great relief.

"And what did you want me for, and when did you become a Bevin boy? You said nothing about it at Club to-night."

"I'll tell you as we go," said Jim. "I've wasted too much time already, but I couldn't stand until now."

He tried to get up, but even with Pru's help he could only stagger to the bed and sit on it.

"You can't now," commented Ken. He gave a push at Jim's chest, whipped off his trousers, and had him tucked into bed before he knew what was happening.

"Now you'll stay there if I have to slug you!" growled Ken threateningly. "If there's anything to be done, Pru and I will do it."

Jim was about to protest, but looking at Ken's face he could see it would be a waste of time. And, boy! did it feel good to be in bed.

Quickly he told them what had happened to him. He couldn't have wished for a better audience. Their goggling eyes and gasps of astonishment and sympathetic horror as he described the shadow that had looked and sounded like an alligator made him feel for the first time that it was good to be in for some excitement even if he *had* got knocked about. As soon as he mentioned the wounded man, Ken broke in.

"Hang on a minute," he said.

He nipped out of the room. Pru just had time to whisper "You were jolly brave, Jim!" and Jim to reply "What about you, you bruiser?" when Ken returned carrying his clothes and a first aid box, and a pyjama jacket which he threw at Jim. He snapped out the light, and said to Jim: "You can talk while we're dressing."

Jim painfully hauled off his shirt, wriggled into the jacket, and continued his story. By the time he had finished his friends were ready.

"Don't worry, Jim," said Ken. "We'll look after your pal – *and* keep mum about it! Dick Rawlings at the garage will help us – he's on all night, and he'll have a rope and lend a car. I'm sure his wife will give the chap a bed. You can go to sleep and don't worry –

Pru'll go to her old bedroom when we get back, and as there isn't room for two in this bed, I'll sleep downstairs on the couch – if there's any of the night left!"

Ken spoke rapidly and decisively, and Jim felt confident that he and Pru could handle the situation, with Dick's help. Jim closed his eyes with a sigh, and was asleep almost before they shut the door.

They crept cautiously downstairs and out of the front door: then they raced for the garage.

"Why do girls bang their knees together and kick their legs up sideways as they run?" wondered Ken aloud.

"Keep your mind on your own legs, Bandy," retorted Pru, forging ahead.

They told Dick enough for him to get out a small van. The young mechanic was a Northerner and betrayed no excitement or surprise. All he said as they drove off was: "Pru, sit on yer brother's lap if yer can't keep yer knobbly knees out o' my gear lever."

"They're very nice knees, Grumpy," protested Pru.

"Ah'll put ye across *my* knee, young woman, if this 'ere is a leg pull."

They had no difficulty in finding the manhole as it was the only one of its type in the street. Dick prized up the cover and led the way into the clammy cavity beneath. He had brought a torch and it didn't take them long to be sure there was no-one there. The

cellars were as Jim had described them, but there was no lamp and the door at the top of the steps was locked but not bolted.

"So ye were havin' me on," growled Dick ominously. He made a dive for Pru to carry out his threat, but stopped as he trod on something springy. It was a sorbo ball; and except for recent grime it looked as if it had been washed.

"We'd better get out o' this," said Dick grimly. He gave Pru a leg up and hauled Ken after him and drove them back to his garage. "This 'ere is a job for the police," he pronounced.

"But the man asked——" said Pru.

"Ah'm tellin' ye."

"He may be Secret Service," suggested Ken.

"We'll talk about it in the mornin'. Now buzz off 'ome – and keep out o' mischief if ye can."

"You'll not ring them up tonight?" begged Pru.

"Not till I've spoke to Jim myself. Now 'op it."

"Thanks, Dick – you're a sport."

They ran off as he turned back to his work. As they approached their street, Ken said, "You cut along home. I'll just see if there's a light in Jim's house and if there is I'll tell his mother not to worry."

"All right," said Pru, yawning. "Don't forget you're sleeping downstairs."

She ran off towards her home. Just before she reached the front door a car drew up beside her. Two men sprang out and seized her. Before she could utter a sound, something soft was pressed over her mouth and nose and she was smothered with a sweet sickly smell. She struggled frantically but was helpless. Just before she lost consciousness she felt her ankles bang against the running-board as she was dragged into the car.

JIM awoke with a start. Someone was climbing in at the window. It was too late to do Pru's guillotine trick, even if he had been in any condition to move swiftly.

He felt for the pear-shaped switch of the light over the bed, and pressed it. The sudden light dazzled him, as it did the intruder. He was standing by the foot of the bed with his hair wetly plastered down and water dripping from it down his face.

It was someone he recognised, someone he knew well, someone he loved and admired.

It was his cousin Ray.

And the reason why his blood froze as he opened his mouth for a shriek which the man's wet hand quickly stifled, was that Ray was dead. He'd been dead two years. His jet aircraft had crashed somewhere in the sea off Iceland, and the wreckage had been found. The report said there could not possibly have been any survivors.

Did ghosts feel as solid as the clammy hands that gripped him?

To be continued next week

GRANDPA

TRY IT YOURSELF

SIZES OF PLATES 4¾" × 6½" OR 3¼" × 4½" MAKE A LID JUST LARGE ENOUGH TO TAKE PLATE. LENGTH OF BOX APPROX 8" (OR 6" FOR A SMALLER SIZE) PRICK PINHOLE AT INTERSECTION-

-OF DIAGONALS ON THE FACE OF CAMERA. PAINT INSIDE AND OUT WITH MATT BLACK. TO USE, COVER PINHOLE, PLACE ON FIRM OBJECT FACING SUBJECT. EXPOSE FOR 10 MINS COVER PINHOLE, REMOVE PLATE IN DARK ROOM & DEVELOP.

SUBJECT MUST BE IN BRIGHT SUNLIGHT. DO NOT TRY TO TAKE PICTURES OF MOVING OBJECTS.

ADVICE ON YOUR PETS

Keeping Goldfish

By Professor Cameron

FUNGUS
LOOKS LIKE STRANDS OF COTTON WOOL.

12 GALLONS OF WATER

YOU CAN KEEP GOLDFISH EITHER OUTSIDE IN A POND, OR INSIDE, IN A SUITABLE AQUARIUM TANK – NOT IN A SMALL GOLDFISH BOWL. THE BEST TANKS ARE RECTANGULAR IN SHAPE BUT THEY NEED TO BE FAIRLY LARGE: THE RULE IS 'ONE GALLON OF WATER TO EVERY INCH (IN LENGTH) OF FISH" TWO GOLDFISH EACH SIX INCHES LONG NEED TWELVE GALLONS OF WATER. KEEP THE TANK AWAY FROM THE SUN AND HAVE SHADE OVER PART OF TANK

WATER PLANTS

WATER SNAILS

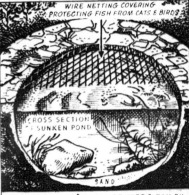

WIRE NETTING COVERING PROTECTING FISH FROM CATS & BIRDS

CROSS SECTION SUNKEN POND

SAND

THE TANK (OR POND) SHOULD BE KEPT CLEAN BY COVERING THE BOTTOM WITH SAND PLANTED WITH PROPER WATER PLANTS. YOUR LOCAL AQUARIST WILL SHOW YOU WHICH TO BUY. PUT RAIN WATER IN AND ALLOW THE PLANTS TO GROW AND THE WATER TO GET REALLY CLEAR BEFORE INTRODUCING FISH

GOLDFISH ARE NOW AVAILABLE AGAIN, BUT BE CAREFUL WHEN YOU BUY ONE TO SEE THAT IT LOOKS HEALTHY. DO NOT BUY ONE WITH DROOPING FINS OR DULL EYES OR WITH FUNGUS (WHICH LOOKS LIKE COTTON WOOL) ON ITS BODY READ GOOD BOOKS ABOUT THE CARE OF FISH.

GOLDFISH FOOD

Bread Crumbs

Chopped Earthworms

Prepared Food

Cooked Peas

Chopped Lettuce

Daphnia

FISH IN PONDS NEED LESS THAN THOSE IN TANKS, BUT SHOULD BE GIVEN A LITTLE PREPARED FOOD AND EARTHWORMS FROM TIME TO TIME. THOSE IN TANKS SHOULD BE FED REGULARLY EITHER WITH A COMMERCIAL FOOD OF GOOD QUALITY OR WITH BREADCRUMBS, CHOPPED EARTHWORMS, CHOPPED LETTUCE AND SMALL AMOUNTS OF COOKED PEAS. IF YOU CAN GET SMALL WATER CRUSTACEANS (SUCH AS DAPHNIA) THESE ARE EXCELLENT.

Golden Orfe

Cat Fish

Water Snails

GOLDFISH ARE 'LEATHER' MOUTHED AND HAVE NO TEETH AND DO NOT DAMAGE OTHER FISH. IT IS BEST TO KEEP THEM ON THEIR OWN OR WITH OTHER HARMLESS FISH SUCH AS THE GOLDEN ORFE OR CATFISH. DO NOT ON ANY ACCOUNT ALLOW STICKLEBACKS OR NEWTS IN THE SAME POND OR TANK. WATER SNAILS ARE USEFUL SINCE THEY ACT AS SCAVENGERS. *John Dyke*

Harris Tweed, EXTRA SPECIAL AGENT

Harris Tweed, EXTRA SPECIAL AGENT

Harris Tweed, EXTRA SPECIAL AGENT

The Case of the Flying Detective

AH, MR. TWEED, GOOD OF YOU TO COME. TODAY I PROPOSE TO MAKE MY LONG EXPECTED ATTEMPT ON THE WORLD BALLOON ALTITUDE RECORD.

GOOD SHOW, PROFESSOR.

AND HERE IS MY NEW BALLOON, FILLED WITH A NEWLY DISCOVERED GAS. BUT I HAVE REASON TO ANTICIPATE SABOTAGE. I SUSPECT THAT DANGEROUS CRIMINALS ARE ON OUR TRACK. THAT IS WHY I'VE ASKED YOU TO COME.

...I THOUGHT THAT WITH YOUR EXPERIENCE YOU MIGHT EXAMINE THE APPARATUS FOR TIME BOMBS AND SO FORTH.

CONDITIONS ARE IDEAL FOR RECORD BREAKING TODAY.

AH, A PERFECT TAKE-OFF!

HOW ON EARTH DID THAT HAPPEN? THE CROOKS HAVE BEEN TOO QUICK FOR US.

LOOK, MR. TWEED, AT LEAST WE CAN TELL OUR HEIGHT... THIS SHOWS IT... IN MILES.

GOSH... I CAN MOVE THE NEEDLE!

CLOUDS, BY JOVE!

PERHAPS WE'LL COME OUT THE OTHER SIDE.

OH DEAR... VANISHED INTO THE CLOUDS... NO MEANS OF TELLING THEIR HEIGHT.

GOOD HEAVENS, THE ALTIMETER SHOWS 15 MILES. WE SHALL FREEZE TO DEATH. QUICK, I MUST REDUCE THE GAS PRESSURE.

NOW I CAN'T STOP THE THING. PHEW, WHAT A SMELL!

THAT'S TORN IT!

HELP! STOP IT!

LOOK... A BALLOON.

LOOKS AS IF IT'S GOT A PUNCTURE.

PERHAPS IT BURST.

IT'S COMING DOWN HERE.

GALA SWIMMING POOL

CONGRATULATIONS, SIR. I HAVE MUCH PLEASURE IN AWARDING YOU THE GALA GOLD CUP FOR THE BIGGEST SPLASH OF THE SEASON!

THAT'S NOTHING, TWEED, YOU HAVE BEATEN THE WORLD ALTITUDE RECORD. SIXTEEN MILES, FIVE FEET TWO INCHES... I HAVE RECOVERED THE ALTIMETER WHICH PROVES IT.

BUT WHAT ABOUT THE SABOTEURS PROFESSOR?

SABOTEURS, MY DEAR CHAP! THERE WEREN'T ANY... I'M GETTING A BIT OLD FOR FLYING AND I THOUGHT YOU WOULD BE JUST THE MAN TO TRY OUT MY NEW BALLOON!

RYAN

CAPTAIN PUGWASH

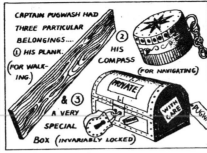

CRICKET COACHING BY LEARIE CONSTAN_

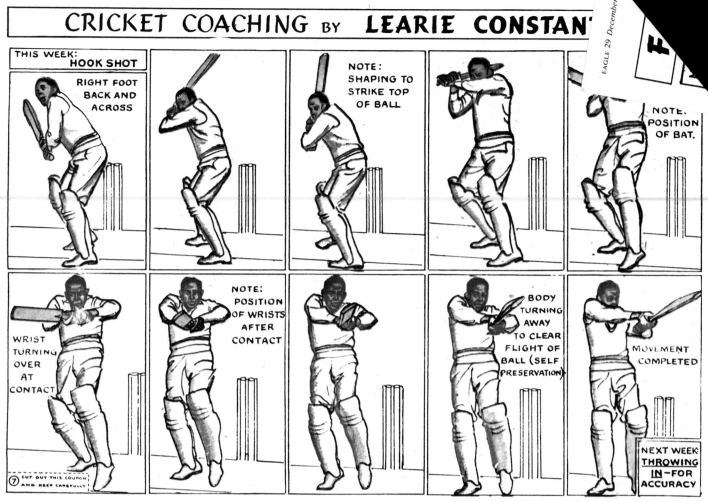

CRICKET COACHING BY LEARIE CONSTANTINE

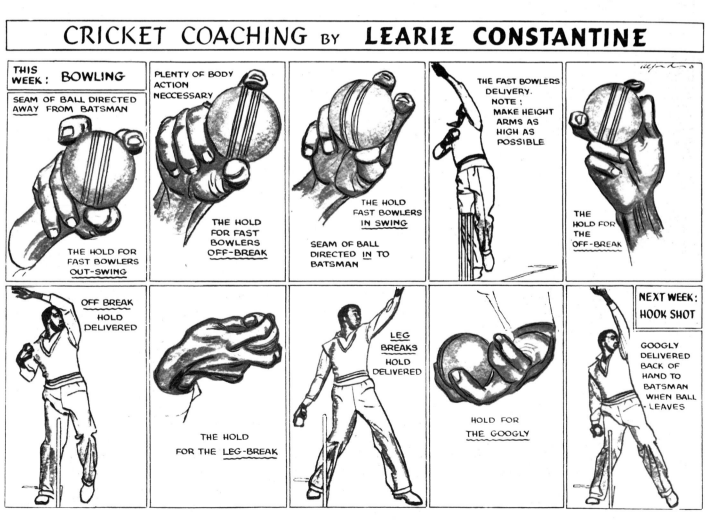

FOOTBALL HINTS BY BILLY WRIGHT
Captain of the Wolves and England

Nº 2. HEADING.

WHEN HEADING A BALL, DON'T JUST LET IT HIT YOU — YOU MUST GIVE A DEFINITE THRUST, AS SHOWN HERE.

THIS SHOWS THE POSITION OF THE FEET IN A STATIONARY 'HEADER'. NOTE HOW THE REAR FOOT IS PLACED TO GIVE THE NECESSARY THRUST TO THE BALL.

YOU SHOULD MEET THE BALL WITH YOUR FOREHEAD, AS THIS IS THE HARDEST PART OF THE HEAD. ALSO, WATCH THE BALL RIGHT UP TO THE MOMENT YOU MEET IT.

BALANCE IS A VERY IMPORTANT POINT IN HEADING — WITHOUT IT YOU CANNOT GET DIRECTION. KEEP YOUR BALANCE BY USING YOUR ARMS LIKE A TIGHT-ROPE WALKER.

THE ART OF HEADING IS TO MEET THE BALL AT THE HIGHEST POINT OF YOUR JUMP. IN THIS WAY, A 5'8" PLAYER CAN BEAT ONE OF 5'11".

ALWAYS HEAD TO ONE OF YOUR OWN MEN — UNLESS IN A TIGHT SPOT.

NEXT WEEK: DRIBBLING.

FOOTBALL HINTS BY BILLY WRIGHT
Captain of the Wolves and England

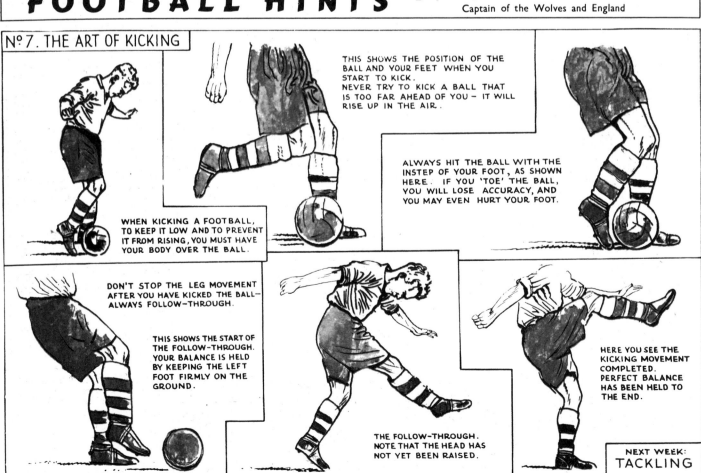

Nº 7. THE ART OF KICKING

THIS SHOWS THE POSITION OF THE BALL AND YOUR FEET WHEN YOU START TO KICK. NEVER TRY TO KICK A BALL THAT IS TOO FAR AHEAD OF YOU — IT WILL RISE UP IN THE AIR.

ALWAYS HIT THE BALL WITH THE INSTEP OF YOUR FOOT, AS SHOWN HERE. IF YOU 'TOE' THE BALL, YOU WILL LOSE ACCURACY, AND YOU MAY EVEN HURT YOUR FOOT.

WHEN KICKING A FOOTBALL, TO KEEP IT LOW AND TO PREVENT IT FROM RISING, YOU MUST HAVE YOUR BODY OVER THE BALL.

DON'T STOP THE LEG MOVEMENT AFTER YOU HAVE KICKED THE BALL — ALWAYS FOLLOW-THROUGH.

THIS SHOWS THE START OF THE FOLLOW-THROUGH. YOUR BALANCE IS HELD BY KEEPING THE LEFT FOOT FIRMLY ON THE GROUND.

THE FOLLOW-THROUGH. NOTE THAT THE HEAD HAS NOT YET BEEN RAISED.

HERE YOU SEE THE KICKING MOVEMENT COMPLETED. PERFECT BALANCE HAS BEEN HELD TO THE END.

NEXT WEEK: TACKLING

LEARN BOXING WITH *Freddie Mills*

LESSON 1.
THE TARGET.
ON GUARD.
THE STRAIGHT LEFT.

FIRST—THE TARGET

TEMPLE
RABBIT PUNCH (A FOUL)
POINT
KIDNEY PUNCH (A FOUL)
MARK (OR SOLAR-PLEXUS)
BELOW THE BELT (A FOUL)
RIGHT! NOW FOR THE FIRST POSITION...

ON GUARD

THIS IS HOW YOUR OPPONENT SHOULD SEE YOU. SQUARE ON YOUR LEFT FOOT—ON THE BALL OF YOUR RIGHT, AND SLIGHTLY CROUCHED. →

LEFT FOOT TOWARDS OPPONENT. RIGHT ARM ACROSS CHEST. ELBOWS WELL TUCKED IN. THE FEET—A WALKING PACE APART.

—READY FOR **THE STRAIGHT LEFT TO THE POINT**

THE START. WATCH THOSE FEET. LEFT FOOT REACHING FORWARD.

⇧ 'FULLY EXTENDED' PISTON MOVEMENT. THE FEET HAVE NOW SLID UP INTO THE 'ON GUARD' POSITION.

AND HERE IS AN ACTUAL SHOT FROM MY FIGHT WITH ENRICO BERTOLA—BUT THIS IS A STRAIGHT LEFT TO THE MARK. NOTICE THE FEET ARE WIDER APART AND REMAIN SO WHEN FULLY EXTENDED. →

NEXT WEEK PARRYING THE LEFT LEAD

CRICKET WITH THE MASTERS BY Patsy Hendren

LEN HUTTON ON PLAYING FORWARD

Patsy Hendren gave you some sound batting advice last week, and he also had some nice things to say about me. What he did not tell you was that he deserves a share of the credit for the record Test score I made in 1938, for it was Patsy who looked after me on the morning of the last day when only thirty-five runs separated me from the highest Test score ever made, and I was as nervous as a kitten. "Don't worry," Patsy told me, "just imagine that you are playing an ordinary innings, and you'll get 'em." And so I did.

How was it done? I can't tell you. But I do know that I would not have done it, or in fact played for England in any Test, had I not made a study of the basic principles of batting that Patsy mentioned last week.

A comfortable, tidy stance, with the left shoulder pointing towards the far wicket, and hands gripping the bat the same distance from each other as from the top of the handle. Left foot in line with the leg stump, pointing towards cover, and right foot pointing towards third man. Weight of the body shared equally between comfortably spaced feet.

There are only two strokes in batting, back and forward, and the two strokes I am going to describe to you are the basis of all the brilliant variations such as the drive, the cut and the hook.

First, the forward shot, played to a medium paced ball pitched well up to the batsman on, or just outside the off stump, and similarly just outside the leg stump. Patsy's student, Ray, is demonstrating these two shots in the pictures below, and very well he is doing them, too.

For both shots get your stance right first, with your eyes toward the bowler. Then begin your backlift with the bat straight behind you as you shift your weight from the left to the right foot. At the top of the back lift, your elbows should be well away from your body to give maximum freedom of movement. Then as you come down with your bat, you should move your left leg forward towards the pitch of the ball, your toe pointing in the direction you intend making the stroke, to the off or on side.

At the time of impact your weight should be fully on your left leg, left knee bent, and head well down over the bat.

Next week we will talk about "playing back".

RAY DEMONSTRATES PLAYING FORWARD TO THE OFF SIDE

1. Stance very good, eyes toward bowler. Hands together cuddling bat, feet evenly balanced. **2, 3.** Good, straight back lift. **5.** Note left foot advancing towards mid-off ready for impact in **7.** Here Ray has his bat a little wide, but he corrects himself in **8.** Here he has elbows well up, head down over ball, commencing the follow through. **9.** This shows the "further follow through". Note Ray's perfect balance after the stroke – there is not a shiver in him, and you could not push him over.

PLAYING FORWARD TO THE ON SIDE

1. Again a good stance. **2.** Ray is lifting his bat correctly above the off stump, and, **3,** advancing his left leg ready to play. **4, 5.** Left leg advances still further to make impact firmer. **8.** Impact. So far the stroke has been good, but as Ray plays the ball towards mid-on you can see that he has not lifted his right heel sufficiently to get full reach, and his left knee should be bent a little more to keep the ball down. The faults are slight, and it is evident that Patsy has a winner in Ray!

JOURNEY INTO AN UNDISCOVERED WORLD

by MACDONALD HASTINGS

"Eagle" Investigator's First Assignment

"DO you read Dan Dare?" said the Editor.

"You bet I do," I said.

"Then why can't you do something like that in real life?"

"What . . . Me? Fly to Venus?"

"You haven't got to fly to Venus. Think of all the exciting adventures waiting for you right here in the world."

"Such as?"

"Well, you could make a parachute jump, for instance. Tell our readers what it's like to bale out."

"I can tell them that now. I've done it; and it's awful."

"Then what about shooting a man-eating lion, or arresting a dangerous criminal or . . . I've got it . . . suppose you make a journey into some unknown territory?"

"The only place left in the world I can think of, which is still relatively unknown," I said snootily, "is the bottom of the sea."

"But that's a splendid idea," said the Editor.

"Is it?" I said.

"Why not?"

"I can think of several good reasons why not. It might be very difficult."

"Difficulties are made to be overcome," said the Editor firmly. "As the Eagle's investigator, you must obviously make a journey to the sea-bed. Now where's the best place to go? The Mediterranean?"

"I suppose so. At any rate, it's warm there."

"All right, off you go. And don't come back till you've got to the bottom of it."

The Frogmen

So I went. First, I called on my friend M. Maurice Vignon, who is an important representative of the French Government in London, and an expert I always consult when I have an assignment on the Continent.

"It's ridiculous," I said, telling my story, "but that's what the Editor wants me to do."

"It isn't ridiculous, my dear boy," said M. Vignon. "It's a splendid idea."

"You, too," I said miserably.

"I will send you to the best man in all France. You will go to Juan les Pins on the Cote d'Azur and meet M. Alexandre Barache of the Hotel Juana. He will introduce you to the Club de la Mer."

"What's that?"

"The Frogmen of France. They will take you to the bottom of the sea."

"As easy as that?"

"Oh, no, it is difficult. It is dangerous, too, my friend. But danger is the spice of sport."

"I see."

"It is a very exclusive club I am introducing you to. It is new, very new. So far, only a few Frenchmen belong to it. You will be one of the first Englishmen to be admitted to the secrets of the sea."

"What sort of apparatus do I use? Am I let down to the bottom in some sort of diving suit?"

"But no. This is a new sport. You will wear a light breathing tube in your mouth, a bottle of compressed air on your back, a pair of goggles and - *voila!* - you are all set to explore the wonders of the deep."

On the evening that I arrived in Juan les Pins I was taken to a café where the ordinary tourists seldom go. In a cubby hole behind the service bar I was introduced to a little group of broad-shouldered, sun-tanned men lounging about, like Mediterranean pirates, on heaps of gear salted and roughened by the sea. They were the members of the Club de la Mer, men who were so soon to be my friends in adventure: Alexandre Barache, the President, whom I had heard about in London; Maleville, the Vice-President, leaning back on a five-foot Roman vase which he himself had recovered from the sea; Laporte, laughing Laporte, the crazy boy and one of the best divers in the club; and Louis Dehoux, "Lulu," who himself was to take me on my underwater journey.

"Lulu" wasted no time. Then and there, he opened a wooden box and showed me the new portable equipment, called the "Scaffendre," which has made it possible for men without diving suits to explore the sea-bed.

In principle, the "Scaffendre" is based on the wartime frogman's suit. But the equipment worn by frogmen is too dangerous for civilian use. The frogmen have to work in secret so it is essential that no air bubbles betray their movements. Consequently, the frogmen breathe pure oxygen which they use again and again as it passes through a chemical filter. But pure oxygen is dangerous stuff for the lungs. It can easily do serious damage. The "Scaffendre" gets round the danger by using ordinary compressed air.

The apparatus was developed immediately after the war by a French naval officer, Jacques Yves Cousteau, together with two friends, Cagnan and Dumas, as a substitute for the clumsy old-fashioned diver's suit. The old-fashioned diver, with his helmet, leaded boots, lifeline and pumping machinery, can only move with difficulty in the circumscribed area where he has been lowered from a specially-equipped ship. But, with the "Scaffendre," the diver is naked and free, and carries only a bottle of compressed air on his back.

Nearly Drowned

As the Frenchmen explained to me the origins of the "Scaffendre", there was a hiss of escaping air as "Lulu" opened the tap of one of the compressed air bottles which were decked in triangular piles round the club's headquarters. Into my mouth he put a rubber device like a boxer's gum shield.

"Now breathe," he said. "Breathe in through the mouth slowly. *Doucement. Doucement.*"

The compressed air, coming to me through a corrugated rubber tube, tasted sweet and rubbery.

"Now breathe out again strongly. No, stronger."

I pushed the bad air out of my lungs through a valve in the apparatus. The bad air passed through, making a noise like the bark of a seal.

"*C'est bon*," said "Lulu," with a satisfied nod.

"Is that all there is to it?"

"That's all," said "Lulu."

But I didn't believe him. And I was right. The first time I tried to use the "Scaffendre" in a shallow pool among the rocks, I nearly drowned myself. It didn't help that, as I went under water for the first time, I heard a party of English tourists telling each other that they wouldn't be surprised if I never came up again. "Lulu," swimming all around me under the water, like a playful dolphin, saw that I was in trouble and helped me out.

"Better tomorrow," he said, patting me on the shoulder as I lay panting on a rock. The next day, and the next, the lessons went on.

At last, I got the hang of it. "Lulu" decided that the time was ripe for me to make my first real dive to the sea-bed.

We put out in a little white motor boat the following afternoon.

At last he found the place we wanted. The anchor went overboard. And, on the deck of the motorboat, I stripped and got ready to follow it.

WANTED - ADVENTURES

HERE is the first article by our new Special Investigator appointed to undertake dangerous and exciting adventures for EAGLE readers. His reports will appear in EAGLE every few weeks.

Have YOU any suggestions as to what he should do? He is prepared to go anywhere, to do anything that can reasonably be done, and is not merely fantastic or completely foolhardy. Also we don't want him to have to go away to the ends of the earth for too long, as there are so many things for him to do here.

If you have adventures that you want him to undertake or any questions you want to ask him write to Macdonald Hastings, c/o EAGLE, 4 New Street Square, London, E.C.4.

First, I tightened a belt, weighted with lead, round my middle. The reason for the lead is to counter-balance the buoyancy of the diver's body in the water. Without it, you'd have to be a very powerful swimmer indeed to get to the bottom. Next, I wetted my diving goggles and adjusted them over my nose and eyes. The purpose of the goggles is to protect the nose and keep the eyeballs clear of the pressure of the sea; wetting them, and wiping the glass with spittle, is a trick to prevent clouding. "Lulu" heaved the iron bottle of compressed air on to my back, and dropped the two-way corrugated breathing tube over my head. I waggled my frog-feet to check that the flappers were fitted firmly and took a deep breath through my nose to make sure that the mask was airtight. All was well. Turning on the air-tap on my back I clenched my teeth on the mouthpiece of the breathing tube.

I raised my thumb to indicate that I was ready. They put out the ladder and, flip-flopping clumsily on my frog-feet, with the compressed air bottle bumping heavily and uncomfortably between my shoulders, I went over the side of the boat.

As I slipped into the sea, the thirty-five pounds of metal that I was carrying seemed to lose its weight. I was lying comfortably on my face on the surface looking down through the plate-glass of my mask into the sun-shafted blueness of the world under the sea.

As I porpoised down, using my frog-feet like paddles to gain depth, I bit hard on to the rubber mouth-piece and concentrated on trying to remember everything that "Lulu" had told me.

"Breathe slowly," he said, "so that the supply of air isn't used up too quickly."

"Lulu" himself can make one bottle of compressed air last for half-an-hour. I wanted to make sure that mine lasted at least fifteen minutes. And, if the air ran out, I had to remember to turn on the emergency tap in the base of the bottle that would give me another five minutes to get to the surface.

On To Ocean Bed

I knew when I had dived fifteen feet because the pressure on my ears increased uncomfortably. "Lulu" had warned me it would happen. When you dive under the sea, your ears react to the increased pressure in exactly the same way that the air pressure affects you when you go up in an aircraft. But, although the pressure in the sea increases the deeper you go, there is no perceptible difference from fifteen feet, when you begin to feel it, until you get down beyond one hundred and twenty feet. The great thing is to clear the pressure early.

"Lulu" told me that, if my ears were hurting, I should rest and swallow saliva until the sensation eased. So I drifted through the clear water to the place where I could see the anchor cable of our boat. I caught on to it with one hand and hung there, in mid-water, swaying on the rope like a piece of weed.

Then I saw "Lulu" himself, with a harpoon gun, sailing past me on his way down to the ocean bed. His limbs were moving like a ballet dancer's; and, as he went by, he gave me a slow wave of greeting and gestured encouragingly towards the bottom.

I felt an almost irresistible wish to talk to him; but, fortunately, I had the good sense to keep my mouth tightly shut on the breathing tube. Letting go of the anchor rope I followed "Lulu" in the tail of the white chain of bubbles rising out of the valve on his back. When I looked up, I saw the floppy bubbles from my own valve piling up like soap-suds over my head. In the silence of the underwater world, all I could hear was the precious air hissing out of my bottle. It reminded me that I was probably using up my reserves too quickly. I breathed more slowly and, watching the white body of "Lulu" snaking among the rocks underneath, I tried to imitate his own casual movements. At last, with my ears singing, I closed my hand on a patch of weed on the ocean bed.

It was quite light. The water, greenish-blue, glittered with mineral fragments, like diamonds, which I had stirred up from the bottom. The sunbeams reached through the clear water and danced over a strange new landscape which, wonderfully, I have been one of the first to see.

The place we were in was a rocky paradise with forests of waving green and brown weed, sandy dells, barnacled caverns, precipitous cliffs, translucent underwater fields and misty blue horizons.

Underwater Forest

As I rolled gently on the ocean bed, keeping my position by grasping a handful of red seaweed growing out of a rock, a shoal of tiny fish, with golden heads and pink bodies swam slowly past me. I followed them along the edge of a forest of waving green flags until I came to a sandy clearing where another fish, a larger one which I guessed was of the perch tribe, came out to have a look at me. With slow deliberation, he swam straight at me and, when I put out my hand, he let me touch him. Afterwards, I tried to catch a fish. But, although I got my palm round one, he flashed clear.

I began to learn that the places to look for the fish – fish as lovely and colourful as precious stones in a blue jewel box – were in the gaps and cavernous holes among the rocks. They sailed out to have a look at me with solemn-eyed interest.

Almost with surprise, I suddenly realized that, in the rough landscape of the sea-bed there are no obstacles for the explorer. When I came to a precipice, I slipped peacefully over the top of it into the valley below. I moved the weeds aside to swim through forests. And, when I came to a hill, I simply let my own buoyancy in the water carry me over the top of it.

I saw "Lulu" swimming round purposefully among the rocks looking, as he told me afterwards, for lobsters and crayfish. But there were none there that day and no fish big enough to be worth shooting with the powerful spring harpoon gun which "Lulu" was carrying with him. But, instead, he found a torpedo, a sinister relic of the war.

I have no notion how long I was on the ocean bed. The bottle on my back stopped hissing. And when I tried to draw in air through the mouthpiece, I caught my breath with alarm.

For a moment I panicked. Then grim necessity brought me to my senses. I turned the emergency tap in the base of the bottle. With a feeling of almost unbearable relief, I tasted the good air again. With unmannerly haste, I reached for the surface.

For the gallant Frenchmen who were with me, our dive was a disappointment. They wanted to take me to a rocky paradise, under a lighthouse, to show me the wreckage of Roman triremes and the remains of Phoenician trading ships. But "Lulu" decided that the swell there was too strong for a novice like me to make a successful dive. We're going treasure-hunting next time.

And what treasures must be waiting for the explorer on the bed of the Mediterranean!

Frogmen under water

For five thousand years that sea has been the busiest shipping route of the world. The Egyptians, the Carthaginians, the Romans, the Greeks, the Barbary· pirates all sailed their oared-galleys on its blue waters. And because the Mediterranean is tideless, and free from underwater currents, the probability is that the ships and their cargoes are still where they settled down on the ocean-bottom.

City of Gold

Already, the experts of the Club de la Mer have gone down 250 feet to the ocean bed; 120 feet is nothing to them. For long dives they take a battery of three bottles which means they can remain in deep water over an hour.

They have recovered complete amphora, the huge earthenware vases in which the ancients used to carry oil, grain and wine. They have found lead anchors from Phoenician ships, signs of a submerged Roman settlement and the wreckage of vessels sunk over two thousand years ago. So far, only a handful of pioneers have been exploring one small area of the Mediterranean. There is almost no limit to the possibilities of discovery in this hitherto inaccessible world. They are talking now of a submerged city off the island of Pantalleria where the monuments are made of solid gold.

After my dive, we all went back to the headquarters of the Club de la Mer where I was initiated as an active member, one of the first Englishmen to be honoured. I was appointed the official London representative and presented with a club badge to wear in the lapel of my coat.

The badge of the Club de la Mer is the signal flag in the International Code for the letter "M": a white cross on a blue base. The "M", of course, stands for "Mer." In the corner of the badge is a single red spot representing "One." So the flag reads "First Under the Sea." As the Eagle's representative, I'm very proud of it.

The Club de la Mer is an association of brave men with a fine rule. The rule of the Club is the rule of the sea; that members

EAGLE 9 April 1954

The p... saved, but the ... with the wreckage in ... an hour one of the members of ... Mer found the wreck and recover... jewels.

But, apart from dives to explore the unknown bed of the sea, the great sport of the Club de la Mer is underwater hunting with special harpoon guns fired with a spring. Later on I hope that I'm going back to hunt the big game fish for you under the sea in Corsica. Where we were diving this time it's not considered sporting to spear the fish because they are too small. The big game fish are the ones the members of the Club de la Mer like to hunt.

I'm sure that you would like to have a chance to make a dive yourself. But I'm afraid that (1) the equipment for deep-sea diving is very expensive: it costs about £100; (2) the sea in Britain is, generally speaking, too cold (about 61 degrees in summer by comparison with 77 degrees in the Mediterranean). Nevertheless, I've brought back to Britain a special new gadget which can be used to look into the water at the seaside or in rivers over here. Another week I'll tell you all about it; that is, if the Editor doesn't kill me in the meantime.

I saw a notice "Don't Disturb" outside his door the other day, and I've got a sneaking suspicion that he's been thinking up new ways of frightening the life out of me. Next thing, I suppose, he'll be wanting me to make an escape from a submerged submarine!

The End

MAKE YOUR OWN TOBOGGAN for 6'10½d.

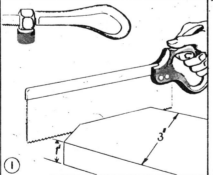
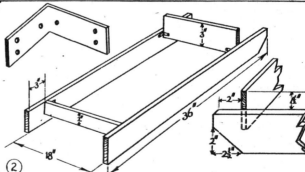
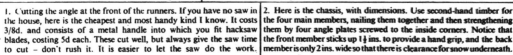

RIGHT at the beginning of this series, which will run in EAGLE from time to time, I will make three promises:

1. I won't suggest any job which the average EAGLE reader can't quite easily do.

2. I won't suggest expensive materials, and with each job I will provide a price list.

3. I won't suggest the use of tools which you haven't got, or can't quite easily get.

To begin with, then, this toboggan. It is strong but light, and it is very easy to make. *H. P. Matthews*

1. Cutting the angle at the front of the runners. If you have no saw in the house, here is the cheapest and most handy kind I know. It costs 3/8d. and consists of a metal handle into which you fit hacksaw blades, costing 5d each. These cut well, but always give the saw time to cut – don't rush it. It is easier to let the saw do the work.

2. Here is the chassis, with dimensions. Use second-hand timber for the four main members, nailing them together and then strengthening them by four angle plates screwed to the inside corners. Notice that the front member sticks up 1½ ins. to provide a hand grip, and the back member is only 2 ins. wide so that there is clearance for snow underneath.

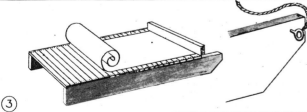

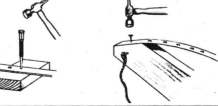

PRICE LIST

7 ft. 6 ins. 3 in. x 1 in. timber (second-hand)	2s 0d
1 ft. 6 ins. 2 in. x 1 in. timber (second-hand)	5½d
Empty box	6d
4 Angle brackets, 3½d each	1s 2d
¾ in. screws for angle brackets, 2½d doz. ...	5d
Hoop iron, nails, etc. about	1s 6d
	6s 10½d

3. The chassis boarded over. For cover boards use wood from empty grocery boxes. One sixpenny box will provide plenty. Drive the nails well home so that there's no chance of tearing your clothes. I've shown a strip of old carpet being nailed over the boards with strong tacks; this is not really necessary, but adds a little something the others may not have. The tow rope is attached to screw eyes as shown.

4. I suggest that the runners are shod with hoop iron. (Try the biggest local ironmonger for this.) This prevents wear and gives you a smoother, faster ride. Here you see a nail punch being used to make the holes for the nails while the iron is laid on a solid block of wood. If you haven't such a punch it will cost about a shilling and will last for ever. Finally, if you're in any doubt as to whether a toboggan is worth making when it may only be used for a week or two each year, forget it. There's no reason why you shouldn't fit wheels to it and use it for all sorts of things throughout the year. If you live in the country it will be just the thing for hauling branches or logs.

BEHIND THE SCENES

A Conference with the Editor about an adventure I'll be telling you soon. With me and Mr Morris are the Assistant Editor, Ellen Vincent, and the Art Editor, Michael Gibson

THIS is EAGLE'S 4th Birthday issue. It's really Special Investigator's fourth birthday, too, because although my first adventure wasn't published until number 27, Marcus Morris gave me my marching orders in that same exciting week when he passed the page proofs of the first issue.

I was in an airliner on my way to dive to the bottom of the Mediterranean, my first assignment for EAGLE, as Marcus Morris was on the line sending the message which, to an editor, is as exciting as the moment when a captain orders his ship to clear for action:

"O.K. to print!"

Now the great gravure presses at Liverpool have been running so long that there must be a lot of you who can't even remember the day when EAGLE spread its wings for the first time.

I have to kick myself to remember that when Marcus Morris and I sat down to plan this feature, I'd never even heard of *Dan Dare*. And, if I'd guessed half the things Marcus Morris was going to let me in for in the next four years, I'd have kicked myself out of his office the same day.

But I didn't. So here I am, coming up for the fourth time to wish myself many happy returns of the day. And to share them, not only with Marcus Morris, but with the whole editorial staff of EAGLE.

You'll remember we awarded the first Special Investigator jack-knife to Reader Peter Rutland, of Burton-on-Trent, for the letter in which he said that he himself would like to know how E.S.I.'s adventures are arranged.

I told him at the time that it's a team job which keeps a lot of people, besides me, jolly busy.

In fact, it's rather like the army, where they say it takes ten men to supply one soldier in the actual fighting line. If you include the compositors who set the type and the machine minders, as well as EAGLE'S editorial staff, it takes really dozens of people to keep me in action.

The Editor is the man in charge of operations. He's the General who decides where I'm to go and what I'm to do, at a conference when the contents of the whole paper are planned.

Usually, we're handling four adventures at the same time. While I'm on my travels collecting a new one, my secretary is already busy making the arrangements and working out my programme for the next one. Meanwhile, in EAGLE office, the Art Editor is laying-out the page (which means arranging pictures and type) for another, and the Assistant Editor is making the final corrections for the printers on a fourth.

And don't forget that, wherever I am, there's a photographer, too. Quite often, his job is more exciting than mine.

A few weeks ago, when you saw me at the helm of a fast Motor Torpedo Boat, I wonder if you asked yourself how it was possible to take the photograph.

What happened was that Chris Ware, the photographer, jumped off our boat on to a rusty hulk anchored in the Solent. Then I put the Motor Torpedo Boat past him at full speed. I ran so close that the wake from the M.T.B. nearly washed Chris Ware overboard. He managed to jump clear, on to what was left of the superstructure of the old hulk, just in time.

Another time, when I was riding in Canada as a cowboy, Chris Ware stood his ground while I galloped a horse straight at him. He didn't take the photograph until I was right on top of him and, although the horse's hooves missed him by inches, he never flicked an eyebrow.

Sometimes, in spite of all our careful arrangements, things go wrong. When we went out to the Longstone Lighthouse, the head-keeper thought we were pirates because the sea had been so rough that we ourselves got out to the lighthouse before

To get the pictures of the fastest ship the Royal Navy's got, Chris Ware had to jump on to an old hulk moored in the Solent.

they could get out the message to him that we were coming.

On some of the jobs with an element of risk to them, I have to sign a paper called "a blood chit", saying that, if anything happens to me, I've got nobody to blame but myself.

But, whatever we plan, wherever we go, everybody knows EAGLE.

Often, when I'm going aboard an aircraft early in the morning to fly on a special assignment for you, the Customs Officers and the airport officials recognize me. Then, if they've got children of their own, they ask me what I'm up to next. But I always keep that a secret because we can never be quite sure that everything is going to work out the way we want it to.

Once I spent three days in the North Sea, without taking my clothes off or going

Next Week's Adventure: Here is Chris Ware photographing me roasting in a steel works!

to bed, trying to catch a big tunny. But we couldn't find the fish.

Another time, in Canada, I wanted to shoot the rapids in a canoe. But I couldn't persuade the Indians to lend me a canoe. Like the Oxford crew last week, they weren't worrying about me; all they were concerned about was that I might hole the canoe on the rocks.

But when everything goes well, as it often does, it makes up for all the disappointments. Then, if I'm out of touch with the office, I'll send a signal like this one cabled to Marcus Morris from the Far North of Canada:

SPECIAL INVESTIGATOR REPORTING FROM THE 62nd PARALLEL. HAVE FOUND GOLD, CONTACTED MOUNTED POLICE PATROL, AND HIRED DOG TEAM. ALL WELL.

One way and another, it's an exciting life. And now I've got to get cracking. No time for birthday parties. I'm on the trail of adventure again.

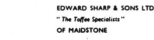

One of the "blood chits" signed when on a special assignment with the Royal Navy

You can watch me roasting in a steel works next week!

Mac Hastings (Eagle Special Investigator) goes

in search of the

Little Yellow Men

ROME

BOAC ARGONAUT FLIGHT
LONDON AIRPORT   CAIRO   KHARTOUM

ENTEBBE

FLIGHT PLAN

By B.O.A.C. Argonaut Flight and Central African Airways, from London Airport to the Kalahari in the Bechuanaland Protectorate

HE'S been a cowboy and an engine-driver; he's been a knife-thrower's and a crack shot's target; he's ridden the Cresta, joined the fire brigade, flown an aircraft, driven a Centurion tank and been on patrol with the Mounties in the snows of the Far North of Canada.

He's dived to the bottom of the sea, made a submarine escape, joined the circus, been hooked into a helicopter, driven a racing car, mined for gold, roasted in a steel works, and ridden with the Household Cavalry.

He's Macdonald Hastings, Your Own Special Investigator, the man who never says "No" to danger.

But everything he's done in the past is nothing to the adventure that Mac is setting out on now. He needs all the luck you can wish him this time. And he'll be reporting, if he comes through, the most exciting real-life story you've ever read. It's for "Eaglers" only.

LOOK OUT FOR EXCITEMENT!

IT'S Lewis, not the Editor of EAGLE – who, heaven knows, has got enough to answer for already – who must take the blame for this adventure.

Major Lewis Hastings is my favourite uncle (or was) and it's his responsibility because, ever since I was a schoolboy, he's been working on me against the day when I should follow in his footsteps the elephant's tracks, the buffalo's spoor and the lion's trail.

For the record, in case you never hear from me again, I'm on my way to the land of Cecil Rhodes, Dr Livingstone and Baden Powell; to the country of big-game hunters and explorers; of thirsty veldt, hippo pools and crocodile swamps; and of everything that crawls and roars and stamps under the African sun.

I haven't a clue what it's going to be like. All I can tell you is that Lewis has lent me his own big-game rifle – his Jeffreys .404 – with the comment that I shall probably be glad of it.

"It's used to looking trouble in the eyes," he says, "and, so far, it's never missed."

I shall try to keep out of trouble; but I shall hold on tight to the rifle. My job this time, as Your Own Special Investigator, is to penetrate into the wilds of the Kalahari in the Bechuanaland Protectorate. If you want to know where that is, you'll find it in the very centre of Southern Africa where the Continent narrows down towards the Cape.

What I'm going for is to see whether I can bring back for you, and for the anthropological department of the Natural History museum, a record of the most primitive men in the world today. I'm setting out in search of the yellow Bushmen of the Kalahari, looking for a disappearing race of men who live now as Prehistoric Man lived in the Stone Age.

To find the little yellow men, I've got to say goodbye to civilization and search them out in what, I'm told, is one of the most untamed, unexplored, and pitiless terrains in the world. I hope I won't make a mess of it.

Lewis has done everything he can to help me. I'm on my way with a personal introduction to Sir Godfrey Huggins, the Prime Minister of the Federation for Rhodesia and Nyasaland. I've got Lewis's big-game rifle, too, which has never missed. It ought to bring me luck.

But I don't mind telling you that my heart is in my mouth. I'm on my way to a land six times the size of Britain, where the sun, so they say, beats down like a slap in the face. Even now, the Kalahari is still largely unexplored. Even now, it's an untamed land where the important people aren't men but buffaloes; it's still the private hunting territory of lion, leopard, giraffe and cheetah, the stamping ground of a million antelope.

"Don't pay too much attention to the map," Lewis says. "You could pass over most of the places marked on it and never know you were there. That lake, for instance, called Ngami. You'll maybe be driving over it in a lorry a few weeks from now."

"Then why is it marked as a lake?"

"It *was* a shallow lake when Livingstone discovered it nearly a hundred years ago. Since then, it's dried up into a grassy plain. That's typical of the Kalahari. You're going into a country which man has never conquered and in which even Nature has never made up its mind."

"What do you reckon my chances are of finding the little yellow men?"

"I can only tell you that during the many years I was hunting and soldiering hereabouts, I saw the Bushmen twice. Once, in the German-West campaign in the First World War, I came across one asleep by the side of a giraffe he'd killed with a poisoned arrow. Another time, I found a family of them when I was on a hunting expedition. We discovered their meat hung up in the trees and we waited until they were sufficiently hungry to come up to us."

"What are they like?"

"You can't mistake the Bushmen when you find them. They're pygmies, yellow in colour, not black, with odd hair that grows in tufts on their heads. They're wanderers without homes and without property; and the real Bushmen are as wild as the animals they hunt for a living."

"How many Bushmen are left?"

"Nobody has ever had a chance to count them; maybe a thousand altogether, in an area of about 350,000 square miles."

"At one time, they spread all over Southern Africa. They were driven out by the Bantus, and subsequently by the coming of the white man. In the end, the only place where they could exist in peace was in the parts of Africa like the waterless Kalahari, where other men feared to live."

"But how do the Bushmen survive?"

"That's what you're going to the Kalahari to find out."

"What's the climate like?"

"When you are there it will be well into the hundreds. This is the hottest season. But it's the time, just before

The man who started it all, Major Lewis Hastings, M.C.

the rains, when the cover has been burnt down by bush fires, and you find the game moving towards water. Where the game is, your little yellow men will be."

We sat together, Lewis and I, in front of a blazing fire in the smoking room of a London club. Outside, the rain was sluicing through the gutters, making a dismal tattoo against the windows. And I was sitting there, staring into the red hot caverns in the coals, wondering what my chances were of finding the little yellow men in the sun-baked waste called the Kalahari.

The map had never looked so big and I don't think that I have ever felt so insignificant.

"Do you realize what you've taken on?" I kept on telling myself. But my air passage to Africa was already booked.

EAGLE CLUB

AND EDITOR'S PAGE

13 *April,* 1951

The Editor's Office
EAGLE
4 *New St. Square, London,* E.C.4

THE time has gone so quickly during the last year that it is difficult to realise that we are now celebrating EAGLE's first birthday.

We little thought a year ago, when the first issue went to press, how widely EAGLE would have spread, and how firmly it would have become established among readers of all ages.

It has been a most exciting time, and one of the best things in it has been the contact we have made with you, our readers – both by way of letters of which we get a great number each week, and also through the various expeditions which EAGLE Club has organized.

We wish we could have given you in celebration of our birthday a bumper number with more pages and many new features. Unfortunately, the paper situation is so difficult that we are only able to give you the usual number of pages, but we have tried to include one or two features of special interest. And on this page we have some specially important announcements to make, which will appeal particularly to Club members.

We are going to celebrate our birthday in four ways.

1 BIRTHDAY PARTIES

We are arranging big birthday parties in six of the biggest towns in the British Isles, to which we are inviting selected members of EAGLE Club. They will take place every day during the week beginning April 23rd, and they will be held at Glasgow, Newcastle, Manchester, Birmingham, Bristol and London.

In each of these places there will be a party and entertainment, and I shall be present at each of them, together with Frank Hampson, our *Dan Dare* artist.

We wish it was possible to invite all Club members living in these towns, but there are so many of you that this is quite impossible. So will those of you who live in or near any of these six towns write in to me saying that you would like to be invited. All letters should reach us not later than 17th April.

On the 18th April the letters will be put in a big drum, and I shall pick out one hundred for each town. Those who are chosen will then receive an official invitation telling them where and when the party is to be held. Address your letters to PARTIES, EAGLE Club, Colley House, London E.C.4.

2 PRESENTS

We are going to do something for those who do not win an invitation to the parties. We shall be sending out nearly 3,000 gift parcels to Club members in all parts of the country. These 3,000 will be chosen by ballot.

3 SPECIAL COMPETITION

Here is a special competition open to all our readers. There will be £50 in prizes, but instead of sending money to the winners we are going to give them the choice of a really good piece of sports equipment. There will be 10 prizes awarded. The winners will have the choice of a cricket bat, football, tennis racket, hockey-stick, lacrosse stick.

Here is the competition:- I want you to imagine that these EAGLE characters meet together – DAN DARE, DIGBY, P.C. 49, JEFF ARNOLD, HARRIS TWEED and his boy, and TOMMY WALLS. Write down the conversation that you think might take place between them.

Send your entries to BIRTHDAY COMPETITION, EAGLE, Colley House, London E.C.4, giving your name, address, age and Club number (if any).

4 MORE PRIZES

As this is our Birthday issue we are also for this week doubling the number of prizes for competitions in Competition Corner which you will find on page 5. There will be 24 prizes for each competition, and these, too, are open to all readers.

In addition to these four Birthday extras, we hope you will like the two Special Announcements on this page – and take part in them.

MUG OF THE YEAR

IT was very difficult to decide from among all the MUG awards we have made, the one who deserved the special honour of being MUG OF THE YEAR.

You will see on this page the decision we finally reached. We are inviting John Grimes to London and offering him a holiday at EAGLE's expense. He will also be presented with a special certificate and badge.

We shall, of course, be continuing our MUG Awards during next year, choosing one each month as MUG of the Month. In 1950 MUGS of the Month were, you remember, taken on a holiday to Italy.

EAGLE CLUB PLANS

WE are making lots of plans for Club activities during the coming year – organizing, on an even bigger scale, the various schemes we have carried out during the past year. For example, local visits, holidays at home and abroad, and so on.

We hope we shall get a great many more members of EAGLE Club during the next year. Because of all the things we are planning to do for members, we have had to decide to put up the subscription to the Club to 2/- instead of 1/6. This increase will date from today, so those of you who have not yet joined and want to do so should write to EAGLE Club, Long Lane, Aintree, Liverpool 9, giving your name, address, age and school, and enclosing a Postal Order for 2/-.

Those of you who are already members of EAGLE Club will shortly be receiving from me a special illustrated Report giving an account of our activities so far. This will contain a form for rejoining the Club for another year. So if you are already a member, do not write in to renew your membership until you receive this Report from me.

FORTNIGHTLY COMPETITION

THIRDLY, you know that we have during this last year been running special competitions *for Club members.* We have now decided to have them once a fortnight instead of once a month to give many more of you a chance of taking part in the visits to London and the other prize-winning expeditions we organize.

Here is the first Fortnightly Competition. This is for Club members only. It should appeal particularly to those of you who are interested in motor sports, and there is a thrilling prize.

I want you to write a short story of which the plot deals with some form of motor or motor-cycle racing. The story can be any length up to 2,000 words. Prizes will be awarded for the best written and most interesting.

The senders of the six best entries will have the thrill of being *flown* to the Isle of Man to see the Senior International Tourist Trophy Motor Cycle Race – one of the world's fastest. In addition, we shall choose three prize-winners who live in the Isle of Man.

Send your entries to Fortnightly Competition, EAGLE, Colley House, London E.C.4, to reach us not later than 25th April, giving your name, age, address and Club number.

BERTRAM MILLS Circus will be appearing at Colchester from April 23rd to 25th and we are taking a party of 20 members of EAGLE Club, free of charge, to see the show on April 23rd at 4.30 p.m. This is for members living within 5 miles of Colchester, and those of you who would like to go should write as soon as possible to "Circus", EAGLE Club, Colley House, New Street Square, London E.C.4, giving your name, address and Club number. The first 20 applications opened will be chosen.

Yours sincerely,
MARCUS MORRIS

MUG OF THE YEAR

JOHN GRIMES
7 Beach Grove, Cleaton Estate, South Shields

Why has thirteen-year-old John Grimes been chosen as MUG of the year? Because he is a first-class example of the sort of person the MUG's badge exists to honour.

John is a cripple and the eldest of a family of six. Many household responsibilities fall upon him as his mother is not too fit. But it was the way he responded to an especially testing time that marks him out as a hero of everyday life. John was working hard to try to qualify for Grammar School Entrance. His mother went sick with quinzy and pneumonia and his brother, Mike, with pneumonia. John stayed away from school to look after them and the home. He stayed up with his brother all night sometimes. He was with him when he died. He tended his mother all night too. Yet, even under this strain – which lasted for weeks – John did what he could to prepare himself for Grammar School Entrance. He was back at school in time for the examination and, out of 500 pupils, he alone gained a special place at Corby Hall School, Sunderland.

Always thoughtful for others, John reacts to difficulties by putting out a greater effort to overcome them. Our heartiest congratulations, John!

TWO SPECIAL ANNOUNCEMENTS:

FIRST:

EAGLE FAMILY DAY

WE have decided to make April 14th every year (the day on which EAGLE first came out) into EAGLE FAMILY DAY.

The idea is that on this day EAGLE readers should think especially of their own families – parents, brothers, sisters – and resolve to do everything they can to make the day happier for their family.

Most of you will know that for hundreds of years there has been Mothering Sunday when children do what they can to help their mothers, and perhaps give them a small gift of violets or a simnel cake as a sign of their love.

EAGLE FAMILY DAY has the same idea behind it. I am not going to suggest exactly what you should do for your families each April 14th. It is up to you to think how you can help them most. But it should be more than just being ordinarily useful about the house – helping with the washing up and so on – which you probably do anyway.

There are no prizes being awarded for EAGLE FAMILY DAY, but I hope as many of you as possible will write in to me and tell me what special thing you have done on April 14th. The first EAGLE FAMILY DAY is, of course, tomorrow, so you won't have much time to think what you are going to do, but write and tell me about it.

AND:

EAGLE CHRONICLERS

A JOB FOR EVERYONE

WE feel that EAGLE and its readers should play their full part in the Festival of Britain this year. We are, therefore, launching on a nation-wide scale, a brand new scheme to enable *you* to play *your* part, and we hope that all of you will join in. Our EAGLE *Chroniclers Scheme* is something which can last for a very long time, and which can be of real benefit to future generations.

This is how it works:-

How is it that you know that King Alfred burnt the cakes, and that Lady Godiva saved Coventry from excessive taxation? It is only because someone at the time who lived near where these incidents happened took the trouble to write them down, and their records have been passed on to us. But thousands of similar events, which would have been of great interest to us, have been lost because there was no one to chronicle them.

During this Festival of Britain year especially, a great deal of local history may be made. Need the record of all this be lost, or can we EAGLE readers help in chronicling it for the future?

Forming a Group

We suggest that *Eaglers* in the same school or the same district should form a group, and together plan to produce a Chronicle of their own town or district or village. They should invite some one older (perhaps their headmaster or headmistress) to act as Editor-in-Chief, and give advice.

Then each member of the Group, who would be known as EAGLE Chroniclers, should be entrusted with one particular part of the Chronicle. Here are some of the subjects into which it could be divided:-

1. Brief historical notes on your District, including local Notables and Folk Lore.
2. Interesting Architecture of the District.
3. Local Government activities.
4. Plans of your District (with details of population, rates, roads, transport, etc.).
5. Social Life of District (Youth Organizations, Institutes, Literary Societies, etc.).
6. Local Flora and Fauna.
7. Local Art (drawings of beauty spots, etc.).
8. Local Sport (1951 records, teams, etc.).
9. Festival Activities of the District. Notable visitors, etc.

These subjects could easily be divided up into smaller sections, or you may be able to think of many more subjects to deal with. Every section could be illustrated with photographs and drawings.

Twelve Prizes

When you have collected all the material together, you should then hand it over to the one in your school or district who is the best "pen-man", who could write it out neatly.

EAGLE will give a prize to the 12 groups who produce the best Chronicle.

This scheme of EAGLE Chroniclers is something in which almost everyone can take part, because it does not matter how big your group is. All you have to do in the first place is to call a meeting of EAGLERS you know and make your plans.

When you have formed your group, the one of you who is appointed as Chairman should write in to me telling me what district you are going to cover. We will give you all the advice and help we can. Later on we shall make arrangements for all the Chronicles produced to be judged to find the 12 prize-winners. We shall, of course, give you plenty of time to make your Chronicle and shall not start the judging until the autumn.

THE GREAT ADVENTURER

THE GREAT ADVENTURER

JERUSALEM 1900 YEARS AGO SAUL of TARSUS HAS INCITED THE MOB TO STONE STEPHEN — A NAZARENE (CHRISTIAN)

WE MUST ROOT OUT ALL THESE STUPID NAZARENES

STOP THEIR PREACHING — THROW THEM INTO PRISON!

THE NEXT DAY SAUL MAKES HIS WAY TO THE HOUSE OF CAIAPHAS, THE HIGH PRIEST . .

SAUL OF TARSUS, SIR

AH, COME IN, SAUL

I WAS VERY PLEASED WITH THE WAY YOU HANDLED THAT STEPHEN BUSINESS YESTERDAY, MY BOY!

AND NOW, I UNDERSTAND, YOU WANT TO GO AND STOP THE SPREAD OF THIS NEW NAZARENE BELIEF IN DAMASCUS?

I CAN STAMP IT OUT IN DAMASCUS, SIR, IF YOU WILL GIVE ME YOUR COMMISSION TO GO THERE & ARREST ANY NAZARENES I FIND!

IT'S DONE, SAUL — YOU SHALL GO! BUT FIRST I SUGGEST THAT YOU QUESTION SOME OF OUR NAZARENE PRISONERS — YOU MAY PICK UP SOMETHING USEFUL

COME ON OUT, YOU NAZARENE SCUM — THERE'S A GENTLEMAN TO SEE YOU!

IT'S SAUL OF TARSUS!

HERE ARE THE WRETCHES YOUR HONOUR

THE GREAT ADVENTURER

THE GREAT ADVENTURER

LISTEN, RUTH — WE HAVE SOME VERY IMPORTANT NEWS — BEND CLOSER SO THE GUARD WON'T HEAR!

·JERUSALEM· 1900 YEARS AGO. IN THE PRISON COURTYARD RUTH, *A NAZARENE (CHRISTIAN)* IS TAKING FOOD TO THE NAZARENES IN THE CELLS

SAUL OF TARSUS IS GOING TO DAMASCUS TO-MORROW TO PERSECUTE THE NAZARENES THERE

YOU MUST TELL PETER TONIGHT TO TRY AND GET WORD TO THEM

THAT NIGHT RUTH GOES TO THE SECRET MEETING OF THE NAZARENES

SO IT'S DAMASCUS NOW, IS IT? WE'LL SEND A WARNING BY THE NEXT CARAVAN.

THERE WON'T BE TIME, PETER HE'S LEAVING IN THE MORNING AND WILL BE RIDING HARD — YOU KNOW SAUL— HE'LL BE USING THE BEST HORSES HE CAN FIND!

HE WON'T HAVE ONE AS GOOD AS MY FARA

YOU'RE RIGHT BARNABAS— FARA IS A FINE HORSE

AND THE ROMAN GUARDS AT THE DAMASCUS GATE ARE USED TO SEEING ME RIDE IN AND OUT

I'M PRETTY SURE I CAN GET THROUGH WITHOUT A PASS

BUT SUPPOSE YOU RUN INTO SAUL? HE KNOWS YOU — YOU WERE BOYS TOGETHER

I WON'T BUMP INTO MASTER SAUL I'LL TAKE THE EASTERN ROAD THROUGH JERICHO

NEXT MORNING

KEEP YOUR EYES OPEN BARNABAS — THAT JERICHO ROAD IS THICK WITH BANDITS!

FRANK HAMPSON

THE GREAT ADVENTURER

JERUSALEM 1900 YEARS AGO

AN ARMED CAVALCADE SWEEPS OUT OF THE CITY AS SAUL OF TARSUS RIDES TO DAMASCUS TO PERSECUTE THE NAZARENES (CHRISTIANS) THERE

HALT — WE'LL STOP AT THIS INN FOR THE NIGHT.

WHAT'S WRONG WITH SAUL? HE'S HARDLY SPOKEN SINCE WE STARTED — AND IF YOU SAY ANYTHING HE BITES YOUR HEAD OFF!

LOOK AT HIM THERE BROODING.

HE'S BEEN LIKE THAT EVER SINCE THAT CHAP STEPHEN WAS STONED.

AND SINCE HE QUESTIONED THOSE NAZARENE PRISONERS.

I THINK THERE'S SOMETHING STRANGE HAPPENING TO HIM — IN HIS HEAD.

AH WELL WE SHOULD WORRY WHATEVER IT IS! DON'T SUPPOSE HE'LL RAISE OUR PAY!

NIGHT FALLS ON THE INN

BUT AWAY TO THE EAST UNKNOWN TO SAUL, BARNABAS RIDES THE DANGEROUS EASTERN ROAD IN A BID TO WARN THE DAMASCUS NAZARENES

TIRED FARA?

I'M AFRAID WE MUST PUSH ON...

BUT I'LL WALK FOR A SPELL...

... AND WE'LL PROBABLY BE ABLE TO REST UP FOR A COUPLE OF HOURS IN THE MORNING.

THE GREAT ADVENTURER

THE GREAT ADVENTURER

ROMANS!

BARNABAS, RIDING TO DAMASCUS, TO WARN THE NAZARENES THERE AGAINST SAUL OF TARSUS HAS BEEN CAPTURED BY BANDITS. SUDDENLY THE BANDITS CAMP IS ATTACKED BY A ROMAN PATROL

STEADY FARA—THIS MAY HELP US!

MERCY!

ALRIGHT—TAKE THE REST OF THEM PRISONER—THEY'LL MAKE FOOD FOR THE GALLEYS!

HELLO—WHO'S THIS?

WE FOUND HIM TIED UP SIR—HE CLAIMS HE WAS CAPTURED AND ROBBED BY THE BANDITS LAST NIGHT

I'M A CITIZEN OF JERUSALEM, CENTURION—TRAVELLING TO DAMASCUS ON A LAWFUL JOURNEY WHEN I WAS SET UPON BY THESE MEN

HM ALRIGHT, UNTIE HIM & GIVE HIM HIS HORSE BACK

YOU'LL HAVE TO COME WITH US TO THE FORT AT CAPERNAUM AND SHOW YOUR PASS TO THE LEGATE

MY PASS!!

SORRY, CENTURION—CAN'T STOP NOW

HEY!

THE GREAT ADVENTURER

DAMASCUS AT LAST!

1900 YEARS AGO.
SAUL OF TARSUS ARMED WITH THE HIGH PRIESTS COMMISSION TO ARREST ALL NAZARENES (CHRISTIANS) DRIVES HIS MEN ON UNDER THE HOT SYRIAN SUN.

PERHAPS WE'LL GET SOME REST NOW

NOT IF I KNOW SAUL — WE'LL BE CHASING NAZARENES AS SOON AS WE REACH DAMASCUS

YOU'D THINK THE WHOLE WORLD DEPENDED ON US GETTING THERE. I'VE NEVER RIDDEN. SO HARD IN MY LIFE!

OH — HE CAN'T BEAR TO THINK OF ANY NAZARENES SLIPPING THROUGH HIS FINGERS!

AAAH!

WHAT IS IT?

IT'S A THUNDERBOLT

IT'S THE END OF THE WORLD!

IT'S A VISITATION

HELP!

SAUL'S STILL THERE IN THE MIDDLE OF IT!

HE — HE'S TALKING!

IT'S FADING NOW . . . . . .

WHAT'S THE MATTER WITH HIM?

MEANWHILE, ON THE EASTERN ROAD, BARNABAS GALLOPS ON IN HIS BID TO WARN THE DAMASCUS NAZARENES.

CORTEZ, CONQUEROR OF MEXICO

FOR A MONTH CORTEZ SAILS WESTWARD – AND THEN . . .

SEÑOR CORTEZ! THERE'S LAND AHEAD

A STRANGE LAND IT SEEMS. THE NATIVES OF CUBA NEVER BUILT ROADS OR HOUSES LIKE THOSE.

THEY'RE COMING ABOARD. TREAT THEM WELL, ALL OF YOU.

SEND FOR THE SOLDIER, GERONIMO. HE SPEAKS INDIAN DIALECTS. PERHAPS HE CAN TALK TO THESE PEOPLE.

I CANNOT UNDERSTAND A WORD, SEÑOR CORTEZ.

WAIT! WHO HAVE WE HERE?

YOU'LL UNDERSTAND ME, WHITE STRANGER. I HAVE LEARNT SOME OF YOUR DIALECT FROM A NATIVE WHOSE CANOE WAS BLOWN ON TO OUR COAST SOME YEARS AGO.

WHAT COUNTRY IS THIS? WHO IS ITS RULER?

THE EASTERN SHORE OF THE AZTEC KINGDOM OF OUR EMPEROR, MONTEZUMA.

HIS EMPIRE STRETCHES FIVE HUNDRED MILES WESTWARD TO ANOTHER OCEAN. HE LIVES IN THE CITY OF MEXICO AND HAS MORE THAN A MILLION MEN.

IT IS DANGEROUS FOR US TO TREAD THE SOIL OF THIS GREAT EMPIRE.

ALL THE MORE REASON FOR US TO APPEAR BOLD. GET THE SOLDIERS ON LAND AT ONCE.

CORTEZ, CONQUEROR OF MEXICO

UNAFRAID OF MONTE-ZUMA, CORTEZ LANDS ON THE MEXICAN COAST

THAT COLUMN OVER THERE— PERHAPS THEY COME FROM THE EMPEROR.

IT IS LED BY TWO NOBLEMEN FROM THE ROYAL COURT.

THEY BRING GREETINGS FROM MONTEZUMA AND ASK WHENCE YOU COME

FROM ACROSS THE SEA. OUR KING IS THE MOST POWERFUL IN THE WORLD.

NO KING IS AS GREAT AS MONTEZUMA. BUT HERE ARE A FEW GIFTS FOR YOUR RULER.

I ACCEPT THEM GRATEFULLY

BY SAINT JAGO! IT'S NEARLY ALL MADE OF GOLD.

THE VERY EYES OF THE BIRDS ARE RUBIES!

BUT THERE IS ONE OTHER MATTER..

MONTEZUMA DOES NOT WISH TO HAVE WHITE MEN IN HIS COUNTRY. YOU MUST LEAVE AT ONCE. FAREWELL.

WHAT NOW, HERNANDO? AFTER THE EMPEROR'S WARNING, OUR MEN WILL BE SCARED TO REMAIN HERE.

YOU ARE RIGHT. THEY FEAR THE AZTEC ARMIES.

I'LL FORCE THEM TO REMAIN HERE. SERGEANT, MARCH THE MEN ALONG THE COAST AND SEE THEY DO NOT COME BACK UNTIL SUNSET.

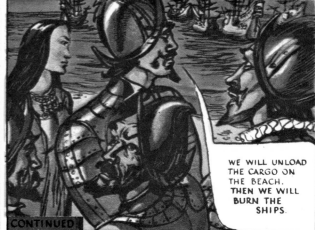

WE WILL UNLOAD THE CARGO ON THE BEACH. THEN WE WILL BURN THE SHIPS.

CONTINUED

CORTEZ, CONQUEROR OF MEXICO

THE SOLDIERS FEAR MONTEZUMA AND WISH TO SAIL AWAY. TO STOP THEM, CORTEZ BURNS THE VESSELS AFTER UNLOADING THE CARGOES

THE MEN ARE IN SIGHT, CORTEZ SOON THEY WILL REACH CAMP.

PERHAPS THE AZTECS ATTACKED THE CAMP.

AYE, WHO ELSE WOULD HAVE BURNED OUR VESSELS?

WHAT HOPE OF ESCAPE NOW?

ESCAPE? OUR ONLY ESCAPE WILL BE DEATH.

THOSE VESSELS LEAKED. NEVER COULD WE HAVE RETURNED TO HISPANIOLA IN THEM. LET US GO FORWARD INTO MONTEZUMA'S KINGDOM.

CORTEZ IS RIGHT. LET US RISK IT.

CORTEZ PERSUADES HIS MEN TO FOLLOW. THEY MARCH INLAND.

YOUR PEOPLE ARE FRIENDLY, MARINA. NO DANGER HERE

AHEAD IS THE CITY OF CHOLULA WHOSE CITIZENS ARE TREACHEROUS

WHAT BEAUTY! NEVER HAVE I SEEN SO FAIR A CITY.

THE INHABITANTS WILL WELCOME YOU, BUT REMEMBER MY WARNING.

MARINA SAYS THERE IS DANGER FOR US IN THIS CITY.

SHE MUST BE WRONG. THESE PEOPLE ARE VERY FRIENDLY.

LET US RID OUR CITY OF THESE SPANIARDS.

THERE IS DANGER, CORTEZ! THE CITIZENS SAY YOUR MEN HAVE GROWN CARELESS. YOU WILL BE ATTACKED AT DAWN TOMORROW.

FAITHFUL MARINA! YOU WERE RIGHT AFTER ALL.

CORTEZ, CONQUEROR OF MEXICO

MARINA HAS WARNED COR-TEZ THAT THE WARRIORS OF CHOLULA ARE PREPARING TO ATTACK THE SPANIARDS AT DAYLIGHT.

WE WILL OPEN THE GATES AND MARCH TOWARDS THE OPEN COUNTRY. BE READY TO DEFEND YOURSELVES... NOW, FORWARD!

THE PYRAMID, OLEA! THESE STONES ARE BEING HURLED FROM ITS SUMMIT. TAKE MEN AND ATTACK THE WARRIORS ON TOP

KEEP CLOSE TOGETHER! DRIVE THEM OVER THE EDGE!

THE PYRAMID IS CLEAR, HERNANDO.

WELL DONE, OLEA. NOW LET US GET CLEAR OF THE CITY BEFORE THEY ATTACK AGAIN.

I WILL STILL MARCH TO THE CITY OF MEXICO, MARINA.

BEYOND THOSE MOUNTAINS LIES THE CITY. DO YOU DARE PASS THROUGH THEM, SENOR CORTEZ?

I WILL NOT TURN BACK, AND MY MEN WILL GO WITH ME.

WE WILL DIE BEFORE WE REACH THIS CITY OF WHICH SENOR CORTEZ SPEAKS.

BY MY OATH! I AM NEARLY DEAD ALREADY OF THIS COLD.

COURAGE JOSE! MARINA SAYS WE ARE NEAR THE SUMMIT. SOON WE SHALL ACTUALLY SEE THE CITY OF MEXICO.

IF I AM NOT FROZEN TO DEATH BY THEN, HERNANDO!

LOOK! THERE LIES OUR PROMISED LAND!

CORTEZ CONQUEROR OF MEXICO

CORTEZ AND HIS MEN REACH MEXICO

MONTEZUMA? HE WILL NEVER ATTACK US!

AND TO THINK WE WERE AFRAID OF ENTERING THIS COUNTRY!

WHY HAS MONTEZUMA CHANGED HIS MIND, MARINA? ONLY A WHILE AGO HE THREATENED US AND NOW EVERYONE IS FRIENDLY.

YOU SO QUICKLY DEFEATED THE AZTECS AT CHOLULA THAT MONTEZUMA BELIEVES YOU ARE GODS.

BEHOLD OUR REWARD, JOSE, FOR THE DANGERS WE HAVE FACED.

THE CITY THAT FLOATS LIKE A LOTUS FLOWER ON THE WATER.

THE EMPEROR HIMSELF IS COMING TO MEET YOU. GO FORWARD ON FOOT, CORTEZ. TO GREET HIM.

WELCOME TO MEXICO, O STRANGER

GREETINGS, O ROYAL MONTEZUMA.

ONE OF MY PALACES IN THE CITY SHALL BE YOUR HOME. THIS CHIEFTAIN WILL LEAD YOU TO IT. I SHALL SPEAK WITH YOU LATER.

A MAGNIFICENT HOME FOR US, HERNANDO. I NEVER SAW AS BIG A SPANISH CASTLE.

MONTEZUMA COMES TO STAY WITH CORTEZ AT THE PALACE AND THEY BECOME GOOD FRIENDS. BUT THE PEOPLE OF MEXICO GROW JEALOUS.

OUR EMPEROR IS TOO FRIENDLY WITH THESE STRANGERS.

I HEAR HE HAS GIVEN THEM PRESENTS OF GOLD AND SILVER.

THE WHITE MEN BEHAVE AS IF THEY OWNED OUR CITY.

OUR WARRIORS ARE BEING SMUGGLED DAILY INTO THE CITY FROM THE MAINLAND.

WE HAVE THESE SPANIARDS LIKE RATS!

THEY WILL NEVER ESCAPE ALONG THE CAUSEWAY... THEY WILL DIE IN OUR FIRST ATTACK.

CORTEZ, CONQUEROR OF MEXICO

THE AZTECS OF MEXICO GROW JEALOUS OF THE SPANIARDS' FRIENDSHIP WITH MONTEZUMA. THE YEAR IS 1520

WHY SO FEW PEOPLE ABOUT? PERHAPS MARINA SPOKE THE TRUTH WHEN SHE WARNED US THAT THE PEOPLE WERE PLOTTING TO KILL US.

I DO NOT LIKE THESE EMPTY STREETS. THERE IS MISCHIEF ABOUT, HERNANDO.

DEATH TO THEM!

DEATH!

DEATH!

WE WILL ATTACK AT NOON. EVERY WARRIOR IN THE CITY WILL JOIN US. DEATH TO THESE WHITE STRANGERS.

TO ARMS! TO ARMS! HO, GUNNERS! PREPARE YOUR CANNON. THE AZTECS ARE UPON US!

THEY WILL ATTACK AGAIN IN A MINUTE. WHERE IS CORTEZ?

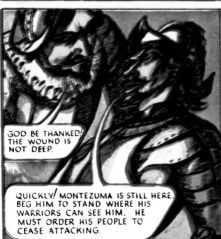

GOD BE THANKED! THE WOUND IS NOT DEEP.

QUICKLY! MONTEZUMA IS STILL HERE. BEG HIM TO STAND WHERE HIS WARRIORS CAN SEE HIM. HE MUST ORDER HIS PEOPLE TO CEASE ATTACKING

STOP! I COMMAND YOU STOP! THESE SPANIARDS ARE MY FRIENDS. I HAVE PROMISED THEM SAFETY IN OUR CITY. STOP!

THESE MADMEN HAVE KILLED THEIR OWN EMPEROR, JOSE.

AND NOW THEY WILL NOT STOP UNTIL THEY HAVE KILLED US AS WELL.

CORTEZ, CONQUEROR OF MEXICO

95

A FAMOUS BRITISH EXPRESS — THE "ROYAL SCOT"

A four-cylinder 4-6-2 Pacific Locomotive, Class "7", hauling the "Royal Scot" on her daily journey from Euston, London, to Glasgow. Total weight in working order 161½ tons.

KEY TO HOW IT WORKS

1. Steam injector forces water from tender into boiler. 2. Clock valves admitting water to boiler. 3. Regulator rod from driver's cab. 4. Steam rises to this dome and is admitted, by regulator valve to steam pipe. 5. Steam pipe to superheater. 6. Superheater. 7. Steam passes back into boiler via these pipes inside a flue and returns superheated. 8. Superheater flue pipes. 9. Tubes from firebox which heat the water. 10. Superheated steam pipe to cylinders. 11. Piston valves which control steam alternately either side of piston. 12. Piston of one of the forward inside cylinders (on the forward stroke). 13. Double exhaust blast pipe from all four cylinders. 14. Double chimney. 15. Outside cylinder. 16. Inside connecting rods to leading driving axle. 17. Cranks of leading driving axle. 18. Outside connecting rod and cranks of second driving axle. 19. Walschaert's gear for driving piston valves of outside and inside cylinders. 20. Water level above firebox. 21. Firebox supported by stays above. 22. Firebrick arch. 23. Fire door. 24. Mechanical lubricators. 25. Sandbox fillers. 26. Steam sand pipes for avoiding wheel slip on greasy rails. 27. Water pick-up scoop (raised). 28 Water uptake to dome which deflects it downwards into tender. 29. Air escape vent. 30. Ordinary water filler for tender. 31. Water capacity, 4,000 gallons. 32. Coal capacity, 10 tons.

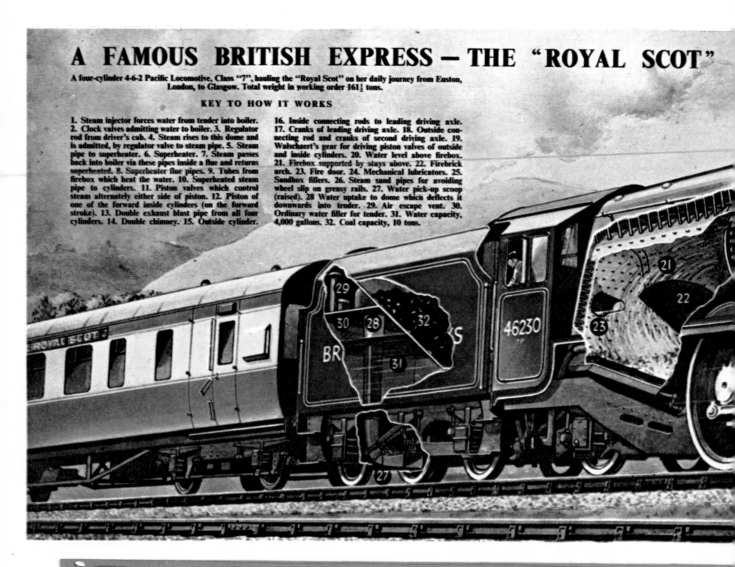

KEY TO PARTS

1. Rudder. 2. Starboard propellers. 3. After starboard engine-room. 4. Control platform. 5. Forward starboard engine-room. 6. Oil fuel tanks in double bottom. 7. After starboard boiler rooms. 8. Boiler uptakes to after-funnel. 9. Turbo-generator room. 10. Forward starboard boiler rooms. 11. Boiler uptake to fore-funnel. 12. Oil fuel tanks. 13. Tourist cabins. 14. Tourist dining-room and galley. 15. First-class cabins. 16. Navigating bridge. 17. Motor-driven lifeboats (26 in all). 18. Air intake vents. 19. First-class hall and library. 20. Main staircase and lifts. 21. First-class swimming pool. 22. First-class restaurant. 23. Barber's shop and Doctor's consulting room (under). 24. First-class lounge. 25. First-class saloon and ball-room. 26. First-class smoking-room. 27. Main galley and pantries. 28. Cabin-class cabins. 29. Lift. 30. Cinema-theatre (seating 380). 31. Verandah grill-room. 32. Cabin-class smoking-room. 33. Cabin lounge. 34. Staircase and lift. 35. Refrigerated stores. 36. Cabin-class swimming pool. 37. Baggage lift. 38. Crew's quarters. 39. Docking bridge.

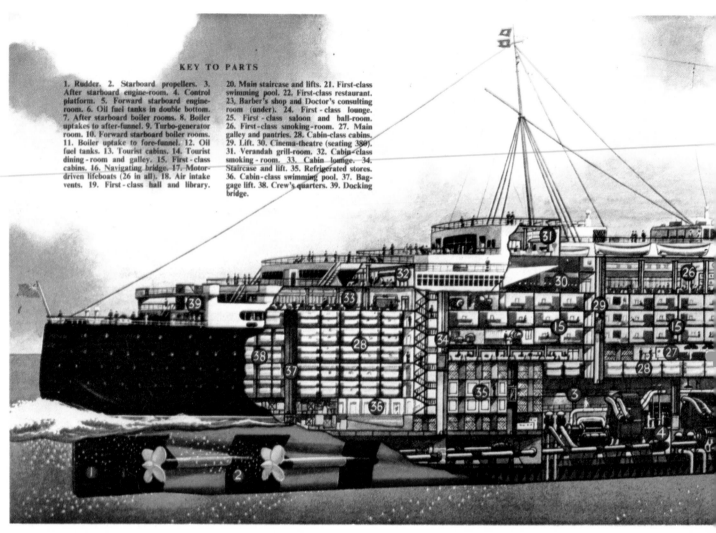

HE WORLD'S LARGEST LINER – THE "QUEEN ELIZABETH"

stateliest ship in being" aptly describes this wonderful 83,673-ton British luxury liner. She is feet long and 118 feet in width. She carries a crew of 1,100 and has accommodation for 2,300 passengers, and has a speed of 29 knots.

THE WORLD'S FIRST JET AIR LINER

Britain leads the world with the opening of the first regular jet air line by the 36-seater De Havilland Comet of B.O.A.C. The service is between London and Johannesburg, South Africa, a distance of 6,724 miles. The Comet will cover this in 23 hours 40 minutes, including stops for refuelling. We show it here passing low over the famous Victoria Falls, near Livingstone. The Comet will cruise at about 40,000 feet (seven miles) at 450 miles per hour. It is powered by four De Havilland Ghost 50 turbo-jet engines, each of 5,000 lbs static thrust.

It is interesting to recall that EAGLE published on 5th May, 1950, our artist's impression of the Comet as it might appear in what was then the future.

KEY TO ONE OF THE FOUR TURBO-JET ENGINES

(1) Air inlet to compressor. (2) Centrifugal air compressor. (3) Combustion chamber and flame tube, where the compressed air is mixed with fuel and ignited. (4) Turbine wheel, driven by the hot gases. The wheel, in turn, drives the compressor by the central shaft. (5) Electric starting motor and engine driven accessories. (6) Cone, against which jet thrust reacts. (7) Jet orifice; 5,000 lb static thrust.

KEY TO OTHER NUMBERS

(8) Captain. (9) First Officer or Engineer. (All the

H.M.S. EAGLE
THE NEW WONDER AIRCRAFT CARRIER OF THE ROYAL NAVY

It is fitting that in the second birthday number of EAGLE we introduce the first and exclusive drawing of Britain's latest and largest aircraft carrier, with some of her crew spelling out her name on the flight deck.

H.M.S. Eagle has a displacement of 45,000 tons and the four sets of steam turbines give her a speed of 31½ knots. She is 803 ft. 9 ins. long and 112 ft. 9 ins. wide. The enormous area of flight deck is equivalent to over two acres.

The great hangars can accommodate over 100 aircraft. This space could stow 263 double-deck buses. The full crew is 2,750 men.

Armament consists of 16-4.5 in. high-angle dual-purpose guns and 60-40 m.m. Bofors anti-aircraft guns. The ship has the first operational squadron of jet aircraft to go into service with the Navy-Supermarine Attackers of 800 Squadron.

H.M.S. Eagle is indeed a fine ship. *In another issue of EAGLE we shall show one of the Attackers.*

KEY TO ABOVE DECKS

(1-1) Aircraft catapults. (2-2) Forward 4.5 in. guns. (3) Forward aircraft lift. (4-4) Multiple 40 m.m. anti-aircraft guns. (5) 5 ton mobile crane. (6) Flight control bridge. (7) Navigating bridge. (8) Fire control director towers. (9-9) Radar gun control apparatus. (10) Tripod mast with radar navigating scanner. (11) New type funnel. (12) Funnel uptakes from boiler room. (13) Single 40 m.m. guns. (14) Aircraft safety barriers lowered (six in all). (15) Aircraft safety barrier raised. (16) Single 40 m.m. guns. (17-17) Gunnery directors. (18) Multiple 40 m.m. anti-aircraft guns. (19) Fire control director towers. (20) Aerial masts. These are lowered outboard when flying is in progress. (21) Life saving Carley floats. (22) Flight deck centre line, marked off every 20 feet. (23) Supermarine Attacker jet aircraft parked on flight deck. (24) Aircraft and boat crane. (25) After aircraft lift (lowered). (26-26) After 4.5 in. guns. (27) Arrester wires (16 in all), to assist in pulling up landing aircraft, engage them with a hook on the tail. (28) Round down landing lights.

KEY TO BELOW DECKS

(29) After upper hangar. (30) After lower hangar. (31) Twin balanced rudders (port side). (32) Port propellers. (33) After port engine room. (34) Forward port engine room. (35) Ward room. (36) Officers' baths. (37) Torpedo room. (38) After boiler room. (39) Oil fuel tanks. (40) Forward boiler room. (41) Auxiliary machinery. (42) Aero-engine room. (43) Bakery. (44) Forward lower hangar. (45) Forward upper hangar. (46) Crew space and wash places.

THERE IS A SPECIAL MESSAGE FOR READERS ABOUT H.M.S. EAGLE ON PAGE 11

Simple explanation of how the atomic reactor would provide power in the form of steam.

A Tubes of "Uranium 235" – the fuel.

B Heavy water tank wherein the uranium atoms are exploded by neutrons, generating great heat.

C Cooling fluid drawing-off heat.

D Fluid pump.

E Cooling fluid passes through the heat converter and turns distilled water into steam again.

F Distilled water supply from condensers.

G Steam outlet to turbines.

H Graphite to retain neutrons.

J Thick protective shield to prevent radiation.

LUCK OF THE LEGION

The Shadow of THE SCIMITAR

Sergeant 'Tough' Luck, Corporal Trenet and Legionnaire Bimberg are stationed at Fort Lebel – a Sahara outpost. When a sentry disappears mysteriously from the walls, the C.O. – busy with private matters – orders Luck to investigate. A rope cast from outside the fort whirls over the parapet and catches the Sergeant in a noose. Luck frees himself, reports to the C.O., and warns him that the dreaded Touareg are the trouble-makers.

STORY BY GEOFFREY BOND. DRAWN BY MARTIN AITCHISON

I DON'T WANT YOUR TOM-FOOL THEORIES, SERGEANT! THE TOUAREG HAVE NEVER BEEN KNOWN TO ADVANCE SO FAR NORTH – WHY SHOULD THEY DO SO NOW?

I CAN'T ANSWER THAT, SIR – YET. THE POINT IS, WHAT MEASURES ARE WE GOING TO TAKE?

I'LL LET YOU KNOW IN THE MORNING – TOO MUCH ELSE TO THINK ABOUT NOW! DON'T EXPECT THERE'S ANYTHING TO WORRY ABOUT REALLY

NOW – WHAT IS IT TO BE? THE FIRING-SQUAD FOR YOURSELF AND ANY OTHER MUTINEERS – OR ACCEPTANCE OF MY COMMAND?

YOU GIVE ME NO CHOICE, SIR – BOTH MEAN DEATH! HOWEVER, I AM BOUND TO OBEY...

Later...

COMPANY READY TO MOVE OFF, MON OFFICIER! WILL YOU GIVE THE COMMAND?

NO, MON SERGENT – THIS IS YOUR OPERATION AND YOU ARE IN CHARGE. I SHALL REMAIN IN FORT LEBEL UNTIL YOUR RETURN.

THIS PLACE IS IMPREGNABLE – I CAN HOLD IT SINGLE-HANDED AGAINST EVERY TOUAREG IN NORTH AFRICA

HE'S EITHER VERY BRAVE OR OUT OF HIS MIND

THE ATOMIC SUBMARINE

artist's impression, exclusive to EAGLE, of the atomic submarine of the future, based on
...ntific facts.

...es nuclear energy by exploding "Uranium 235" atoms (the fuel) with neutrons in a nuclear
...atomic reactor.

...m each exploded atom two neutrons are thrown off (the fission process) which in turn explode
...more atoms and so on. An ounce of "Uranium 235" in heavy water will produce an enormous
...unt of atomic power in the form of heat. By passing a cooling fluid through the atomic reactor
...heat is converted into steam in a specially protected chamber and used to drive the turbines,
which in turn drive the propellers.

The reactor tank is surrounded by a thick layer of graphite to retain the neutrons, and
the whole is heavily shielded against radiation.

Such a submarine would be able to do 30 knots and have a displacement
of 2,000 tons. If sufficient oxygen could be generated chemi-
cally for the crew, the vessel could travel submerged
for thousands of miles with no danger of
running short of fuel.

KEY TO THE NUCLEAR PROPULSION

(1) Atomic or nuclear reactor. (2) Heat converter.
(3) Heavy shielding to prevent radiation. (4) "Uranium 235" fuel store, also shielded. (5) Gangway
past shielding. (6) Steam supply to turbines. (7)
Steam propulsion turbines. (8) Port propeller.

(9) Turbo-generators and chemical oxygen generator. (10) Condensers where exhaust steam is con-
densed back into distilled water. (11) Distilled
water pump to heat converter; thus the water and
steam go round in a closed circuit.

KEY TO OTHER PARTS

(12) After port hydroplane. Hydroplanes are used
for diving and surfacing. (13) Rudder. (14) Hydroplane and steering machinery. (15) Escape hatches.
(16) Marker buoy. (17-17) Retractable 20 m.m.
anti-aircraft guns. (18) Radio and radar room.
(19) Fresh water tanks. (20) Only small battery
space necessary. (21) Section of outer hull containing main water ballast tanks. (22) Control
room. (23) Main hatch. (24) Periscopes lowered
into well under control room. (25) Surface steering

position. (26) Streamlined conning tower to reduce
underwater resistance. (27) Anti-fouling wires.
(28) Galley. (29) Athwartships secret homing torpedo tubes. (30) Commander's cabin. Officers'
ward room on starboard side. (31) Compressed air
bottles for blowing water ballast tanks when rising.
(32) Crew's quarters. (33) Torpedo room. (34)
Secret detection gear. (35) Port torpedo tubes.
(36) Forward port hydroplane. (37) Torpedo load-
ing hatch.

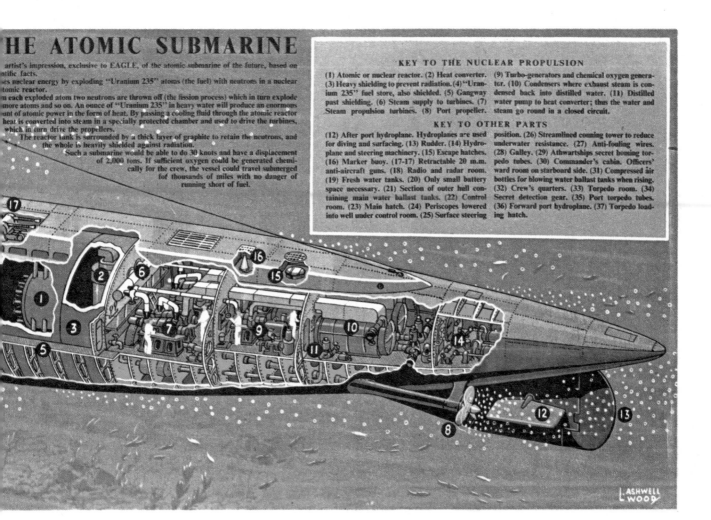

R SPACE-SHIP

In this special EAGLE feature, on our fourth birthday issue, we endeavour to show what the super spaceship of the future may be like, based on many scientific facts already known. Such a ship may take a hundred years or less to develop, or it may take a thousand; no one can say exactly how long; but ultimately men will link our Earth with the new worlds that now lie waiting for the first human footsteps.

The ship depicted here would only operate from satellite space stations orbiting round the earth. It would not land on the planets, but would get into an orbit round them and launch a ferry rocket which would descend to the surface.

KEY TO HOW IT WORKS.
(1) Cosmic ray recorder. (2) Upper control room. (Crew equipped with magnetic boots to overcome lack of gravity.) (3) Air lock and flexible coupling for connection to satellite space station. (4) Lower control room. (5) Double skin. (6) Aerials. (7) Radar room. (8) Oxygen bottles. (9) Crew's quarters and living accommodation. These run through the centre of the ship. (10) Retarding or braking rockets in use as the ship nears the orbit of a planet for launching the ferry landing rocket. (11) Ferry landing rocket being launched. Crew in space suits. (12) Landing 'legs'. (13) Booms with controls inside. (14) Control rods for propellant tanks. (15) Propellant tanks from which electrically charged particles are fed to ion propulsion rockets. (16) Positive and negative storage cells. (17) Observation blisters. (18) Spaceship is entirely constructed of light pressed-steel framework. (19) Cargo and supplies. (20) Observation gallery. (21) Berth for ferry landing rocket. (22) Generators supply electrostatic energy. (23) Gas turbines driving generators. (24) Gas-cooled atomic pile, supplying energy to gas turbines. (25) Atomic re-action shielding. (26) Rocket feed from propellant tanks. (27) Ion rockets. (28) Ion electrostatic acceleration chamber which discharges rearwards electrically charged particles. These produce the thrust for propelling the ship at 200,000 m.p.h. at full acceleration. They are shown shut off here, as the ship is being slowed down by the braking rockets forward. (29) Rocket nozzles. (30)-(31) Steering rockets.

KEY TO SATELLITE STATION (Below) (A) Earth orbiting satellite space station. (B) Parabolic reflector collecting sun's heat for power. (C) Moored earth ferry rocket, bringing supplies and crew. The spaceship would be assembled here by men working in space suits, the parts being brought up from Earth. (D) Radar equipment in touch with the Earth and the spaceship. (E) Interplanetary spaceship departs.

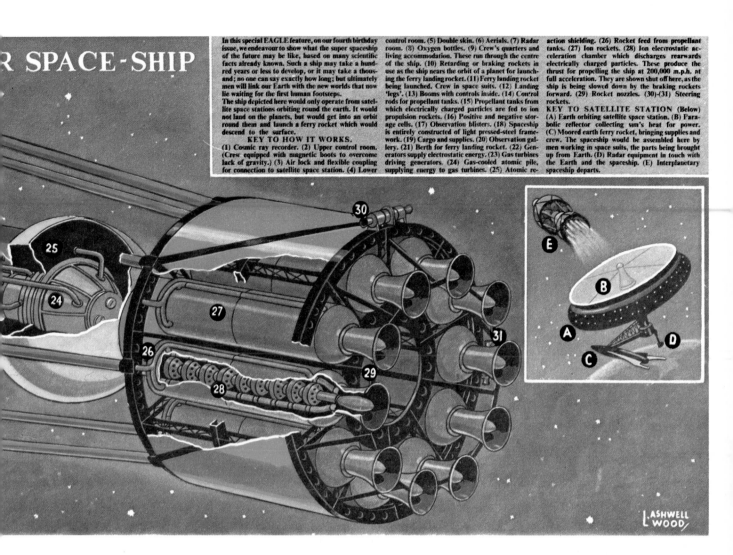

L. ASHWELL WOOD

THAT'S THE IDEA, TAFFY! GET THE FIREWORKS READY — JUST IN CASE!

AH, THERE YOU ARE, MON BRAVE! A LEGIONNAIRE WISHES TO SPEAK TO YOU

THAT I WILL, SERGEANT BALH — THOSE TOUAREG WILL GET THE ROCKET IF THEY TURN UP, LOOK YOU!

THIS IS A FINE TIME FOR INTERVIEWS! WHO IS HE AND WHAT DOES HE WANT?

HIS NAME'S PAVLOS — HE WOULD NOT SAY WHY, BUT HE INSISTED ON SEEING YOU HE'S OVER THERE

ant Luck orders the ... in the open desert.

THERE WAS A LITTLE MAN AND HE HAD A LITTLE PAN AND THE BANGERS WERE MADE OF HORSE, HORSE HORSE

AND HE'S ... DIERS IN THE ... THAT, IF WE GO ... REASON — THIS ... ATE WARS!

LOOK — THERE THEY ARE! TOUAREG! AUX ARMES! AUX ARMES!

ISHKABIBBLE! OUT OF THE FRYING-PAN, INTO THE FIRING-LINE — WAIT FOR ME!

THE MORRIS MINI-MINOR AND AUSTIN SEVEN

By turning the engine sideways across the car to give a bigger proportion of passenger space, and using small wheels to minimize the intrusion of the wheel arches into the interior, the designers of the B.M.C. baby cars have managed to provide generous passenger and luggage space in cars only 10 ft. long. Both cars are identical except for badges, front grilles and interior trim, and use a 848 c.c., 34 nett b.h.p. version of the B.M.C. 'A' series engine fitted, for example, to the Morris Minor 1000.

The four-speed gearbox is below instead of behind the engine, enclosed in an enlarged engine-sump. Power drive is taken directly to the front wheels via short universally-jointed half-shafts. The radiator faces to the left instead of forward, and air is forced through it by the engine-driven fan to exhaust through louvres in the wheel arch. Suspension is independent on all four wheels, a new type of rubber springing being used in conjunction with the usual telescopic shock-absorbers for damping. Front-suspension units are incorporated in the complete engine-gearbox-transmission assembly, and the trailing link rear-suspension units are mounted on a special frame which is bolted as a unit to the rear of the body.

A single wide door each side opens on to the interior, the front seats tipping forward to give access to the wide rear seat. Considering the small overall dimensions of the cars, the luggage boot is of useful size, and may be utilized to the full by the purchase, as an extra, of a smart set of three fitted cases. All four seats are flanked by large metal wells in the doors and body sides, providing ample storage space for parcels, etc. There is additional space beneath the rear seat to accommodate two specially-shaped picnic baskets, also available at extra cost. To complete the excellent provision for small items, there is a parcel shelf right across the front bulk-head below the windscreen, and another behind the rear seat back. A conventional dash is dispensed with in favour of a single central instrument cluster.

Despite their limited size and small-diameter wheels, the B.M.C. twins are fully-fledged cars – as distinct from the 'bubble car' fraternity – performance and handling being distinctly better than that of their conventional '8 h.p.' contemporaries. Maximum top speed is about 72 m.p.h.; 50 m.p.h. can be reached from a standstill in 17 seconds, and 60 m.p.h. can be reached in third gear. Fuel consumption varies according to whether or not full use is made of the very considerable performance, but the car should average 45-50 m.p.g. on a quiet run.

KEY TO NUMBERED PARTS: (1) Side-facing radiator. (2) 848 c.c. engine-gearbox unit. (3) Carburettor and air-cleaner. (4) Distributor. (5) Generator. (6) Coil. (7) Instrument cluster (with speedometer, fuel contents gauge, oil pressure warning light, main beam warning light, and ignition light). (8) Wiper motor. (9) Windscreen washer bottle. (10) Screen sprays. (11) Front sub-frame. (12) Front wheel damper. (13) Rubber spring and suspension linkage housing (through which passes shaft drive to front wheels). (14) Gear lever. (15) Parcel tray. (16) Hand-brake. (17) Door parcel boxes. (18) Rear parcel wells. (19) Door lock pull-cord. (20) Sliding windows in doors. (21) Direction indicators' lever. (22) Tipping front seats. (23) Rear seat. (24) Storage space beneath rear seat. (25) Rear parcel shelf. (26) Optional fitted luggage in boot. (27) Luggage boot lid, retained in open position by cables, provides platform for extra cases. (28) 5½-gallon petrol tank and filler. (29) Spare wheel. (30) Rubber mat covers wheel and boot lid. (31) 12v. battery in boot. (32) Exhaust pipe and silencer. (33) Rear suspension unit and sub-frame. (34) Small diameter (5.20 x 10 in.) tubeless tyres are a noteworthy feature.

PRINCIPLE OF THE SUSPENSION SYSTEM: This is shown in the two diagrams below. As the front wheel (A) moves up and down, 'wishbone' arms hinge about point (B), compressing and pulling strut (C) and rubber spring (D). At the rear, movement of the swing arm (E) is transmitted via strut (F) to rubber spring (G).

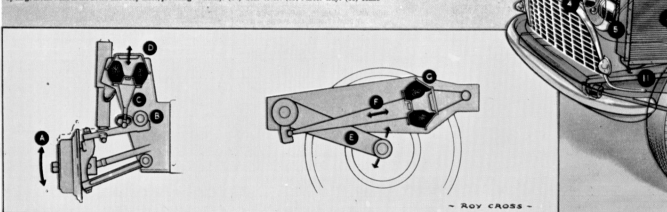

~ ROY CROSS ~

LUCK OF THE LEGION

The Shadow of THE SCIMITAR

Sergeant 'Tough' Luck, Corporal Trenet and Legionnaire Bimberg are stationed at Fort Lebel – a Sahara outpost. Stavil, a sentry, disappears, and Luck discovers that the dreaded Touareg are at work. Captain Bavasc, the mad C.O., makes Luck take the garrison into the desert to search for them. At sundown the company bivouacs, and Pavlos, a friend of Stavil, threatens Luck. Suddenly, the Touareg are sighted. The Legionnaires are alerted . . .

STORY BY GEOFFREY BOND: DRAWN BY MARTIN AITCHISON

. . . and settle down to wait for the impending attack.

DON'T FIRE UNTIL THE SERGEANT GIVES THE ORDER, MES ENFANTS.

THAT MEANT TRIBESMEN

RIGHT, MES ENFANTS! NOW – FIRE!

REMEMBER HULTON'S BOYS AND GIRLS EXHIBITION AT OLYMP

COST AND CONTENTS
The Morris Mini-Minor is shown in the drawing. Standard price of both cars is £496 19s. 2d., including purchase tax. The de luxe versions, priced at £537 6s. 8d., have the following extras: bumper over-riders, opening rear windows, windscreen washers, ashtrays, lights in the rear bodyside parcel wells, floor carpeting, two-tone leather-cloth seat covering, foam-rubber cushions and chrome wheel-trims.

Our Painting Competition

Here is a selection from the best paintings in our recent National Painting Competition. Throughout, the standard was very high indeed and gained the admiration of the judges. See Editor's letter for full list of winners.

GROWING SHADOWS by Paul Scholey (age

MARKET by Douglas John Boyd (aged 16)

IN HARBOUR by Malcolm Dunnett (age

INDUSTRIAL LANDSCAPE *by John Braben (aged 11)*

THE CRESCENT *by Jeremy David Annett (aged 14)*

TRAFALGAR SQUARE
by Frank Elsey (aged) 15

Walls ice cream *Presents* **TOMMY WALLS** *The Wonder Boy*

STORM NELSON — SEA ADVENTURER

THE BLUE PEARL MYSTERY

BEGINNING TODAY

Personal Column

THE SILVER FLEET SERVICE: British ex-Naval Officer, fully equipped for any sea enterprise, offers services in any ocean. Investigation, exploration, treasure trove. Distance no object. Now in Pacific. APPLY: Storm Nelson. Box 6790. London.

If anyone finding a sma... please contact...

AHOY THERE, SKIPPER!

STORY BY EDWARD TRICE: DRAWN BY RICHARD E. JENNINGS.

HULLO, SPANNER. WHAT'S THE FLAP?

RIGHT—HEAVE TO—I'LL COME ALONGSIDE.

A SIGNAL, SIR—SOUNDS LIKE A JOB.

GOOD OLD DON! LAST I HEARD HE WAS SAILING ALONE ROUND THE WORLD—WONDER WHAT'S SO URGENT?

LOST HIS TIN-OPENER, P'RAPS.

HEY, BASH—STOP STOOGING! GET BACK TO "SILVER SPRAY" AND LOAD ON—WE'RE SAILING!

BASH ON!

THE "SILVER SPRAY," FLAGSHIP OF THE SILVER FLEET, MAKES READY TO SAIL.

SWING 'ER OVER, HAPPY M' LAD.

IT'S A RUM RENDEZVOUS—100 MILES IN THE MIDDLE OF NOWHERE.

WE WINNA GET THERE BY MIDNIGHT. TRUST A FRIEND OF STORM'S TO CUT THINGS FINE!

ALL RIGHT, LADS. KEEP RADAR WATCH, JONAH. WHEN WE GET NEAR, BASH AND I'LL FLY ON AHEAD IN "SILVER HAWK."

MIDNIGHT—ABOARD THE "SILVER SPRAY."

McCANN CALLING—TWO WEE CRAFT RIGHT BELOW.

OKAY, BASH! CIRCLE—I'LL FIRE A FLARE.

THERE SHE IS—DEAD ON COURSE AND DEAD ON TIME—BUT SHE'S ALONE AND...

...SHE'S EMPTY!

STORM NELSON — SEA ADVENTURER

CONTINUING —

THE BLUE PEARL MYSTERY

CRUISING WITH HIS SILVER FLEET IN THE S. PACIFIC, STORM KEEPS A MID-OCEAN RENDEZVOUS WITH AN OLD SHIPMATE, DON KENYON, BUT FINDS AN EMPTY BOAT, THE WORD "LACUNA" SCRAWLED IN BLOOD, AND A BLUE PEARL. GOING ASHORE TO REPORT, KIT IS AMBUSHED BY THUGS. HIS CREW RACES TO HIS RESCUE...

CONTACT!

THANKS, LADS!

LET 'EM GO — I'M ALL RIGHT!

I SPOKE TOO SOON, SPANNER — IT'S GONE! — THE BLUE PEARL! — SO THAT'S WHAT THEY WERE AFTER — NOW YOU LADS FIND OUT WHAT YOU CAN ABOUT KENYON — SEE YOU LATER!

AT THE POLICE STATION...

AH, M'SIEU NELSON — IF WE ACTED EVERY TIME A SAILOR HAD A FIGHT, LIFE WOULD BE BUSY INDEED!

KNOW ANYTHING ABOUT BLUE PEARLS?

HEY — WHAT'S SO FUNNY?

THERE IS NO SUCH THING, M'SIEU! — IT'S A NATIVE FABLE. SOMEONE HAS BEEN PULLING THE LEG — YES?

IT DIDN'T *FEEL* LIKE THAT, M'SIEU L'INSPECTEUR — BY THE WAY, DOES THE NAME "KENYON" MEAN ANYTHING TO YOU?

AH YES — THAT WAS SAD — HE IS DEAD! — VOILA!

TAHITI G.

LONE YACHTS-MAN LOST KENYON WRECKED ON TAGA REEF

LATER — IN THE CABIN OF THE SILVER SPRAY...

...BUT THAT NEWSPAPER WAS DATED A WEEK *BEFORE* KENYON SENT US THAT SIGNAL! — AND WHAT DID YOU CHAPS PICK UP BESIDES BLACK EYES?

KEPT AS CLOSE AS A CLAM ABOUT IT...

KENYON WAS PEARL FISHING AWA' IN THE TUAMOTU ISLANDS.

HIS AGENT'S A CHINESE — LING SOO — AT THE BACK OF THE TOWN.

GOOD OH — I'LL PAY HIM A VISIT!

RECKON I'D BETTER COME WITH YOU THIS TIME, SIR!

THERE'S THE PLACE — BETTER WAIT HERE WITHIN HAIL, SPANNER.

HELLO THERE — ANYONE ABOARD!

MURDER

CONTINUED.

STORM NELSON — SEA ADVENTURER

THE BLUE PEARL MYSTERY

CONTINUING—

CRUISING WITH HIS SILVER FLEET IN THE S. PACIFIC, STORM AND HIS COMPANIONS — SPANNER, BASH, JONAH McCANN AND HAPPY — KEEP A MID-OCEAN RENDEZVOUS WITH AN OLD SHIPMATE, DON KENYON, BUT FIND AN EMPTY BOAT, THE WORD "LACUNA" SCRAWLED IN BLOOD, AND A BLUE PEARL. ASHORE THE PEARL IS STOLEN. KENYON HAS BEEN REPORTED DROWNED. STORM VISITS KENYON'S AGENT BUT FINDS HIM MURDERED

WARNED BY THE PARROT, STORM DIVES IN TIME....

PHEW! — LARKING AGAIN?

WATCH OUT — BEHIND THAT CURTAIN!

WHOEVER HE WAS, HE'S SCARPERED, SIR?

AND THAT'S WHAT WE'RE DOING SPANNER — COME ON.

FULL AHEAD BOTH, SIR — HERE COME THE JOHNNY DAMS!

QUICK WORK — THEY MUST HAVE BEEN TIPPED OFF.

RECKON SOMEONE WANTS BLUE PEARLS PRETTY BADLY, SIR.

OR TO COVER UP KENYON'S TRACKS!

SILVER FOAM

LATER — ABOARD SILVER SPRAY.

HAVE YOU PLOTTED BACK THE COURSE OF KENYON'S BOAT YET, BASH?

YES — HE COULD HAVE TAKEN OFF FROM HERE...

TUAMO

MAKEMOTU

THEN THAT'S WHERE WE'RE GOING.

ACTION STATIONS! — THE JOHNNY DAMS ARE HERE, SIR — PERMISSION TO REPEL BOARDERS?

NO — LET 'EM COME ABOARD.

I UNDERSTAND CAPITAINE THAT YOU FOUND THE LATE M'SIEU KENYON'S BOAT — I HAVE A WRIT ATTACHING IT FOR DEBT.

TOO BAD — IT'S MINE BY SALVAGE — MAY I SEE YOUR WRIT?

Il faut donc rendre le bateau immédiatement. Deposé par *Lucius Lacuna*

M. LUCIUS LACUNA, Perle Bleu, MAKEMOTU, Les ÎLES TUAMOTU.

LACUNA!

I REGRET M'SIEU L'INSPECTEUR, THAT THIS SHIP IS BRITISH TERRITORY — I MUST ASK YOU TO LEAVE — WE SAIL IN FIVE MINUTES FOR MAKEMOTU TO CALL ON MR. LACUNA.

MEANWHILE, ON MAKEMOTU...

TO LONDON — URGENT — CABLE FULL DOSSIER ON EX-NAVAL OFFICER STORM NELSON AND HIS SO-CALLED SILVER FLEET.

THE SILVER FLEET IS SIGHTED, TUAN LACUNA.

AAAAAH — CAPTAIN NELSON IS WELCOME — REMEMBER THAT, NUMBAT!

RICHARD E. JENNINGS

I GET TIRED OF GLOBE-TROTTING ENGLISHMEN WHO THINK THEY OWN THE SEA!

STORM NELSON — SEA ADVENTURER

CONTINUING —
THE BLUE PEARL MYSTERY

CRUISING IN THE S. PACIFIC WITH HIS SILVER FLEET AND HIS COMPANIONS — SPANNER, JONAH MᶜCANN, BASH AND HAPPY — STORM KEEPS A RENDEZVOUS WITH AN OLD SHIPMATE, DON KENYON. HE FINDS A SMALL EMPTY BOAT, A BLUE PEARL, AND THE NAME "LACUNA" SCRAWLED IN BLOOD. THE PEARL IS STOLEN. THE BOAT IS CLAIMED BY A "MR LACUNA", SO STORM DECIDES TO VISIT HIM ON MAKEMOTU ISLAND...

THE ISLAND OF MAKEMOTU.

MUST'VE COST A PACKET TO BUILD A VILLA UP THERE!

STORY BY EDWARD TRICE. DRAWN BY RICHARD E JENNINGS.

...AND IN THE VILLA, LACUNA SURVEYS THE APPROACHING SILVER FLEET...

SCHOONER — SPEEDBOAT — HELICOPTER — HAH — AND KENYON'S DINGHY IN TOW — QUITE A LITTLE ARMADA!

ON THE JETTY — LATER.

I'LL BE BACK WITH THE DAILY ORDERS, SPANNER, AS SOON AS I'VE CHECKED ON THIS JOKER, LACUNA

MR LACUNA BIDS YOU WELCOME, CAPTAIN NELSON!

THANKS — BUT I'LL MAKE MY NUMBER WITH THE AUTHORITIES FIRST!

MR LACUNA *IS* THE AUTHORITIES! — THIS WAY PLEASE.

MY *DEAR* NELSON! HOW GLAD AM YOU'VE COME — ANY FRIEND OF POOR KENYON'S IS DOUBLY WELCOME. SEE! EVEN ZAGGA, MY CHEETAH, IS PLEASED TO SEE YOU.... ...QUIET, ZAGGA!

AT THE VILLA...

AS WE'RE ALL BEING SO FRIENDLY, P'RAPS YOU'LL START BY TELLING ME WHAT HAPPENED TO KENYON?

PRRRR PRRR

ALAS — MANY HAVE SOUGHT THE BLUE PEARLS OF MIA MOTU — ALL HAVE PERISHED. I BEGGED HIM NOT TO TRY!

LIKE THE OTHERS, HE WAS WRECKED AND DROWNED

WAS HIS BODY RECOVERED?

NO — BUT *THIS* WAS — FROM THE BELLY OF A SHARK!

D. KENYON 5846

MEANWHILE, ON THE "SILVER SPRAY", MOTHER-SHIP OF THE SILVER FLEET...

HOW ABOUT SOME HARPOON-FISHING? SWITCH ON THE ECHO-SOUNDER, JONAH, AND SEE IF THERE ARE ANY FISH AROUND.

GOSH BASH, YE'RE A LAZY GOWK! YE'LL BE ASKING THE PUIR WEE SEA CREATURES TO RADIO THEIR POSITIONS NEXT!

JONAH SWITCHES ON THE ECHO-SOUNDER — A DEVICE USED TO DETECT OBJECTS UNDER THE WATER

LAWKSAMUCKY! SOME O' THAE FISH MUST BE AS BIG AS SUBMARINES!

UNDERNEATH THE "SILVER SPRAY", THE PRESSURE HATCH OF THE SUB SLOWLY OPENS...

117

STORM NELSON — SEA ADVENTURER

CONTINUING —

THE BLUE PEARL MYSTERY

CRUISING WITH HIS SILVER FLEET IN THE S. PACIFIC, STORM NELSON AND HIS COMPANIONS — JONAH McCANN, BASH, SPANNER AND HAPPY — KEEP A MID-OCEAN RENDEZVOUS WITH DON KENYON. BUT FIND AN EMPTY BOAT, A BLUE PEARL, AND THE NAME "LACUNA" SCRAWLED IN BLOOD. THE PEARL IS STOLEN. NELSON VISITS LACUNA, WHO CONFIRMS THAT KENYON DIED PEARL-FISHING OFF MIA MOTU.

MEANWHILE, BASH CALLAGHAN, THE FLEET'S PILOT, GOES FISHING....

HERE GOES FOR A FISH SUPPER.

HURRY, BASH — I JUST GOT A PING ON A BIG ONE — RIGHT UNDERNEATH US NOW.

STORY BY EDWARD TRICE. DRAWN BY RICHARD E JENNINGS.

WITH HIS COMPRESSED-AIR PIPE CUT, BASH STRUGGLES BACK TO THE SURFACE...

... WHILE, AT LACUNA'S VILLA......

AS MAYOR, MAGISTRATE, POLICE CHIEF AND CORONER, I WISH YOU A *PEACEFUL* STAY ON OUR LOVELY ISLAND, CAPTAIN NELSON.

THANKS, LACUNA — BUT I SAIL AT DAWN FOR MIA MOTU TO FIND OUT WHAT *REALLY* HAPPENED TO KENYON!

THEN I FEAR YOU WILL SHARE HIS FATE! MIA MOTU IS AN ANGRY GODDESS — A DESOLATE VOLCANO IN AN UNCHARTED MAZE OF CRUEL REEFS.

DON'T WORRY — I'M NOT THE TYPE TO DROWN — *NOR WAS KENYON!* — SO LONG.

STORM & SPANNER RETURN TO THE SILVER SPRAY.

HOW WAS THIS FELLOW, LACUNA, SIR?

JUST A FAT LUMP OF SOFT SOAP... HELLO, WHAT'RE BASH AND JONAH DOING, I WONDER?

BASH MET A TWO-LEGGED SWORD-FISH WHO SLIT HIS WIND PIPE!

THE FROGMEN AREN'T FRIENDLY IN THESE PARTS, SKIPPER!

FROGMEN! UNDER THE SHIP — I'M GOING DOWN TO HAVE A LOOK.

STORM PUTS ON THE SHALLOW DIVING-GEAR

A LIMPET MINE STUCK ON THE KEEL! BETTER GET THIS UP ON DECK — QUICK!

A NEAT LITTLE JOB! THE PROP. WINDS UP AS WE GO THROUGH THE WATER AND EXPLODES IT WHEN WE'RE NICELY OUT AT SEA. NO WONDER LACUNA WAS SO SURE WE WOULDN'T COME BACK!

MAYBE THAT'S WHAT HAPPENED TO KENYON, SIR?

IN THE VILLA.

L. REPORTING TO M—ONE. N. SAILS AT DAWN. PRECAUTIONS TAKEN AS WITH K.

THAT NIGHT, THE SILVER SPRAY HAS A VISITOR —

SILV

STORM NELSON — SEA ADVENTURER

CONTINUING—

THE BLUE PEARL MYSTERY

CRUISING WITH HIS "SILVER FLEET" AND HIS COMPANIONS—SPANNER, BASH, HAPPY AND JONAH McCANN—IN THE S. PACIFIC, STORM KEEPS A MID-OCEAN RENDEZVOUS WITH DON KENYON. HE FINDS AN EMPTY BOAT, A BLUE PEARL, AND THE NAME "LACUNA" SCRAWLED IN BLOOD. THE PEARL IS STOLEN. MR LACUNA CONFIRMS THAT KENYON DIED PEARL-FISHING OFF THE VOLCANO-ISLAND OF MIA MOTU. RETURNING TO THE "SILVER SPRAY", STORM FINDS A MYSTERIOUS FROGMAN HAS FIXED A LIMPET-MINE TO THE KEEL OF HIS SHIP...

WHEN WAS THE MINE SET TO EXPLODE, SPANNER?

AVERAGING 12 KNOTS, I'D SAY AFTER ABOUT TWELVE HOURS SAILING, SIR.

TOLD BY EDWARD TRICE DRAWN BY RICHARD E. JENNINGS.

STORM LOOKS IN THE CHART ROOM.

WHERE WOULD TWELVE HOURS AT 12 KNOTS TAKE US, BASH?

LOOK, STORM— IT TAKES US JUST SHORT OF...

MIA MOTU!

SECTION K

SOMEBODY SEEMS VERY ANXIOUS TO STOP US GETTING THERE!

MEANWHILE, ON DECK, HAPPY—THE KANAKA BOY— HAS TURNED IN FOR THE NIGHT.

ZZZZZZ

W-W-WET FOOTPRINTS!

A G-G-GHOST! — OR A THIEF!

OOUCH!

WHAT ON EARTH? HEY, BREAK IT UP YOU TWO!

HIM THIEF, TUAN STORM!

NO, I'M NOT — I'M A STOWAWAY!

PACK IT UP YOU TWO — NOW, WHO ARE YOU?

I'M KERFUFFLE! MR KENYON WAS MY FRIEND—LACUNA LOCKED ME UP WHEN HE HEARD YOU WERE COMING— BUT I ESCAPED!

SEARCH PARTY COMING ABOARD, SIR.

WHY, IT'S LACUNA'S LAD, NUMBAT— IN A DIFFERENT HAT!

ME POLICE—THIS BOY ESCAPE—I TAKE HIM BACK— BY ORDER!

DON'T LET 'EM TAKE ME!

SORRY, I GIVE ORDERS HERE!... HE STAYS ON BOARD.

COME — OR I TAKE!

LEMME GO!

NO, YOU DON'T!

STORM NELSON — SEA ADVENTURER

THE BLUE PEARL MYSTERY

CONTINUING —

CRUISING WITH HIS SILVER FLEET AND HIS COMPANIONS — SPANNER, BASH, JONAH McCANN AND HAPPY — IN THE S. PACIFIC, STORM KEEPS RENDEZVOUS WITH DON KENYON. HE FINDS AN EMPTY BOAT, A BLUE PEARL AND THE NAME "LACUNA" SCRAWLED IN BLOOD. THE PEARL IS STOLEN. LACUNA CONFIRMS THAT KENYON DIED PEARL-FISHING OFF MIA MOTU. LATER, A LIMPET-MINE IS FOUND ON THE KEEL OF THE "SILVER SPRAY". KERFUFFLE, A YOUNG FRIEND OF KENYON'S, ESCAPES FROM LACUNA AND COMES TO STORM FOR HELP. LACUNA'S SERVANT, NUMBAT, TRIES TO FETCH KERFUFFLE BACK . . .

WE'LL HAVE SOME BETTER MANNERS FROM YOU IN FUTURE, NUMBAT — NOW GET BACK TO LACUNA AND TELL HIM THE BOY STAYS WITH ME!

TOLD BY EDWARD TRICE: DRAWN BY RICHARD E. JENNINGS.

AS DAWN BREAKS, THE SILVER SPRAY STANDS OUT TO SEA . . .

ON THE BALCONY OF LACUNA'S VILLA . . .

THEY'VE SAILED — YOU'RE A BLUNDERING DOLT, NUMBAT! FIRST YOU LET THE BOY ESCAPE — THEN YOU LET NELSON TAKE HIM.

THAT BRAT, "KERFUFFLE", IS DANGEROUS — WE'LL FOLLOW THEM IN THE SUBMARINE! THIS TIME THERE MUST BE NO SURVIVORS!

MY NAME, HAPPY XMAS — I BORN XMAS DAY ON XMAS ISLAND — WHY YOUR NAME, "KERFUFFLE"?

THAT'S WHAT MY DAD SAID FIRST TIME HE SAW ME — "MY, WHAT A KERFUFFLE!"

HEY, KERFUFFLE — CAPTAIN WANTS YOU ON THE BRIDGE!

SILVER SPRAY

HOW DID YOU COME TO BE ON LACUNA'S ISLAND?

I STOWED AWAY FROM AUSTRALIA TO FIND MY DAD WHO WAS LOST AT SEA.

ONE NIGHT THERE WAS A T'RIFIC BANG AND THE SHIP BEGAN TO SINK — EVERYONE HAD GONE BUT ME — I SAILED ON A RAFT TO A DESERT ISLAND WHERE MY FRIEND MR KENYON FOUND ME.

ROBINSON CRUSOE JUNIOR, EH? DID KENYON GIVE YOU ANY MESSAGE FOR ME?

HE SAID, IF I EVER MET YOU, TO TELL YOU HE WAS "A-ONE".

"A-ONE" — WONDER WHAT DON MEANT? · · · OF COURSE — I'VE GOT IT — MEANS HE'S CONSIDERED "A-ONE AT LLOYD'S" OF LONDON — PERHAPS THEY'LL KNOW WHAT HE WAS DOING.

STORM ENTERS THE SIGNAL OFFICE . . .

JONAH — SEND A SIGNAL TO LLOYD'S OF LONDON — "CAN YOU STATE KENYON'S ASSIGNMENT — MAY BE ABLE TO HELP."

SOME HOURS LATER . . .

SHIP AHOY!

NO, IT'S NOT — IT'S MIA MOTU!

ONE MILE ASTERN — INSIDE LACUNA'S SUB . . .

THAT LIMPET-MINE IS DUE TO BLOW THEM UP SOON — IF ANYTHING GOES WRONG WE'LL SURFACE AND SINK 'EM BY GUNFIRE!

WE'VE INTERCEPTED THE REPLY FROM LLOYD'S TO CAPTAIN NELSON'S SIGNAL, M'SIEU LACUNA!

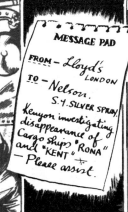

MESSAGE PAD

FROM — Lloyd's LONDON

TO — Nelson. S.4. SILVER SPRAY.

Kenyon investigating disappearance of Cargo ships "RONA" and "KENT" — Please assist.

ON SILVER SPRAY, STORM RECEIVES THE MESSAGE . . .

EVER HEARD OF A SHIP CALLED THE "RONA" — OR THE "KENT"?

YES! "KENT" WAS THE SHIP I STOWED AWAY ON — "RONA" WAS MY DAD'S SHIP!

In the end Storm rescues Kenyon who proves to be Kerfuffle's father. Lucana, his crew and submarine are blown up.

BRAND NEW MYSTERY STORY BEGINS TODAY

The Boy with a future – but no past!

MARK QUESTION

Story by ALAN STRANKS : Drawn by HARRY LINDFIELD

WATERLOO STATION, LONDON—MARCH, 1957...

LONDON— AT LAST!

BUSTLE HIM WHILE I SNATCH HIS WALLET, CONGER!

HEY!

WATCH YOUR STEP, CLUMSY!

STRIKE ME PINK, CONGER— LOOK WHO HE IS! WE'VE STRUCK A GOLD-MINE IN THAT KID!

TO TAXI

AND I DON'T AIM TO LOSE IT! COME ON, SNUFFLE!

IT CAN'T BE GONE — I HAD IT A FEW SECONDS AGO!

LOOK OUT!

HE STEPPED OUT RIGHT IN FRONT OF MY LORRY! I DIDN'T HAVE A CHANCE!

RING NINE-NINE-NINE AND CALL AN AMBULANCE— LIVELY!

O.K., OFFICER!

HE'S BEEN SKITTLED! IF THIS HADN'T HAPPENED, HE WOULD'VE LED US STRAIGHT TO...

WE'LL FOLLOW THE AMBULANCE. I GUESS WE'RE THE ONLY ONES IN LONDON WHO KNOW THAT KID'S IDENTITY!

THE MYSTERY BOY LIES UNCONSCIOUS IN HOSPITAL FOR MANY DAYS — THEN, THREE WEEKS LATER ...

I'M 'DOC' STEELE! MIND IF I ASK YOU A FEW QUESTIONS?

FIRE AWAY, DOC—BUT, IF IT'S ANYTHING ABOUT MY PAST, I'M AFRAID YOU'LL ONLY DRAW BLANKS...

... I'VE HAD THE POLICE HERE EVERY DAY FOR A FORTNIGHT NOW, TRYING TO FIND OUT WHO I AM—BUT THEY KNOW JUST AS MUCH AS I DO!

I JUST DON'T REMEMBER ONE SOLITARY THING ABOUT MY PAST.

'AMNESIA' WE CALL IT—FANCY NAME FOR LOSS OF MEMORY...

...YOU'RE IN FINE PHYSICAL SHAPE, YOUNG 'UN, AND WE NEED THIS BED. WHAT ABOUT SHARING MY PLACE UNTIL THE POLICE GET A LINE ON YOU?

I'D LIKE THAT!

HERE ARE THE DETAILS OF THE CASE, DOCTO!

WE'LL NEED A NAME FOR YOU, UNTIL WE LEARN YOUR REAL ONE!

NAME
ADDRESS
AGE

NOTHING BUT QUESTION MARKS, EH? I GUESS ALL YOU'VE GOT TO DO IS TURN THAT BACK TO FRONT AND CALL ME 'MARK QUESTION'!

MARK QUESTION — *GREAT NEW MYSTERY STORY!*

The Boy with a future — but no past!

A mystery boy arrives in London. His wallet is stolen by Snuffle and Conger. Knocked down by a lorry, he wakes up in hospital — his mind a blank — and assumes the name 'Mark Question'. 'Doc' Steele offers Mark, now recovered, a home . . .

Story by **ALAN STRANKS**: *Drawn by* **HARRY LINDFIELD**

WELL, HERE WE GO — A BOY WITHOUT A PAST, AND A DOCTOR MINUS AN ARM!

HOW DID IT HAPPEN, DOC?

A WAR SOUVENIR. FROM NOW ON, YOU'LL BE MY LEFT ARM!

I'LL TRY, DOC!

THERE HE GOES, SNUFFLE!

'THE GOLDEN BOY' — EH, CONGER?

SNUFFLE AND CONGER WATCH THEM LEAVE.

COME ON! WE'VE WAITED WEEKS OUTSIDE THAT HOSPITAL, AND WE DON'T WANT TO LOSE HIM.

THE NEWSPAPERS SAY HE DOESN'T REMEMBER A THING ABOUT HIS PAST. I GUESS WE'RE THE ONLY ONES WHO REALLY *KNOW*!

ONLY A FEW STEPS FURTHER, MARK!

WAIT, DOC! LOOK AT THIS!

I'VE GOT A HOME NOW — THANKS TO YOU, DOC — BUT I NEED A JOB.

WHY NOT TRY YOUR LUCK?

SMART BOY WANTED APPLY WITHIN

SO, YOU'RE MARK QUESTION, EH? THAT'S A STRANGE NAME! I'M MR FEATHERS — I'LL PAY YOU TWO POUNDS A WEEK AND ALL THE BIRD-SEED YOU CAN EAT!

I'LL TAKE IT, SIR — AND REPORT FOR WORK FIRST THING IN THE MORNING!

SHAKE HANDS WITH A WORKING MAN, DOC!

CONGRATULATIONS, MARK! NOW COME AND SEE YOUR NEW HOME . . .

WE'RE IN LUCK, CONGER!

SURE! FANCY HIM TAKIN' A JOB WITH OLD FEATHERS!

LATER . . .

HERE'S TO THE FUTURE, MARK! I GUESS THERE ARE LOTS OF PEOPLE WHO'D BE GLAD TO FORGET THE PAST.

BUT I *WANT* TO KNOW ABOUT MYSELF, DOC . . . WHO I AM — WHERE I LIVED — IF I HAD ANY FAMILY — AND I'LL NEVER REST UNTIL I FIND OUT!

WELL, NOW WE *KNOW*, CONGER . . . WHERE HE WORKS — WHERE HE LIVES . . .

AND *WHO HE IS!* BUT WE'RE NOT TELLING ANYBODY UNTIL WE'RE GOOD AND READY!

WHAT IS THE MYSTERY OF MARK QUESTION — AND WHY ARE CONGER AND SNUFFLE SO INTERESTED IN 'THE BOY WITHOUT A PAST'?

MARK QUESTION — *EAGLE's NEW MYSTERY SERIAL*

The Boy with a future — but no past!

Mark Question is the mystery boy who took this strange name because, following an accident, he cannot remember his own. He is living with 'Doc' Steele, who looked after him in hospital. Mark has taken a job at Mr Feathers's pet shop . . .

Story by **ALAN STRANKS:** *Drawn by* **HARRY LINDFIELD**

YOU LOOK AFTER THE SHOP, MARK, WHILE I PACK THIS SPECIMEN.

WHAT *IS* THAT QUEER-LOOKING ANIMAL, MR FEATHERS?

AN *ORNITHORHYNCUS*, MY BOY — OTHERWISE, AN AUSTRALIAN DUCK-BILLED PLATYPUS! IT HAS FUR, WEBBED-FEET, AND A DUCK'S BILL—IT LAYS EGGS, NURSES ITS YOUNG AND CAN LIVE EITHER ON LAND OR IN WATER.

GOLLY! THAT MUST BE THE MOST MIXED-UP CREATURE IN THE WORLD!

DING

I'M A PRETTY MIXED-UP CREATURE MYSELF — NOT KNOWING WHO OR WHAT I AM!

HULLO, THERE! TELL MR FEATHERS THAT WE'VE COME TO COLLECT THAT 'PLATYPUSSY' HE'S BEEN STUFFING FOR PROFESSOR CARRACUL!

YES, SIR!

BETTER GET OLD FEATHERS' MONEY READY!

I WONDER IF THAT KID'S FOOLING EVERYBODY ABOUT LOSING HIS MEMORY — HE LOOKS SMART ENOUGH TO ME!

AS CONGER CLOSES HIS WALLET, SOMETHING FALLS UNNOTICED TO THE FLOOR!

HANDLE THAT CAREFULLY—IT'S A VERY RARE SPECIMEN!

LEAVE IT TO US, GUV'NOR!

PROFESSOR CARRACUL WOULD SKIN US ALIVE IF WE DAMAGED HIS PRECIOUS 'PLATYCAT'!

THE PROFESSOR HAS BEEN SENDING ME A LOT OF WORK RECENTLY — BUT I CAN'T SAY I LIKE HIS MEN . . .

IT TAKES ALL SORTS TO MAKE UP THE WORLD, SIR!

AS MARK GETS ON WITH HIS WORK, SOMETHING ON THE NEWLY-SWEPT FLOOR CATCHES HIS EYE . . .

HULLO! WHAT'S THIS?

JINGS! THIS IS A PHOTOGRAPH OF ME!

THAT NIGHT, MARK TALKS OVER HIS DISCOVERY WITH 'DOC' STEELE . . .

I HAD JUST SWEPT THE FLOOR BEFORE THOSE MEN CAME IN, SO ONE OF THEM MUST HAVE DROPPED IT!

THIS IS YOU ALL RIGHT, MARK — BUT THAT SNOW BACKGROUND COULD BE IN SWITZERLAND, CANADA, AUSTRIA —ANY OF A DOZEN PLACES.

IF THOSE MEN WORK FOR PROFESSOR CARRACUL, HE'S SURE TO KNOW WHERE THEY LIVE. COME ON, DOC — LET'S FOLLOW UP THIS CLUE WHILE IT'S STILL HOT!

WILL MARK CATCH UP WITH HIS MYSTERIOUS PAST? SEE NEXT WEEK!

MARK QUESTION— *THE NEW EAGLE MYSTERY HERO*

The Boy with a future — but no past!

Mark, the mystery boy who lost his memory, finds a photograph of himself in Mr Feathers's pet shop, where he works. He is certain it was dropped by Conger and Snuffle, two men who called to collect a stuffed platypus specimen for Professor Carracul. Mark reports his find to 'Doc' Steele, and they call on the Professor . . .

Story by **ALAN STRANKS**: *Drawn by* **HARRY LINDFIELD**

YOU'RE TOO LATE—WE'RE JUST CLOSING!

WE WANT TO SEE PROFESSOR CARRACUL!

IT'S VERY IMPORTANT, SIR!

YOU'RE IN LUCK— HE'S WORKING LATE TONIGHT. COME THIS WAY!

WHO *IS* THIS PROFESSOR CARRACUL, DOC?

ONE OF OUR GREATEST AUTHORITIES ON ZOOLOGY, MARK.

AND IN THE MEANTIME...

A PITY TO SPOIL MR FEATHERS'S PERFECT SPECIMEN OF A PLATYPUS, BUT IT CAN'T BE HELPED..

TWO VISITORS TO SEE YOU, PROFESSOR!

FOOL! HOW MANY TIMES MUST I TELL YOU TO KNOCK?

GIVE ME TWO MINUTES AND THEN SHOW THEM IN!

VERY GOOD, SIR!

MARK AND THE DOC ARE WATCHED BY SNUFFLE AND CONGER . . .

HE'LL SEE YOU IN A MOMENT.

THANKS!

!

GOSH—IT'S THAT BOY, CONGER!

WHAT THE DICKENS IS *HE* DOING HERE, SNUFFLE?

"GORILLA SAVAGE!" (CAMEROONS)

IN HIS OFFICE, CARRACUL HASTILY STUFFS THE PLATYPUS WITH A DIAMOND NECKLACE...

A FEW MOMENTS LATER . . .

THE BOY IS QUITE SURE THAT THIS PHOTO WAS DROPPED BY YOUR MEN, PROFESSOR.

A VERY INTERESTING STORY, DOCTOR STEELE, BUT I DON'T SEE HOW I CAN HELP.

CAN'T WE SEE THOSE MEN AND ASK THEM?

OF COURSE! THEY'RE IN THE STOREROOM, PACKING SPECIMENS FOR DESPATCH TO FOREIGN MUSEUMS — WE DO QUITE A LOT OF THAT SORT OF WORK.

SEND CONGER AND SNUFFLE TO MY OFFICE, PLEASE!

THERE'S A GAPING HOLE IN THAT PLATYPUS!

NOW WHY ON EARTH HAS HE DONE THAT?

MARK'S SHARP EYES HAVE SEEN SOMETHING WHICH WILL LEAD HIM STILL FURTHER ALONG THE DARK AND DANGEROUS ROAD IN SEARCH OF HIS PAST! MORE NEXT WEEK!

MARK QUESTION — The Boy with a future – but no past!

The story so far

Mark is the boy who lost his memory in a street accident. He works at Mr Feather's pet shop. Two men, Conger and Snuffle, call at the shop to collect a parcel containing a stuffed platypus for Professor Carracul. Later, Mark finds a photograph of himself on the floor. Convinced that the two men dropped it, Mark takes his friend 'Doc' Steele – with whom he is living – to see the Professor at his office, in the hope that he can assist in following this clue to Mark's mysterious past . . .

Story by **ALAN STRANKS**
Drawn by **HARRY LINDFIELD**

CONGER AND SNUFFLE WILL BE HERE IN A MOMENT.

I SAY—WHO'S BEEN MUCKING ABOUT WITH THIS PLATYPUS? IT WAS PERFECT WHEN IT LEFT MR FEATHERS'S SHOP!

LEAVE THAT ALONE, YOU INTERFERING BRAT!

SORRY, SIR! I DIDN'T MEAN ANY HARM.
I CANNOT *STAND* BOYS WHO MEDDLE!
NOW *WHY* DID CARRACUL BLOW UP LIKE THAT?

A FEW MOMENTS LATER . . .
I'VE NEVER SEEN THIS BEFORE IN MY LIFE!
ME NEITHER!
WELL, THAT SETTLES THAT! SORRY WE CAN'T HELP, DR STEELE!

I'M CERTAIN THOSE MEN DROPPED THIS PHOTO—IT *COULDN'T* HAVE GOT THERE ANY OTHER WAY.
MARINE HALL
I RECKON THEY'RE THE UGLIEST SPECIMENS IN THIS MUSEUM!

WHY DID PROFESSOR CARRACUL SLASH THAT PLATYPUS SPECIMEN?
THERE'S SOME MYSTERY HERE, MARK—AND MAYBE WE'LL SOLVE IT!

MEANWHILE . . .
WHAT HAVE YOU TWO BEEN UP TO?
N-NOTHING, SIR!

YOU MUST HAVE DONE *SOMETHING* TO BRING THAT BOY SNOOPING AROUND HERE! WHO IS HE?
THE KID WHO WORKS AT OLD FEATHERS'S SHOP. THAT'S ALL I KNOW—HONEST, PROFESSOR!

I'VE DISCOVERED THE FINEST METHOD IN THE WORLD FOR SMUGGLING STOLEN JEWELLERY ABROAD. IF YOU TWO IDIOTS RUIN IT, I'LL . . .
NOT LIKELY, GUV'NOR—WE KNOW WHICH SIDE OUR BREAD'S BUTTERED!

I HAVE INVITED LORD HUBBARD TO DINE WITH ME TONIGHT. HE HAS THE WORLD'S FINEST COLLECTION OF RUBIES . . .
WE'LL BE AT *HIS*!

SO, WHILE HE'S AT *YOUR* PLACE . . .
AND WHEN LORD HUBBARD GETS HOME . . .
HE'LL FIND HIS CUPBOARD IS BARE! HA-HA-HA!

IN THE MEANTIME, AT DOC STEELE'S FLAT . . .
I'VE GOT TO FIND OUT WHO I REALLY AM, DOC—AND I'M CERTAIN SNUFFLE AND CONGER KNOW! BUT HOW DO I PROVE IT?
I'M A DOCTOR, NOT A DETECTIVE, MARK—BUT, MAYBE, I CAN DIG A PLAN OUT OF MY LITTLE BLACK BAG WHICH WILL ANSWER THAT QUESTION.

MARK QUESTION — The Boy with a future — but no past!

Mark Question is the mystery boy who lost his memory in an accident, and took this strange name because he cannot remember his own. Mark finds a photograph of himself on the floor of Mr Feathers's pet shop, where he works. He is certain it was dropped there by Conger and Snuffle, two men who are employed by Professor Carracul at the National Museum. With his friend 'Doc' Steele, Mark calls at the Museum, but Conger and Snuffle deny any knowledge of the photograph. When Mark and Doc have left, by no means satisfied, Carracul plans a little 'job' with Conger and Snuffle. At Doc Steele's flat...

Story by ALAN STRANKS
Drawn by HARRY LINDFIELD

THOSE MEN WERE LYING, DOC!

IF THEY *KNOW* WHO YOU ARE, WHY SHOULD THEY HIDE IT, MARK?

THAT'S WHAT I MEAN TO FIND OUT!

SLEEP ON IT, CHUM! WE'LL TALK IT OVER AT BREAKFAST. I'M ON NIGHT-DUTY AT THE HOSPITAL — I'LL BE HOME ABOUT EIGHT. GOODNIGHT!

THERE'S 'BIG BEN' STRIKING ELEVEN! I JUST *CAN'T* SLEEP WITH ALL THIS ON MY MIND!

MIDNIGHT...

SNUFFLE AND CONGER *DID* DROP THAT PHOTO — SO THEY *MUST* KNOW SOMETHING ABOUT ME...

ONE O'CLOCK...

IT'S NO USE LYING HERE TOSSING AND TURNING — PERHAPS A SPOT OF FRESH AIR WILL HELP ME SLEEP...

MARK IS NOT THE ONLY ONE WHO IS WIDE AWAKE — FOR, AT PROFESSOR CARRACUL'S HOUSE...

THANK YOU FOR AN EXCELLENT DINNER, PROFESSOR CARRACUL — NOW I REALLY MUST GO!

NO HURRY, MY DEAR LORD HUBBARD... AH, THERE'S THE TELEPHONE! EXCUSE ME WHILE I ANSWER IT...

AND, AT LORD HUBBARD'S HOUSE...

O.K., GUVNOR! YOU CAN LET HIS LORD-SHIP COME HOME NOW — HE'LL FIND HIS CUPBOARD BARE OF SPARKLERS!

I SEE! IF YOU BRING THEM TO THE MUSEUM, I SHALL BE VERY GLAD TO LOOK AT THEM...

THAT WAS A BIG-GAME HUNTER FRIEND OF MINE. HE HAS BROUGHT BACK SOME VERY VALUABLE SPECIMENS FROM AFRICA, AND WANTS MY ADVICE ON HOW TO DISPOSE OF THEM.

INTERESTING JOB, YOURS, PRO-FESSOR! WELL, GOOD-NIGHT — AND THANKS AGAIN!

THAT OLD FOOL'S DUE FOR A SHOCK WHEN HE GETS HOME! NOW I MUST GO DOWN TO THE MUSEUM QUICKLY...

MEANWHILE, MARK'S AIMLESS FOOTSTEPS HAVE TAKEN HIM TO THE PLACE WHICH HE FEELS SURE HOLDS A CLUE TO HIS FORGOTTEN PAST...

IT ISN'T ANY FUN TO BE NO-ONE! I'M *SURE* CONGER AND SNUFFLE KNOW THE SECRET OF MY PAST!

HOLD HARD, SNUFFLE!

IT'S *HIM* — IT'S THE YOUNG...

QUIET! WHAT THE DICKENS IS *HE* DOING HERE AT THIS TIME OF NIGHT?

MARK QUESTION The Boy with a future – but no past!

Mark Question is the boy who lost his memory, following an accident. He works at Mr Feathers's pet shop and lives with 'Doc' Steele, who attended him in hospital. Mark is sure that the secret of his past is known to Snuffle and Conger, two unpleasant types who work for Professor Carracul, at the National Museum. He also suspects that Carracul is mixed up in some shady business. One night, unable to sleep, Mark goes for a walk and finds himself outside the Museum, just as Snuffle and Conger return from a big jewel robbery arranged by their sinister boss, Carracul . . .

Story by **ALAN STRANKS**
Drawn by **HARRY LINDFIELD**

THERE'S CARRACUL'S CAR, CONGER! WHAT'LL WE DO?

STAY UNDER COVER TILL WE SEE WHAT THAT KID'S UP TO!

THAT'S PROFESSOR CARRACUL! WHAT'S HE DOING HERE AT THIS TIME OF NIGHT?

ARE SNUFFLE AND CONGER HERE?

NOT YET, SIR—I'VE BEEN STANDING BY TO LET THEM IN...

THIS CALLS FOR A SPOT OF SLEUTHING!

NO DOUBT ABOUT IT, SNUFFLE—THAT KID'S SPYING ON CARRACUL!

HE CAN'T HAVE COTTONED ON TO OUR LITTLE GAME, CONGER!

WE CAN'T TAKE ANY RISKS—I'M GOING TO DEAL WITH HIM NOW! YOU STAY HERE!

I'LL HIDE BEHIND ONE OF THESE PILLARS UNTIL HE COMES OUT...

HEY!

GET INTO THE CAR AND KEEP HIM QUIET WHILE I REPORT TO THE BOSS!

I DON'T LIKE THIS A BIT!

A FEW MOMENTS LATER...

IT'S THE SAME KID WHO CAME HERE ABOUT THAT PHOTOGRAPH OF HIM-SELF — HE WAS SNOOPING AROUND OUTSIDE. I'VE PUT HIM IN YOUR CAR WITH SNUFFLE.

YOU BUNGLING FOOL! THERE'S ONLY ONE THING TO DO NOW...

THIS IS THE BIGGEST HAUL WE'VE EVER MADE—AND I'M NOT LETTING ANY YOUNG WHIPPER-SNAPPER SPOIL IT! GET RID OF HIM— AT ONCE!

MARK HAS TUMBLED HEADLONG INTO BIG TROUBLE! WATCH OUT FOR SUPER THRILLS NEXT WEEK!

127

MARK QUESTION — The Boy with a future – but no past!

Mark Question, who lost his memory as the result of a street accident, has been befriended by 'Doc' Steele. Young Mark suspects that two scoundrels, named Conger and Snuffle, hold the key to his forgotten past. Conger and Snuffle are really jewel-thieves working for Professor Carracul, who has discovered a perfect plan for smuggling stolen jewellery abroad. Late one night, Mark sees Carracul furtively entering the National Museum, of which he is the Director. Mark decides to keep watch, but Conger and Snuffle sneak up behind and overpower him. When Conger reports to Carracul, the Professor orders him to dispose of Mark . . .

Story by ALAN STRANKS
Drawn by HARRY LINDFIELD

HOW CAN MARK ESCAPE FROM A WATERY GRAVE? WHERE IS THIS STRANGE-SOUNDING PLACE CALLED STAFFELHAGEN? DON'T MISS NEXT WEEK'S THRILLING CHAPTER, WHEN THE MYSTERY OF MARK QUESTION'S PAST DEEPENS!

JACK o'LANTERN *in* MAN-HUNT

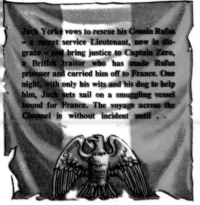

Jack Yorke vows to rescue his Cousin Rufus – a secret service Lieutenant, now in disgrace – and bring justice to Captain Zero, a British traitor who has made Rufus prisoner and carried him off to France. One night, with only his wits and his dog to help him, Jack sets sail on a smuggling vessel bound for France. The voyage across the Channel is without incident until . . .

STORY BY GEORGE BEARDMORE – DRAWN BY ROBERT AYTON

. . . the French coast is sighted – and then . . .

SAIL ON THE LARBOARD QUARTER, SKIPPER! THERE GOES A ROCKET – IT'S THE SIGNAL TO HEAVE-TO

HEAVE-TO? BE HANGED FOR A TALE! SHE'S THE *DEFIANT* – FASTEST REVENUE-CUTTER AFLOAT – AND WE'VE GOT TOO MUCH THAT'S VALUABLE ABOARD. WE'LL HAVE TO RUN FOR IT, MISTER MATE!

SHE'S CLOSING IN ON US, CAP'N

NO MATTER – ONCE WE GET ROUND THE POINT, WE'LL SHOW THEM OUR HEELS. JUST HOPE, MISTER MATE, THAT THEY DON'T OPEN FIRE, FOR WE'RE WITHIN . . .

WE'LL NOT DO IT, SIR – SHE'S FOUND OUR RANGE!

WE MUST RISK IT – IT'S EITHER THAT, OR TEN YEARS IN THE FLEET PRISON!

QU'EST-CE QUI ARRIVE? DO I NOT HEAR A DOG BARK?

OH, LE PAUVRE! SO YOUNG – AND HOW LIKE HE IS TO MY LOST BOY, DROWNED IN THE INDIES THESE TWENTY YEARS GONE!

THANKS BE TO GOD IN HIS MERCY – HE LIVES!

And so Jack comes to France . . .

ONLY A FEW MORE STEPS, MON PETIT, AND I WILL HAVE YOU IN BED . . .

LINCOLN of AMERICA

The life story of Abraham Lincoln

Abraham Lincoln, born at a poor farm in Kentucky in 1809, sees the inhuman way slaves are treated and vows he will stamp out slavery. He becomes a lawyer in 1834, and President in 1861. Lincoln – who now has a wife and son – has only been President for six weeks when the Civil War breaks out, and he finds himself leader of the North (Yankees), who wish to abolish slavery, against the South (Confederates), who are determined to retain their slaves. Saddened by the early defeats of the Northern forces, and by his son's death, President Lincoln refuses to despair. At last the war goes in favour of the North, and when Abraham stands for re-election, he is able to announce that henceforward all slaves are free. Lincoln wins the election and starts his second term of office as President.

STORY BY ALAN JASON: DRAWN BY *Norman Williams*

A MONTH LATER...

MR LINCOLN, SIR, I HAVE EVERY REASON TO THINK THE SOUTH WILL SURRENDER!

WONDERFUL NEWS, GENERAL GRANT – THE COUNTRY WILL BE DIVIDED NO LONGER.

AND PEACE WAS SIGNED ON APRIL 9th, 1865, BY GENERAL GRANT (NORTH) AND GENERAL LEE (SOUTH) ...

AND IN THE SENATE...

GENTLEMEN, THE WAR IS OVER! THE REBELS ARE OUR COUNTRYMEN AGAIN – THE FLAG FLIES OVER THE *UNITED* STATES OF AMERICA!

LATER, IN THE **LINCOLNS'** PARLOUR ...

ABRAHAM, I'VE ARRANGED A CELEBRATION PARTY AT THE THEATRE.

AND VERY NICE, TOO!

IT'S GOOD TO RELAX, MARY.

YES, ABRAHAM, AND HOW YOU DESERVE IT.

A FIRST-RATE PLAY, MARY – I'M ENJOYING THIS...

MEANWHILE, A MADMAN MAKES FOR THE BOX ...

NOW HE'S AT MY MERCY!

WHAT THE...! LOOK OUT, MR LINCOLN!

THUS ALWAYS WITH TYRANTS!

HOLD THAT MAN – HE'S SHOT THE PRESIDENT!

LINCOLN of AMERICA

The life story of
Abraham Lincoln

Abraham Lincoln, born at a poor farm in Kentucky in 1809, sees the inhuman way slaves are treated and vows he will stamp out slavery. He becomes a lawyer in 1834, and President in 1861. Lincoln has only been President for six weeks when the Civil War breaks out, and he finds himself leader of the North (Yankees), who wish to abolish slavery, against the South (Confederates), who are determined to retain their slaves. After many defeats, the war goes in favour of the North and, when Abraham stands for re-election, he is able to announce that henceforward all slaves are free. The Civil War ends shortly after the start of Lincoln's second term as President. To celebrate the peace, he and his wife visit a theatre. During the performance, a madman shoots Lincoln and then makes his escape across the stage.

STORY BY ALAN JASON
DRAWN BY NORMAN

MR LINCOLN HAS BEEN SHOT! THERE GOES HIS ASSASSIN— CATCH HIM!

IT'S THAT LUNATIC WILKES BOOTH, AND HE'S GETTING AWAY!

WITH LOVING CARE, LINCOLN IS REMOVED FROM THE THEATRE...

OUR PRESIDENT IS DYING! BOOTH GOT AWAY, BUT HE WON'T GET FAR

7·25 A.M., APRIL 15TH, 1865...

OUR COUNTRY HAS SUFFERED ITS GREATEST LOSS— MR LINCOLN IS DEAD!

VERY SOON AFTER...

BOOTH'S IN THERE! WE HAVE THE PLACE SURROUNDED— NOW WE'LL MOVE IN!

JOHN WILKES BOOTH— COME OUT AND TAKE YOUR MEDICINE, YOU YELLOW ASSASSIN!

AS BOOTH APPEARS IN THE DOORWAY, HE IS SHOT BY AN OVER ZEALOUS SOLDIER...

WHO FIRED THAT SHOT? OUR ORDERS WERE TO TAKE HIM ALIVE!

LET US PRAY FOR ABRAHAM LINCOLN. HE SAW OUR DISTRESS, AND MADE US ALL FREE MEN...

LET US PRAY FOR THE MAN WE IN THE SOUTH FOUGHT— THE MAN WHO TAUGHT US ALL TO LIVE AS BROTHERS...

WITH LINCOLN'S DEATH, AND THAT OF HIS MURDERER, THE STORY THAT BEGAN IN A HUMBLE LOG CABIN AND ENDED AT THE "WHITE HOUSE" IS TOLD. FREE PEOPLES IN ALL PARTS OF THE WORLD HONOUR THE NAME OF ABRAHAM LINCOLN...

1809 1865

THE LOG CABIN WHERE LINCOLN WAS BORN...

THE "WHITE HOUSE", WHERE LINCOLN LIVED AS PRESIDENT.

From **LOG CABIN** **TO** **WHITE HOUSE** THE END

BEGINNING TODAY!

The Travels of MARCO POLO

TOLD BY CHAD VARAH
DRAWN BY FRANK BELLAMY

700 years ago, Venice was so rich and powerful as a centre of world trade that the Imperial City of Constantinople came under its sway, and its Merchant Princes constantly extended the influence of their Republic. One of these nobles was Nicolo Polo who, at a time when his wife was expecting a child, planned to cross the Black Sea to sell jewels to the Chief of the Western Tartars. Before leaving for Constantinople on the first stage of his journey, with his brother Maffeo, Nicolo places his wife in the care of another brother . . .

DON'T WORRY, NICOLO — I'LL TAKE GOOD CARE OF HER FOR YOU.

AND OF MY SON, WHEN HE ARRIVES!

HOW DO YOU KNOW IT'LL BE A BOY, NICOLO?

BECAUSE A GIRL COULDN'T FOLLOW IN FATHER'S FOOTSTEPS! GOD KEEP YOU TILL WE MEET AGAIN, MY DEAREST!

'FATHER'S FOOTSTEPS'. I EXPECT THE CHILD WILL BE WALKING BEFORE I SEE NICOLO AGAIN.

NONSENSE! HE SHOULD BE BACK NEXT YEAR.

SOME MONTHS LATER . . .

THE PHYSICIAN SAYS SHE WON'T LIVE, MY DEAR.

THAT'S WHAT I FEARED. YET, LITTLE MARCO IS AS HEALTHY AS COULD BE.

DEAR GOD, IF I COULD ONLY HEAR FROM NICOLO BEFORE I DIE!

SIR, HERE IS NEWS FROM ABROAD!

A LETTER FROM NICOLO! HE'S WELL . . . HAS DONE SPLENDID TRADE WITH CHIEF BARKA . . . SAYS YOU'RE TO KISS HIS LITTLE SON!

HE'LL START FOR HOME IN SIX MONTHS . . .

SHE IS DEAD! I WILL TAKE CARE OF LITTLE MARCO.

Nicolo and Maffeo do not return to Venice. Their brother discovers next year that they have been cut off by a war between the Western and Eastern Tartars, and have disappeared into central Asia, from which Europeans have never been known to return alive.

15 YEARS LATER (A.D. 1269).

WHAT'S ALL THE EXCITEMENT ON THE CANAL, MARCO?

I'LL GO AND SEE, UNCLE. I DON'T WANT TO MISS ANY FUN!

WHY, THOSE MEN LOOK STRANGELY LIKE UNCLE . . . IF THEY'RE HIS BROTHERS, ONE OF THEM MIGHT BE MY . . .

FATHER!

THE GREAT CHARLEMAGNE

The life story of Charles the Great

After conquering Lombardy, Charles – King of the Franks – subdues the pagan Saxons. In 778 A.D., Charles crosses the Pyrenees, defeats the Moors and makes the people of Northern Spain subject to his rule. Following a number of uprisings, King Charles receives news that the Saxons are preparing a final attempt against him and advances on the rebels, accompanied by Prince Charles, his son. Eventually, the King succeeds in arranging a peace settlement. In 788 A.D., Duke Tassilo, of Bavaria, is convicted of treachery, after which Charles routs Tassilo's allies, the Huns. Wilmodia, the only remaining danger to his Empire, is conquered by Charles in 797 A.D. Two years later, Pope Leo III is driven from the Vatican. The King comes to the Pope's aid and sends him back to Rome with an escort. Wishing to strengthen his position, Leo considers how he can persuade Charles to accept the crown of the Holy Roman Empire.

STORY BY CHAD VARAH.
DRAWN BY NORMAN WILLIAMS.

CHARLES ARRIVES IN ROME IN 800 A.D. AND IS GREETED BY THE POPULACE WITH CHEERS AND ACCLAMATIONS...

LONG LIVE KING CHARLES! BRAVO! HURRAH!

HE AT ONCE HOLDS AN ASSEMBLY AND, AS NO EVIDENCE IS OFFERED AGAINST LEO III, CHARLES RULES THAT THE POPE CAN CLEAR HIMSELF BY OATH...

IN THE NAME OF THE HOLY TRINITY, I SWEAR I AM INNOCENT.

LET NO ONE DOUBT THAT LEO III IS THE LAWFUL POPE.

LATER... THE DAY AFTER TOMORROW IS CHRISTMAS DAY. WILL YOU HONOUR OUR ANCIENT TRADITION AND WEAR THE ROMAN TOGA AT CHURCH?

GLADLY

YOUR COUNTS ARE MORE GORGEOUS THAN YOU TO-DAY, FATHER.

THINK OF THE KING OF KINGS, BORN IN A STABLE THIS DAY — AND YOU WON'T JUDGE PEOPLE BY THEIR TRIMMINGS, MY SON.

CHRISTMAS DAY. 800 A.D.

IN THE CHURCH OF ST. PETER, CHARLES AND HIS SON KNEEL AT THE ALTAR...

THEN, IN FRONT OF THE HUGE THRONG, POPE LEO UNEXPECTEDLY PLACES THE GOLDEN CROWN ON THE HEAD OF THE KNEELING KING.

TO CHARLES AUGUSTUS, CROWNED BY GOD, THE GREAT AND PACIFIC EMPEROR — LONG LIFE AND VICTORY!

HURRAH! HURRAH!

GOD SAVE THE EMPEROR!

LONG LIVE THE EMPEROR CHARLEMAGNE!

HURRAH! HURRAH!

BRAVO!

So, once again, there was an Emperor of the West, and one who has lived in fame as **Charlemagne** – Charles the Great.

THE END

The HAPPY WARRIOR

The true life story of **SIR WINSTON CHURCHILL**

India, 1896. Lt. Winston Churchill has gone to the North-West Frontier to join the Malakand Field Force which is fighting rebel tribesmen. He joins a brigade which advances into the Mamund Valley and soon finds himself engaged in a desperate action with a small company of men. Under withering fire, the company retreats down a hill with its wounded . . .

TOLD BY CLIFFORD MAKINS
DRAWN BY FRANK BELLAMY

PRESS ON WITH THE WOUNDED. I'LL KEEP THE SAVAGES AT BAY !

AIEE !

WINSTON ALONE FACED THE FIERCE PATHAN TRIBESMEN.

MISSED, MY FINE FRIEND ! NOW YOU ARE FOR IT !

THE TRIBESMAN FELL BEHIND A ROCK !

STILL MORE OF THEM ! I MUST MAKE FOR COVER !

AS WINSTON DASHES OVER THE ROCKS, THE BULLETS WHINE AROUND HIM.

SPLENDID WORK !

TO THE BOTTOM OF THE HILL WITH THE WOUNDED ! HURRY !

WINSTON FIRED SHOT AFTER SHOT AS THE COMPANY STRUGGLED DOWN THE HILL.

COURAGE, MEN ! WE'RE NEARLY THERE !

The HAPPY WARRIOR

The true life story of
SIR WINSTON CHURCHILL

June, 1940. The German blitzkrieg on the Western Front has forced Holland and Belgium to surrender and shattered the French Army. The British Expeditionary Force has been evacuated from Dunkirk by thousands of little ships plying the Channel. Winston Churchill repeatedly crosses to France to inspire the French government to fight on. But at a meeting of the Allied War Council near Orleans, the French are ready to surrender.

TOLD BY CLIFFORD MAKINS
DRAWN BY FRANK BELLAMY

GOODBYE! THIS IS A DARK HOUR BUT I AM SURE WE WILL TRIUMPH IN THE END. EVEN IF FRANCE IS OCCUPIED WE WILL STILL WIN THE WAR.

WE SHALL SEE!

POOR CHURCHILL! IN A FEW WEEK'S TIME ENGLAND'S NECK WILL BE WRUNG LIKE A CHICKEN!

On 14th June, the Germans occupied Paris. M. Reynaud, the French Prime Minister, resigned and was succeeded by the aged Marshal Petain who made peace with Adolf Hitler.

IN LONDON...

WELL, THAT'S THAT! THE BATTLE OF FRANCE IS OVER — NOW FOR THE BATTLE OF BRITAIN!

WINSTON, YOU MUST SPEAK TO THE NATION AGAIN — WITHOUT DELAY.

HITLER KNOWS THAT HE WILL HAVE TO BREAK US IN THIS ISLAND OR LOSE THE WAR ... LET US, THEREFORE, BRACE OURSELVES TO OUR DUTIES AND SO BEAR OURSELVES THAT IF THE BRITISH EMPIRE AND ITS COMMONWEALTH LAST FOR A 1,000 YEARS, MEN WILL STILL SAY "THIS WAS THEIR FINEST HOUR"!

MEANWHILE, THE NAZIS REJOICED...

FUEHRER, WITH OUR BASES IN FRANCE THE LUFTWAFFE WILL SHOOT THE R.A.F. FROM THE SKIES!

AND THEN THE INVASION OF ENGLAND! NOTHING CAN STOP US NOW!

IN JULY, THE BATTLE OF BRITAIN BEGAN IN EARNEST. GREAT WAVES OF GERMAN BOMBERS WITH HEAVY FIGHTER ESCORTS CROSSED THE COAST IN DAYLIGHT RAIDS...

ACHTUNG! SPITFIRES!

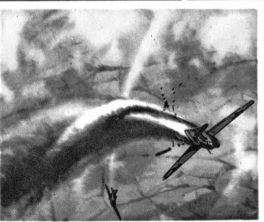

BIGGIN HILL AIRFIELD, KENT. ONE OF THE LEADING FIGHTER STATIONS.

WHAT A SHAMBLES!

LOOK, HERE COMES THE GRAND OLD MAN HIMSELF!

THEY'RE BASHING US ABOUT A BIT, SIR, BUT THEY CAN'T KEEP OUR PLANES OUT OF THE SKY!

THE FATE OF THE COUNTRY NOW RESTS WITH YOU— OUR FIGHTER PILOTS. GOD BE WITH ALL OF YOU!

TO BE CONTINUED.

THE ROAD OF COURAGE

The story of Jesus

BAR-ABBAS IS A THIEF AND MURDERER IF I FREE HIM, WHAT SHALL I DO WITH JESUS CALLED CHRIST?

CRUCIFY HIM!

CRUCIFY HIM!

Pontius Pilate, the Roman Governor, is anxious to get Jesus freed, but the crowd, worked up by the Zealots and Priests, want another Jesus – Jesus Bar-Abbas.

Hoping to placate the Priests and wring mercy from the crowd, Pilate has Jesus scourged. The soldiers give him a mock 'crown' of thorns and a 'royal' robe. Then Pilate brings him before the people again . . .

BEHOLD THE MAN!

SHALL I CRUCIFY YOUR KING?

WE HAVE NO KING BUT CAESAR!

YOU'RE NO FRIEND OF CAESAR'S IF YOU REPRIEVE HIM!

THEY'VE GOT ME, MARIUS I DAREN'T RISK A COMPLAINT TO ROME.

BRING ME THE WARRANT—AND SOME WATER...

I AM INNOCENT OF THE BLOOD OF THIS JUST MAN. THE RESPONSIBILITY IS YOURS..

TAKE HIM AND CRUCIFY HIM!

HE GAVE THEM THE CHOICE, AND THEY CHOSE BAR-ABBAS —BAR-ABBAS!

THEY'RE COMING!

Later, in an upper room, Simon reports to the disciples, who wait with Mary, Mother of Jesus, and Mary Magdalene . . .

THERE'S NO HOPE, THEN

FRANK HAMPSON

Written by MARCUS MORRIS ● *Drawn by* FRANK HAMPSON

THE ROAD OF COURAGE

The story of Jesus

On Calvary, the execution hill just outside Jerusalem, Jesus is prepared for crucifixion with two criminals . . .

FATHER, FORGIVE THEM, FOR THEY KNOW NOT WHAT THEY DO.

As the soldiers gambled for His clothing, in a darkness like an impending storm, Jesus endured the slow agony of the Cross. The Priests of the Temple came out to jeer at their victim, and the people of Jerusalem laughed and mocked at His sufferings, and Jesus gave a great cry: "My God, My God, why hast thou forsaken me?"

HE SAVED OTHERS, BUT HE CAN'T SAVE HIMSELF.

I'LL BELIEVE HE'S THE CHRIST WHEN I SEE HIM COME DOWN FROM THE CROSS!

HO-HO! SO WILL I.

HI, YOU! WHY DON'T YOU SAVE YOURSELF?

COME ON, STEP DOWN!

BE QUIET!

I KNOW HE REFUSED TO TAKE THE WAR-HORSE, BUT PILATE WANTED *ME* UP THERE. HE'S DYING INSTEAD OF ME.

YOU'RE RIGHT THERE. HE'S DYING INSTEAD OF VERY MANY WORSE MEN . . .

TRULY HE MUST BE THE SON OF GOD!

FRANK HAMPSON

Written by MARCUS MORRIS ● *Drawn by* FRANK HAMPSON

THE GREAT SAILOR

The life story of HORATIO NELSON

Admiral Lord Nelson – hero of many past actions, during which he lost the sight of his right eye and had to have his right arm amputated – returns to England in August, 1805, after his fruitless chase of the French fleet to the West Indies and back. England is alarmed by the threatened French invasion, and the Prime Minister, Mr Pitt, entrusts Horatio Nelson with the nation's fortunes at sea. Horatio, aboard the *Victory*, joins his fleet off Cadiz, and waits for the forces of France and Spain – under Admiral Villeneuve – to leave port. Soon, Villeneuve's ships put to sea and – on 21st October, 1805 – the Battle of Trafalgar begins. A French sharpshooter picks off Nelson, and the mortally wounded Admiral is carried below. On deck, Captain Hardy directs a fierce battle . . .

TOLD BY CHRISTOPHER KEYES

CAPTAIN HARDY, SIR, THE ADMIRAL IS CRYING OUT FOR YOU!

I'LL BE DOWN DIRECTLY . . .

HARDY— HOW GOES THE BATTLE?

VERY WELL, MY LORD— WE HAVE TWELVE OR FOURTEEN OF THE ENEMY SHIPS IN OUR POSSESSION.

I AM GOING FAST— KISS ME, HARDY . .

NOW I AM SATISFIED — THANK GOD I HAVE DONE MY DUTY . . .

AT 4·30 IN THE AFTERNOON, ADMIRAL LORD NELSON DIES OF HIS WOUNDS . . .

ON 5TH DECEMBER, THE VICTORY— WITH NELSON'S FLAG AT HALF-MAST—ANCHORS AT SPITHEAD . . .

Then, on a bright January day in 1806, the mortal remains of Vice-Admiral Lord Viscount Nelson, K.C.B., are borne up the Thames from Greenwich to Whitehall Stairs. The greatest sailor the world has known is buried in St. Paul's Cathedral, mourned by the country and the men of the Victory who adored him.

THE END

ALFRED THE GREAT

THE END

THE BADEN POWELL STORY

The True Life Story of the Founder of the Boy Scout Movement. CAPE TOWN, in the year 1903.

At the start of the Boer War, Colonel Baden Powell, nicknamed 'The Wolf', is in command of the town of Mafeking which, inspired by his leadership, resists the attacks of the Boers for seven months. When Mafeking is relieved, Baden Powell, having been awarded the C.B. and promoted to Major-General, forms the South African Constabulary for the purpose of defeating the hard-riding Boer commandos. After a time, the British learn how to master the Boer method of fighting and gradually wear down their opponents. Britain is eventually victorious and peace is signed at Pretoria on May 31st, 1902.

STORY BY ALAN JASON: DRAWN BY

GOOD-BYE TO AFRICA ONCE AGAIN!

In 1903, B.P. leaves Cape Town for England to become Inspector-General, the highest rank in the cavalry.

I WONDER WHAT THOSE BOYS ARE UP TO? I'LL DO A SPOT OF SCOUTING.

Back in England, he strolls through some woods while on leave.

HI! WHAT DO YOU CHAPS THINK YOU ARE PLAYING AT?

STREWTH, GUVNOR! YOU DIDN'T 'ARF MAKE US JUMP—ANYONE 'UD THINK YOU WAS B.P. 'ISSELF!

WHO DID YOU SAY?

BADEN POWELL, MISTER—THE MAFEKING CHAP. HE WROTE THIS 'ERE BOOK.

"AIDS TO SCOUTING", EH! YES, I SEEM TO HAVE HEARD OF IT SOMEWHERE BEFORE!

S'WONDERFUL BOOK, SIR! IT TELLS YOU ALL ABOUT HOW TO TRACK, AN' OBSERVE, AN' READ SIGNS...

SO YOU'RE INTERESTED IN SCOUTING, ARE YOU?

RATHER, GUV! THAT'S WHAT WE WAS PLAYIN' AT JUST NOW.

WELL, DON'T LET ME INTERRUPT YOUR GAME—IT SOUNDS GOOD FUN.

IT IS! YOU OUGHT TO TRY IT SOMETIME, MISTER— YOU'D SOON PICK IT UP!

I THINK THEY'VE GOT SOMETHING THERE. SCOUTING *WOULD* MAKE AN EXCITING GAME FOR BOYS, AND HELP THEM TO BE SELF-RELIANT. I WONDER IF I COULD WORK OUT A SCHEME?

B.P. has been inspecting a mass parade of the Boys' Brigade. He is with Sir William Smith, famous founder of the Boys' Brigade.

YOU'VE GOT A FINE CROWD THERE, SIR WILLIAM. BEST MUSTER I'VE EVER SEEN. I'M QUITE ENVIOUS OF YOU.

YOU'VE NO NEED TO BE. THOSE BOYS IDOLIZE YOU, POWELL. WHY DON'T YOU START A MOVEMENT FOR THEM?

I'D LIKE TO. PERHAPS WE COULD WORK TOGETHER IN SOME WAY?

WHY NOT INDEED? I KNOW—TRY REWRITING THAT SCOUTING MANUAL FOR THE BOYS— THEY'D LOVE IT!

I WILL. AND YOU'VE GIVEN ME THE VERY NAME TOO, SIR WILLIAM— *BOY SCOUTS!*

THE GREAT EXPLORER

The real life story of **DAVID LIVINGSTONE**

David – born in 1813, and a missionary doctor in Africa since 1841 – is not only preaching in parts of the continent never before seen by white men, but is also opening up Africa for more missionaries and traders. After crossing the continent from coast to coast, and suffering terribly from severe bouts of fever, he visits England and finds himself famous. Returning to Africa as a Government explorer, David – with his wife – tries to find a navigable way up the Zambesi. Mrs Livingstone dies, but David stays on in Africa. To the outside world, the great explorer becomes lost because slave-traders steal all his reports. Representing the *New York Herald*, Henry Stanley sets out to find David and, in 1871, he does so . . .

TOLD BY CHAD VARAH
DRAWN BY PETER JACKSON

DOCTOR LIVINGSTONE, I PRESUME?

THE LAMP IN DAVID'S TENT BURNS FAR INTO THE NIGHT, FOR DAVID IS OVERJOYED TO HEAR AND TO SPEAK HIS NATIVE TONGUE AGAIN...

BUT IT IS THE LAST TIME HE WILL DO SO, BECAUSE WHEN AT LAST STANLEY LEAVES FOR HOME, DAVID STAYS BEHIND!

REFRESHED BY THE COMPANIONSHIP OF STANLEY, CHEERED BY THE KNOWLEDGE THAT HIS AIMS AND OBJECTS ARE UNDERSTOOD, DAVID GOES ON WITH HIS WORK UNTIL, ONE NIGHT...

WE CANNOT DISTURB HIM WHILE HE PRAYS.

BUT THIS IS HOW I LEFT HIM HOURS AGO – IF HE SLEEPS, WE MUST PUT HIM TO BED...

HE DOES SLEEP, BUT HE WILL NEVER WAKE AGAIN – THE GREAT MASTER IS DEAD!

DAVID'S FAITHFUL SERVANTS BURY HIS HEART BENEATH A TREE, AND THEN CARRY HIS EMBALMED BODY IN A LITTER OVER A THOUSAND MILES TO THE COAST. THE JOURNEY TAKES SIX MONTHS, BUT FINALLY ENGLAND IS REACHED.

AND SO, ON 18th APRIL, 1874, THE MORTAL REMAINS OF THE GREATEST MISSIONARY OF MODERN TIMES ARE LAID TO REST IN WESTMINSTER ABBEY...

STANDING NEXT TO STANLEY IS JOSEPH MOORE, DAVID'S OLD STUDENT FRIEND...

THIRTY-SIX YEARS AGO, I STOOD WITH LIVINGSTONE ON THIS VERY SPOT. I REMEMBER HIM SAYING THAT HE WAS IN NO DANGER OF BEING BURIED HERE – 'BUT', HE ADDED, 'LET'S PRAY WE MAY DESERVE IT'!

NO MAN HAS DESERVED IT MORE...

...ALREADY HE HAS DEALT THE DEATH-BLOW TO SLAVERY, AND WHEN ONE DAY, GOD WILLING, BLACK AND WHITE PEOPLE LIVE TOGETHER AS BROTHERS, THEY WILL REMEMBER THAT THE MAN WHO SOWED THE SEEDS OF CHRISTIAN LOVE IN AFRICA WAS DAVID LIVINGSTONE – THE GREAT EXPLORER.

THE END

THE SHEPHERD KING

The story of **DAVID**

In the valley of Elah, the Israelite and Philistine armies stand facing one another. From the ranks of the Philistines comes a giant, Goliath of Gath, to terrify the Israelites. Then David, the shepherd boy from Bethlehem, goes out to fight him. He pauses to choose stones from the brook. Goliath, full of contempt, scorns the boy and hurls his spear at David . . .

TOLD BY CLIFFORD MAKINS
DRAWN BY FRANK BELLAMY

COME HERE, BOY, AND I'LL BREAK EVERY BONE IN YOUR BODY!

YOUR WEAPONS ARE USELESS, GOLIATH — FOR THIS IS THE LORD'S BATTLE AND HE WILL GIVE YOU INTO OUR HANDS !

KING SAUL AND THE ISRAELITES WATCH FROM A DISTANCE. THE VALLEY IS SILENT AS A GRAVE . . .

HE'S OVER THE STREAM.

HE'S ABOUT TO DIE !

NOW'S MY CHANCE !

BRITISH BIRDS by George Cansdale PIPITS AND WAGTAILS

THE RATHER PLAIN, SPARROW-SIZED *PIPITS* BELONG TO THE SAME FAMILY AS THE CHEERFULLY-COLOURED *WAGTAILS*, WITH THEIR LONG, CONSTANTLY-MOVING TAILS.

GREY WAGTAIL

The *Pied Wagtail*

DRAWN BY TOM ADAMS

THE *GREY WAGTAIL* HAS THE LONGEST TAIL, AND ITS UPPER PARTS ARE ALWAYS BLUISH-GREY. IT WANDERS ABOUT IN WINTER BUT, IN THE BREEDING SEASON, IT PREFERS SWIFT-RUNNING STREAMS, ESPECIALLY IF THEY ARE SHALLOW AND ROCKY.

THE *PIED WAGTAIL* IS THE ONE WE ALL KNOW, THE 'PEGGY DISHWASHER' THAT LIVES AROUND FARMS AND BUILDINGS AND OFTEN NESTS IN SHEDS AND GARDEN BANKS. IN WINTER, MANY COME TOGETHER IN BIG ROOSTS—SOMETIMES IN REED-BEDS, SOMETIMES IN TREES IN THE MIDDLE OF TOWNS OR CITIES.

YELLOW WAGTAIL

TREE PIPIT

THE *YELLOW WAGTAIL* IS ONLY A SUMMER VISITOR, GENERALLY ARRIVING IN APRIL. IT IS A BIRD OF FIELDS AND MARSHES AND —UNLIKE THE OTHER TWO WAGTAILS, WHICH NEST IN BANKS OR HOLES—THE YELLOW WAGTAIL BUILDS ITS NEST IN THE OPEN.

THE *TREE PIPIT* IS A SUMMER VISITOR AND ALMOST EXACTLY LIKE ITS COUSIN, THE *MEADOW PIPIT*, WHICH STAYS HERE ALL THE YEAR. THE BEST WAY OF SPOTTING IT IS BY ITS LOVELY SONG, MADE WHILE IT DOES A SPECIAL LITTLE FLIGHT FROM A TREE PERCH.

Look around with George Cansdale Salmon Migration

ALTHOUGH SALMON MAY RUN UP FROM THE SEA AT ANY TIME BETWEEN JANUARY AND OCTOBER, THEY LAY THEIR EGGS IN WINTER. THE HEN FISH SCOOPS A HOLE IN THE GRAVEL, IN WHICH SHE LAYS HER EGGS. THE COCK FISH FERTILIZES THEM AND, THIS DONE, THE HEN FISH COVERS THEM WITH GRAVEL. WHEN HATCHED, THE SALMON IS CALLED AN ALEVIN, A TINY CREATURE WITH A SAC UNDER ITS NECK HOLDING ENOUGH FOOD TO LAST IT FOR 6 WEEKS OR SO. THEN IT BECOMES A FRY, THEN A PARR, AND THEN, AT ABOUT THE AGE OF TWO YEARS, A SMOLT, A SILVERY FISH ABOUT 6" LONG. IN EARLY SUMMER, THE SALMON SMOLTS SET OUT ON THEIR PERILOUS JOURNEY TO THE SEA. MANY ARE LOST ON THE WAY. THE SMOLT HAS A NUMBER OF ENEMIES, INCLUDING THE FRESHWATER SHARK—THE PIKE.

SALMON ARE PERHAPS THE BEST KNOWN OF ALL THE FISH THAT MIGRATE. ONE KIND LIVES IN THE ATLANTIC AND SEVERAL OTHERS IN THE PACIFIC, BUT ALL MAKE LONG JOURNEYS TO BREED IN THE RIVER IN WHICH THEY WERE HATCHED.

DRAWN BY BACKHOUSE

IF, AFTER A YEAR AT SEA, THE SALMON RETURNS TO FRESH WATER, IT IS CALLED A GRILSE. IT THEN WEIGHS 3 TO 5 lbs., BUT THE LONGER IT STAYS IN THE SEA, THE BIGGER IT GROWS. THE JOURNEY UP RIVER IS EXTREMELY DANGEROUS. IT MAY BE CAUGHT IN SALMON NETS IN THE ESTUARY, AND IT SNAPS AT THE FLIES AND LURES OF THE FISHERMEN —THOUGH WHY IT DOES THIS IS NOT YET KNOWN, SINCE SALMON TAKE NO FOOD AT ALL AFTER GOING BACK INTO FRESH WATER.

THE JOURNEY UP RIVER IS OFTEN LONG AND DIFFICULT. THE SALMON HAS TO FIGHT ITS WAY PAST RAPIDS, FALLS AND FAST-RUNNING CURRENTS, THOUGH NATURALLY SOME RIVERS ARE EASIER THAN OTHERS.

AFTER SPAWNING, THE PACIFIC SALMON ALWAYS DIES, BUT THE ATLANTIC SALMON MAY SURVIVE. IF IT DOES, IT GOES BACK TO THE SEA AS A KELP, FEEBLE AND EXHAUSTED — BUT EVEN THEN IT MAY STILL FALL VICTIM TO THE FISHERMAN OR TO AN OTTER, AND AN OTTER WILL TAKE A FRESH-RUN SALMON AS WELL AS A KELP.

THE EDITOR'S CHRISTMAS NIGHTMARE

PARDON ME, SIR, BUT HAVE YOU ANY IDEA WHERE WE ARE?

NOT A CLUE, DIG! ALL WE CAN DO IS PRESS ON AND HOPE FOR THE BEST.

LOOK, SIR — SPACEMEN! THE FLEET MUST BE HERE!

IF I FIND THE GALOOT WHO STUCK MY HEAD IN THIS GOLDFISH BOWL, I'LL...

SHUCKS, JEFF! AIN'T ANY USE STANDING THERE CUSSIN'! AIN'T ANYBODY GOT A CAN-OPENER?

I SAY, YOU CHAPS, IS THE CONTROLLER AROUND?

SUFFERIN' SNAKES! MY HOSS!

YEP! SURE 'NUFF. IT IS YOUR HOSS, JEFF. REACH FOR THE SKY, YOU GOLDARNED HOSS THIEVES!

NOW THEN, WHAT'S GOIN' ON HERE?

AH! A STICK UP, EH? O.K., CHUM, IT'S A FAIR COP. YOU'D BETTER COME QUIETLY TO THE POLICE STATION.

HUH! YOU AIN'T A POLICEMAN, MISTER!

NEVER SEEN A LAW OFFICER IN DUDS LIKE THAT, NO SIRREE!

LOOK, SIR, MORE TROUBLE COMING!

THERE HE IS, BIMBERG — THE MAN IN MY UNIFORM KEEP THE REST OF THEM COVERED

YES, SERGEANT LUCK.

I ARREST YOU AS A SPY MASQUERADING IN LEGION UNIFORM.

NONSENSE! I ARREST YOU — FOR IMPERSONATING A POLICE OFFICER.

QUIET! ALL OF YOU!

HOSS THIEF!

BEAVER!

MAMA MIA!

IT IS OBVIOUS WHAT'S HAPPENED. WE ARE ALL IN THE WRONG STORY, THE WRONG CLOTHES AND THE WRONG PAGE.

ONLY ONE MAN COULD CAUSE SUCH A CRIME — FOLLOW ME.

THE EDITOR!

QUIET PLEASE!

YOU ARE GUILTY OF EATING TOO MUCH CHRISTMAS PUDDING, SLEEPING ON DUTY AND LETTING THE ARTISTS RUN WILD — CAUSING CONFUSION AND ALARM TO THE READERS.

FOR THIS YOU ARE SENTENCED TO PROVIDE A SLAP-UP, SUPERSONIC CHRISTMAS DINNER FOR ALL EAGLE CHARACTERS.

MERCY!

FRANK HAMPSON

AND SO...

A MERRY CHRISTMAS, EVERYBODY!

WUFF!

READER'S EFFORTS

Drawn by GORDON THOMPSON (*aged* 14)
9 Monks Brow, Barrow-in-Furness, Lancs.

HERE is the first page of contributions sent in by EAGLE readers and we think you will all agree that they are pretty good. Each contributor will be paid by EAGLE for his effort.

Have *you* written or drawn anything you would like to see published? If so, send it in to the Editor, EAGLE, 4 New Street Square, London E.C.4. Don't forget to include your name, address and age.

THE RIVER

Written by MALCOLM TODD (*aged* 9)
19 Park Grove, Shipley, Yorks.

I am the river
  Flowing down the hills,
Passing open country,
  Passing smoky mills.

I am the river
  With a flow'ry bank,
Goats and sheep and other things
  From my water drank.

I am the river
  Big and swift and strong,
Faster, ever faster,
  I flow along.

I am the river
  Passing nearly all,
Underneath the bridge,
  O'er the waterfall.

I am the river
  Passing near the town,
Joined by little streams
  As I go down.

I am the river
  Nearing the sea,
Watching happy children
  Playing by me.

I am the river
  Entering the dock,
Passing halls and churches
  And the Town Clock.

I am the river
  Entering the sea,
Nothing but waves
  Passing by me.

Drawn by ROGER BRANN (*aged* 14)
40 Mount St. Flats, Devonport, Plymouth.

RIDDLE-ME-REE (1)

(*For answer see foot of col. 4*)

Written by ANDREW SIMPSON (*aged* 15)
452 Lobley Hill Road, Gateshead 11.

My first is in jacket but not in coat,
My second in castle but not in moat,
My third is in fiction and also in fact,
My fourth is in fired but not in sacked,
My fifth is in car and also in cab,
My sixth is in flounder but not in dab,
My seventh is in kernel and also in nut,
My eighth is in open but not in shut,
My ninth is in small but not in big,
My tenth is in date but not in gig.
My whole rides out west and is one of the best.

THE TREE OF DEATH

Written by FRANK BYE (*aged* 14), 86 Storrington Ave., West Derby, Liverpool 11.

When I was in Africa prospecting for gold, one day one of my native luggage-bearers shouted to me that he'd found an old man who was dying, with a poisoned dart in his back, on the ground.

When I got over to him, I gave him a tot of brandy and called my interpreter to ask the man how he came to be like that. I gathered that a tribe, the Andacs who lived in a hidden valley, had wounded him. Then he kept muttering something about the "white tree" until he died, with his swollen tongue lolling out.

I decided that as I had had no luck in my search for gold, I would have a look for the tree of which the man had spoken. But my native-bearers refused to come with me, for the direction which the old man pointed out to me was "tabu" – that is the same as a haunted house is to us in England. So I packed all my belongings, strapped them to my back, told the rest to wait for me, and set off by myself.

After I'd gone about two miles through dense undergrowth, I was beginning to think my quest hopeless. Suddenly I saw a glint of white among the trees. I scrambled towards it and found what I was looking for – a tall white tree! But I could see no valley round about, so I climbed up the tree to get a better look.

At the top was dense foliage and, as I could see no hidden valley, I started to climb down. Suddenly I saw a tunnel in the branches, about four feet high, along which I started to crawl. It seemed that I was crawling for hours, but at last, when the tunnel began to slope downwards, I saw a speck of light, doubled my pace, and reached the end of the tunnel in about five minutes.

It opened into a slope at the bottom of which were some mud huts. Everything was hemmed in by a valley . . . I had found the home of the Andacs! I went down to the huts to get some lodging for the night, and was glad to see that the natives seemed friendly. I explained in sign language what I wanted, which they gave me.

I stayed for a few days being shown round the village, or showing myself what there was to see. But on each of these trips I was aware of a strange sound I can only describe as "Whee-eee-eee-ooo-ooo", sometimes sounding like the wind whistling. Whenever I asked the reason for this noise, the natives were

silent – on all but one day. That particular day everyone seemed to be silent. When I enquired why this was so, they signalled me to go with them. We walked to the outskirts of the village and the strange "Whoo-eee-ooo" noise grew deafening.

Suddenly I was seized by six men who ran with me along a path which led through a marsh. Then . . . I saw it! A swaying tree from which the dreadful noise issued. I was thrown on the ground and one of the natives, whom I had taught some English, explained to me that there was to take place the annual sacrifice to the tree. I was seized again and flung under the branches of the swaying, sighing tree. I was to be the sacrifice!

I was petrified with fear. The tree – if you could call it that – seemed to sense I was there, for the sighing noise rose to a higher pitch, and the branches lowered themselves to surround me!

How to escape – that was the problem. I realized that the leaves of the tree were as dry as bones. In a flash I knew what I would do – I would set fire to the tree! I whipped out a box of matches, struck one and set fire to a branch. In a few seconds the lower branches were aflame and the tree was burning. The natives had moved away. I ran to the marsh and threw myself in it – then all went black . . . I knew no more. . . .

I woke up and found I was back at my camp. My burns had been bandaged. How had I got to the camp? I asked one of my servants, and he told me I had been found in the jungle. But how had I got there? It is still a mystery to me.

The only solution that I can imagine is that I was probably the only "sacrifice" to have escaped the clutches of the sighing tree, and that the natives, impressed by my escape from it, had brought me back through the tunnel into the jungle. The peculiar thing is that I spent a lot of time looking for the "white tree" again . . . I never found it.

RIDDLE-ME-REE (2)
(*For answer see foot of col. 4*)
Written by SHEILA KIRK (*aged* 12)
2 Arnold Avenue, South Wigston, Leics.

My first is in egg but not in bacon,
My second in sad and also mistaken,
My third you will find in English and German,
My fourth in Michael but not in Vernon.
My fifth is in Athens and also in Rome,
My whole is a paper beloved and well-known.

OLD TYTHE BARN, MAIDSTONE.
Drawn by PATRICIA ADAMS (*aged* 15)
5 Greenway, Cherry Orchard Est., Maidstone, Kent.

CLUES
(*For solution see foot of column*)

ACROSS
1 Plan (6).
4 Sing one of sixpence (4).
7 Traitors are often these (6).
8 Thought (4).
10 An adding machine does all this (6 & 2).
13 A builder must first find this (4 & 4).
16 Often called 'Handy' (4).
17 Overseas (6).
18 Pronoun (4).
19 Truly (6).

DOWN
1 Scurry (4).
2 Boss (anag) (4).
3 Valuable dirt (4 and 4).
5 It is bound to come to most of us (3 and 3).
6 Holds tightly (6).
9 Seaside amusement (3 and 5).
11 Amazed (6).
12 French dog (6).
14 Old tax (4).
15 Small whirlpool (4).

By A. WALSH (*aged* 15), 97 Duchy Drive, Heaton, Bradford, Yorkshire.

INJUNS!

Drawn by D. L. WEBB (*aged* 14)
50 Samuel Rd., Fratton, Portsmouth, Hants.

HARRIS TWEED GOES WEST
Drawn by DEREK NEWMAN (*aged* 14)
12 Fletcher Road, Ipswich, Suffolk.

Answers to Riddle-me-rees
(1) JEFF ARNOLD
(2) EAGLE

Solution to crossword

PICTURE REVIEW OF EAGLE'S SECOND YEAR

What has EAGLE been doing in the past year – since our first birthday? Bringing you happiness and interest, we hope, and a strong sense of comradeship between our readers all over the British Isles – and beyond.

Below we look back on some of our second year activities in pictures and hope you will enjoy them.

Dan Dare Recording. At Star Sound Studios in London, Frank Hampson, with son Peter, explains to *Eaglers* how the machine works. This was the first recording of Dan Dare.

Visit to the T.T. Races at the Isle of Man. The Editor and competition winners are photographed before they take their seats in the plane to fly them over to the Isle of Man.

Chat with an Engine Driver. Which is better – to be a passenger or the driver? Here you see the driver and fireman exchanging views with EAGLE readers at Waterloo.

Mug of the Year for 1951. EAGLE sent John Grimes, last year's No. I MUG, to Torquay with his mother for a summer holiday. Here you see John with Mr Hollyer and Mr March of Torquay Corporation.

The Daily Splash! On your mark . . . ready . . . and into the swimming pool was just part of the fun at our holiday camp at Little Canada, Isle of Wight, last summer.

Sampling the soup. Seeing round hotel kitchens can be a hungry business and when the cook says, "Try this, son," *Eaglers* are apt to form a quick queue! It tasted good, too!

See that up there? Cadet W. P. Embleton of the Canadian Pacific *Beaverdell* shows an EAGLE party round the vessel at London Docks.

After Dinner. A good time for quiet reading or for exploring the "log cabin" at our Holiday Camp at Little Canada, Isle of Wight.

On the way to Lords. England's cricketers, Denis Compton, Godfrey Evans and Alec Bedser stopped to have a friendly chat with *Eaglers* before the Test last June.

Film Premiere of *Tom Brown's Schooldays*. John Howard Davies, who played Tom Brown and who is also an EAGLE club member, chats to other *Eaglers* before they see the film premiere at the Gaumont Theatre, Haymarket.

Iceland Visit. Sponsored by EAGLE, Richard Lawrence and Michael Keen went with the British Schools Exploring Society's Expedition to Iceland. Their parents and an EAGLE representative greet them on their return to London.

Christmas Carols at St Paul's. What better end to the year of 1951? St Paul's was filled to overflowing by EAGLE readers and their parents. Our collection was given to the Children's Society and Dr Barnardo's Homes.

Trip in a Helicopter. One of the high spots of our past year was a helicopter trip between Birmingham and London for prizewinners. *Eagler* Terence Ball finds the dashboard pretty exciting, especially with an interested pilot there to explain it all clearly.

A quiet corner. Robin Holloway's father was exhibiting at the Festival Exhibition of the Royal Society of British Arts. Half way round, Tony thought a rest was indicated so he settled to read his EAGLE.

EAGLE SPORTS PAGE · INFORMATION · NEWS
INSTRUCTION

EAGLE GALLERY
OF FAMOUS SPORTSMEN

No. 74   GRAEME HOLE
(South Australia and Australia)

This tall, fair-headed batsman was twenty years old when he made his Test debut against England in 1950-51 and he made an impressive 63 in the second innings of the Fifth Test. He opened the present Australian tour by scoring a century against Worcestershire in his maiden innings in this country.

Besides being a graceful and free-scoring batsman, Graeme is a useful slow-medium off-spin bowler who has taken Test match wickets, and he is also a splendid slip fielder.

LEARN BY WATCHING AT WIMBLEDON

by Geoff Paish
(British Davis Cup International)

On Monday tennis players from all over the world will gather at Wimbledon for the Championships of 1953.

To players and spectators alike, Wimbledon is the magic word in lawn tennis. To play at Wimbledon, and then to win must be every tennis player's ambition: it certainly has been mine.

For those of you who are lucky enough actually to go to Wimbledon, or who can see it on TV, I advise you to spend a lot of the first week watching the players on the outer courts. On the Centre Court one gets a long range view which tends to flatter the play, but at the side of the outer courts one can watch the details of the stroke play more closely.

As you know, since the war players from America and Australia have dominated the championships, and I would suggest that you take the opportunity of watching the young players from those countries – 'Little Mo' Connolly, Ken Rosewell and Lew Hoad for example. Watch their stroke play, their footwork, and the calm, businesslike way they set about winning their matches.

For those of you who are left-handed I suggest you compare the different styles of Drobny, Rose and Larsen, and pick the one that suits you best to follow.

But don't forget the players from Britain who will be giving of their best, and when you get back home try and put into your own play the best of everything that you have seen, so that one day you too may realize that ambition – to play at Wimbledon.

The 31-year-old left-hander **JAROSLAV DROBNY** (above) now ranks as the world's No. 1 amateur. This may be Drobny's last and best chance of achieving his great ambition – to win the Wimbledon Singles title.

BRITAIN'S YOUNG HOPES

Mature **BOBBY WILSON**, 17-year-old Finchley schoolboy (left), lively **ROGER BECKER**, 19-year-old Londoner (centre) and the 'never-say-die' left-hander **BILLY KNIGHT**, 17-year-old Northamptoner.

18-year-old **LEW HOAD** (playing the ball) and fellow Australian **KEN ROSEWELL** (Hoad's doubles partner scored many sensational successes at Wimbledon last year.

ENGLAND v. AUSTRALIA at LORD'S

Paynter and Hammond batting for England against Australia at Lord's in the exciting Test Match of 1938. They set up a record fourth wicket stand of 222.

Of the seventeen Test matches that have been played at Cricket's Headquarters, Australia have won six, England five, and six have been drawn.

The first match at Lord's, in 1884, was memorable for a magnificent innings of 148 by England's A. G. Steel, and for the way G. J. Bonnor, the six-foot-five bearded Australian giant, was caught and bowled by Ulyett off a terrific drive – one of the historic catches of cricket. England won this, and the next match in 1886, by an innings.

A remarkable match took place in 1930. England scored 425. In reply, however, Australia amassed 729 for 6 declared (Bradman 254), their highest total and the highest-ever at Lord's, and they won the match by 7 wickets.

Len Hutton (England)

One of the most exciting of all Lord's Tests was played in 1938. England were 31 for 3 when Wally Hammond was joined at the wicket by left-handed Eddie Paynter, the pugnacious little Lancastrian, and this pair proceeded to set up a record English fourth wicket stand of 222. Out of England's 494 for the first innings, Hammond made 240 in one of the finest knocks of his career. A record crowd of 33,800 people saw Australia make a strong reply of 422 (Brown 206 not out). England were in trouble in the 2nd innings, and half the side were out for 76, when Denis Compton (then 20 years old) came to the rescue. His 76 not out enabled Hammond to declare with the score 242 for 8, leaving Australia 2¾ hours to make 315 runs to win.

In the final innings Don Bradman and Lindsay Hassett stayed grimly to force a draw – Australia 204 for six, with Bradman 102 not out. The Don's fourteenth hundred against England also enabled him to pass Jack Hobbs' record individual aggregate of 3636 runs for the series.

The last time England and Australia met at Lord's was in 1948, when the visitors won by 409 runs, only Denis Compton making a respectable score (53) against fine bowling. It was Lindwall who did most of the damage.

Lindsay Hassett (Australia)

THE KING'S CUP AIR RACE

The start of the third Air Race for the King's Cup in 1924.

This event was first organized by the Royal Aero Club in 1922. That is a long time ago in aerial development: but, indirectly, the race can claim an even longer history, for it succeeded the Aerial Derby, which started in 1912.

Strangely enough, the King's Cup was in one sense less important than the race it succeeded. The Derby was a level race, but its successor was a handicap; and, as manufacturers do not build special machines for handicaps, it had little influence on design. However, to serve its purpose as a sporting event, it had to be a handicap.

In view of this, winning speeds have not always shown the steady increase normal in motor or aerial races. The first win was at well over 100 m.p.h. but: several years later 90 m.p.h. won the trophy, though there were, of course, faster machines competing. In 1935, for instance, a plane owned by the Duke of Kent averaged 209 m.p.h., but finished sixth behind a winner who did 176 m.p.h.

That winner, incidentally, was Tommy Rose, just one of the many pioneers of British aerial development who have taken part in this sporting race.

Fastest winner to date is Alex Henshaw who, in 1938, flew a Percival Mew Gull over a 1,000 mile course at an average speed of 236.25 m.p.h. A similar type of aircraft has been entered for this year's race.

The King's Cup course has varied from year to year, sometimes it's been held on an enormous circuit of Britain. When the race was revived in 1949 the course was shortened to a total length of sixty miles. It was then lengthened to over 100 miles, but now it's back to sixty again.

Last year's race, at Newcastle, was won by Cyril Gregory's Taylorcraft, Class D plus D, at an average speed of 113.5 m.p.h. This year the race will take place at Southend, and challengers for the King George VI trophy must win their place in three qualifying races over three laps of the ten mile course. The Final – the King's Cup race itself – will consist of six ten-mile laps, and a particularly spectacular race is promised.

It is interesting to note that this race is, and always has been, entirely British.

And so we continue to thrill to the race for the King's Cup – classic annual reminder that engineering science is also a sport.

Princess Margaret's Hawker Hurricane 11c fighter, piloted by Group Captain Peter Townsend, D.S.O., D.F.C. rounds a pylon during the 1950 King's Cup Air Race at Wolverhampton. The Hurricane, heavily handicapped, was beaten by 60 yards in a thrilling finish. Townsend sped up to the finishing line but Edward Day, piloting a Miles Hawk Trainer, put his plane into a dive to snatch the victory.

Eagle SPORTS news

INVITES YOU TO JOIN IN OUR CHRISTMAS QUIZ

DENIS COMPTON kicks off with Sporting Halves

Can you recognize the famous sportsman whose friendly grin has been split in half in the picture?

The West Indian cricketers would have little difficulty in solving this problem – they saw a great deal of our 'mystery man' at the batting crease during the summer.

If you're really beaten, you will find the answer printed below.

For a bright start to your party, why not cut out some sports pictures from newspapers and magazines and paste them to thin card. Then cut each piece of card in half and, as each guest arrives, hand him one part of the card and set him the task of finding the holder of the other. It's a splendid way of making introductions.

TOM GRAVENEY

HA! HA! QUIZ

Set by GODFREY EVANS

See if you can fill in the missing letters in these answers to sporting posers. The answers look funny now, but don't let them have the last laugh.

1. – HA – – – – . The Giant of Juventus (pictured).
2. – – – – HA – . She won Britain's first Olympic swimming gold medal since 1924.
3. HA – – – – . Neil is Australia's leading left-handed batsman.
4. HA – – – – – – . British motor racing ace.
5. – – – – HA – . Lancashire and England fast bowler.
6. HA – – – – . A world cycling champion – and he's British.
7. – – – HA – . They play at Craven Cottage.
8. HA – – – – . He also plays at Craven Cottage.

ANSWERS Charles; Grinham; Harvey; Hawthorn; Statham; Harris; Fulham; Haynes.

JOHNNY HAYNES asks

Can YOU score a GOAL?

The ball is at your feet and it's up to you – can you get the ball into goal?

Answer the clues given below by changing just one letter at each step of the pattern. If you do it correctly you can turn BALL into GOAL in six moves.

BALL

It rings	.....	....
Keeps trousers up		
Door-fastening		
Sail in it	.....	....
It's a 'nanny'		

GOAL

Answers: 1. Bell. 2. Belt. 3. Bolt. 4. Boat. 5. Goat.

WHERE ON EARTH?

CALIFORNIA 1

GATESHEAD 5 M
WASHINGTON
HOUGHTON 6 M
2

NEW YORK BOSTON B1192 3

WHIP · MA · WHOP · MA · GATE 4

BAD BARGAIN LANE 5

BREAD · AND · CHEESE · LANE 6

asks Johnny Leach

I've been collecting some more unusual signposts in my table tennis travels around Britain. Yes, Britain – though you could be excused for thinking that Nos. 1, 2 and 3 were only to be found in the U.S.A.

Can you say where each of the six signposts shown are to be found?

ANSWERS

1. Bailey, Herts. 2. County Durham. 3. Lincolnshire. 4 and 5. Both York. 6. Wormley, Herts.

TREVOR BAILEY says FIGURE THIS OUT

A cricket team has two bowlers, Demon and Googly. Before the last match of the season, they have taken 30 wickets between them and their averages are the same. In the last match Demon takes 3 for 24, and Googly 2 for 26. Their averages for the season are now worked out and found in each case to be 4. What are the respective final figures for the season of Demon and Googly?

ANSWER Demon — 15 wickets for 60. Googly — 20 wickets for 80.

CAN YOU BEAT I

WORLD'S GREATEST TENOR

—ENRICO CARUSO (1873-1921)

CARUSO WAS THE 19TH. SON OF AN ITALIAN WAREHOUSEMAN. HIS RECORDINGS ALONE EARNED HIM £600,000 IN ROYALTIES

THE HIGHES...

...RCH STATION, NEW HAMPSHIRE, U·S·A

THE WORLD'S BEST WOMAN HIGH JUMPER

SHEILA LERWILL LEAPT OVER A BAR SET AT 5 FT. 7⅜ INS. TO WIN THE BRITISH TITLE FOR THIS EVENT ON JULY 7TH. 1951.

ENGLAND'S RAREST MAMMAL

THE PINE MARTIN (MUSTELA MARTES) USED AT ONE TIME TO BE FAIRLY COMMON IN ENGLAND. NOW IT IS EXTINCT IN ALL BUT THE WILDEST PARTS OF THE LAKE DISTRICT. THE LARGEST OF THESE MAMMALS ARE 32 INS FROM THE NOSE TO THE TIP OF THE TAIL.

WORLD'S LARGEST AIRCRAFT PROPELLER

THE 8 BLADED CURTIS-WRIGHT 'OCTOPROP' IS OVER 19 FT IN DIAMETER AND IS DESIGNED FOR USE WITH 15,000 HORSE POWER GAS TURBINE AERO-ENGINES.

FOR COLLECTORS ONLY

SHELL COLLECTING
by "The Hobbyist"

Large Snail Shell

SHELLS are so beautiful to look at, and so intricately and perfectly made, that very few people can resist picking them up on a beach and many fine shell collections have started just in that way. Most shells *are* found on beaches or rocks but there is no need to live near the sea to be a shell collector. There are plenty of shells to be found near ponds and lakes, in running streams and even in damp ditches between fields. Shell-bearing animals are called *molluscs* and they include snails and slugs as well as what we commonly call 'shell-fish'. Anybody who studies shells and becomes an expert is called a conchologist (pronounced konk-ol-ogist).

Once you start collecting shells, even the common ones, such as mussels, razorshells, scallops, cockles, whelks and limpets, are worth looking at very carefully. There are at least a dozen kinds of limpet in this country alone! Nearly all shells are fragile and the best place to keep good specimens is in a shallow drawer or large, shallow box divided

Common Whelk

into compartments by strips of cardboard or, better still, by smaller boxes 'nested' so that they fit closely together. For small shells match boxes are ideal. Each box should be lined with a little cotton-wool and if you can get any brightly coloured cotton wool your

shells will look their best. A set of open shelves hanging on the wall is a good place to keep the larger specimens and if you can get hold of any kind of glass-fronted cupboard that is the best place of all to store and arrange shells. A young friend of mine bought a very dirty old cupboard for eight shillings and, after cleaning and painting, it made a first class 'cabinet' for his shells.

If you are collecting shells, read about them and study their shapes in illustrated books or

Fusus Bernicionsis

in a natural history museum. Most public libraries have good reference books on shells and it is often possible to buy very good second-hand books about them for quite a small sum. I bought a Victorian shell book last week, with twenty coloured plates, for three shillings. There is also a King Penguin about British shells which is full of excellent information. Look for shells yourself where and when possible but don't overlook other good sources of supply. Make friends with a fishmonger and there is no knowing what he might be willing to pass on. Missionaries often send home shells for sale at bazaars and one of the best shell 'finds' I ever made myself was in a box of mixed shells I bought for a shilling at a sale of work in aid of missionary funds. You can sometimes find the big, exciting foreign shells in out-of-the-way junk shops where they have been bought in 'odd lots' at house sales but, of course, by far the best way of getting rare or unusual shells of every kind is to have a sailor in the family.

STAMPS – UNIVERSAL POSTAL UNION
by Robert Beck

DURING the last nine or ten months you must have seen stamps from many countries with the words Universal Postal Union somewhere in the design. These special stamps were issued to commemorate the seventy-fifth anniversary of the Convention held by many nations in BERNE, Switzerland, in October 1874.

You will remember that the introduction of our Penny Black established a fixed rate for postage all over Great Britain. By 1860 most countries had done the same, but there was no agreement between nations on a uniform postage rate for letters, parcels, etc., going from one country to another, and many high and varied postal changes had to be made before a letter or any other package reached its destination "abroad".

In 1863 Montgomery Blair, the U.S.A. Postmaster General, sent a circular to all the postal authorities of the world suggesting a meeting to see if they could come to some agreement on universal rates for "foreign" postage. This suggestion was enthusiastically taken up by fifteen nations and a meeting took place in PARIS in May 1863. The exchange of ideas at this meeting led to the calling of the Convention mentioned above at which uniform postal rates for all mail was agreed.

At later meetings of the Postal Congress (as it was now called) many improvements were made. For instance, Congress of 1897 introduced universal colours for the lower values of postage stamps. This still applies today, for our halfpenny is GREEN, our penny stamp is RED, and our two-penny halfpenny is BLUE . . . Now let us look at the same values (for postage) of the U.S.A. . . . the one cent (equals our halfpenny) is GREEN, the two cents (our penny) is RED, and the five cents (our twopenny halfpenny) is BLUE. . . . This agreement of colours has been of great value to Post Office sorters of all countries.

Another Congress met in BERNE in 1900 and a monument was unveiled in the KLEIN SCHANZALL PARK. Our picture of the SWISS stamp illustrates this.

SWITZERLAND. *Showing the Globe Monument in Berne with five men of different nations handing their letter to the next man. Three in set.*

BRITISH COLONIALS. *Design of the lowest value U.P.U. stamps for all the Crown Colonies. Four in each set.*

BELGIAN CONGO. *This attractive stamp is issued by the Congo commemorating the seventy-five years of Universal Postal Union. One in set.*

149

Come and see

HULTON'S BOYS & GIRLS EXHIBITION

OLYMPIA NATIONAL HALL **AUGUST 1-15** 9.30 a.m.-8 p.m. Except Sundays ADMISSION 1/6

LAST year, our Exhibition for boys and girls at Olympia welcomed 227,084 people! This year, with the promise of even bigger and better attractions, we hope even more of you will come and visit this wonderful Exhibition.

It has been specially designed for readers of EAGLE – as well as the companion papers, GIRL, SWIFT and ROBIN. This is the show you'll all want to see, for there are displays and stands to thrill every boy and girl. There will be famous people to meet, and games in which you can join; you will also be invited on to some of the stands to take part in demonstrations. Your visit to our Exhibition will be the highlight of the holidays. Make a date NOW for the whole family – there's something to interest everyone. Bring your friends too – and don't forget, it's HULTON'S BOYS AND GIRLS EXHIBITION at OLYMPIA.

The dates are 1st – 15th August (except Sundays), and the Exhibition is open from 9.30 a.m. to 8 p.m.

Tell your parents about the Exhibition

Admission 1/6

HOW TO GET THERE

TRAINS (Underground)
There will be a special service running from Earl's Court to Olympia

BUSES
9, 27, 28, 49, 73, 91 and 270

GREEN LINE BUSES
701, 702, 704, 705, 714, 716 and 716A

PETS' CORNER

DAN DARE SPACEWALK

Radio Control Launch

Miniature Vickers Valiant

Projection Equipment

RIFLE RANGE

PARENTS' OASIS

CHRISTMAS CAROL SERVICES

This Christmas, as usual, the readers of EAGLE, GIRL, SWIFT and ROBIN and their parents will join with the Editor in Christmas Carol Services throughout the British Isles. There may be a Service near your home. If so, come and join us, bringing your parents and friends. Services will be held at the following Cathedrals and Churches.

St Paul's Cathedral, London . . .	Saturday, 14th December, at 2.15 p.m.
Second Service . . .	Saturday, 21st December, at 2.15 p.m.
St Giles's Cathedral, Edinburgh . .	Tuesday, 24th December, at 3.00 p.m.
Birmingham Parish Church	Friday, 27th December, at 2.30 p.m.
Liverpool Cathedral	Saturday, 28th December, at 4.00 p.m.
Manchester Cathedral	Monday, 30th December, at 2.30 p.m.
St Anne's Cathedral, Belfast . . .	Tuesday, 31st December, at 3.00 p.m.
Bristol Cathedral	Thursday, 2nd January, at 2.30 p.m.
Portsmouth Cathedral	Friday, 3rd January, at 2.30 p.m.
Durham Cathedral	Saturday, 4th January, at 2.30 p.m.

Write at once for your invitations to:- Carol Services, EAGLE, Long Lane, Liverpool 9, enclosing a gummed label clearly addressed to yourself and bearing a 2d. stamp. Don't forget to state which Service you want to attend and how many tickets you require. Applications for tickets will be taken in strict rotation.

SPECIAL NOTES

LIVERPOOL

This year, for the first time, we are holding a Service for our readers in Liverpool.

ST PAUL'S

As always there will be a huge demand for tickets at St Paul's. To avoid disappointment and ensure that so many people are not standing at the back this year, we are holding two Services. Please state your preference, but if tickets are not available for one date we shall send them automatically for the other – **unless you state otherwise.**

PLEASE MAKE SURE YOU CAN COME BEFORE WRITING FOR TICKETS

A BUMPER FREE SUPPLEMENT OF FUN, GAMES AND ADVENTURE!

EAGLE EXTRA

FREE with every issue of EAGLE dated 11th September, 1953

MARVELL of M. I. 5.

THE GOLDEN ARROW AFFAIR.
KIM MARVELL AND "CAUTIOUS" McCAW, ACE SECRET SERVICE TEAM, RECEIVE AN URGENT SUMMONS FROM SIR CLIVE CECIL, CHIEF OF M.I.5.

SIR CLIVE SOUNDED AWFULLY WORRIED, CAUTIOUS. I WONDER WHAT'S IN THE WIND?

TROUBLE, NO DOUBT, KIM! WE'LL SOON KNOW.

STORY BY DAVID CAMERON DRAWN BY NEVIN

WHAT'S THE PANIC, CHIEF?

A TYPE NAMED MARIUS SPANDAU HAS STOLEN THE PLANS OF THE NEW 'GOLIATH' JET BOMBER. HE'S ON THE LOOSE IN LONDON AND TRYING TO BREAK OUT.

ANY DETAILS OF HIS APPEARANCE OR MOVEMENTS?

NONE!—OPERATOR 5 'PHONED IN THIS MORNING TO REPORT HE'D RUN SPANDAU TO EARTH —— HE GOT NO FURTHER THAN GIVING ME THE NAME 'MARIUS SPANDAU' WHEN I HEARD A SHOT AND HE WAS CUT OFF. WE TRACED THE CALL TO A PHONE-BOX, AND FOUND OUR MAN — DEAD!

ALL AIRFIELDS, PORTS AND RAILHEADS ARE BEING WATCHED, WITH THE EXCEPTION OF VICTORIA STATION. THAT'S YOUR TERRITORY, MARVELL. HE MAY TRY TO GET OUT ON THE GOLDEN ARROW EXPRESS. IF HE DOES, IT'S UP TO YOU TO STOP HIM.

NO DESCRIPTION WHATSOEVER? WE'LL NEED PLENTY OF LUCK, CHIEF.

THEY'VE CLOSED THE BARRIER. HERE COMES THE LAST PASSENGER.

WILL PASSENGERS FOR THE GOLDEN ARROW PLEASE TAKE THEIR SEATS IMMEDIATELY.

ALL ABOARD!

HURRY ON, MA'AM!

IF SHE WAITS TO BUTTON HER COAT, SHE'LL MISS THE TRAIN.

VICTORIA STATION

QUITE A GAL, CAUTIOUS! LET'S KEEP HER COMPANY!

IN YOU GET, LADY!

YOU'RE DAFT, MON — WAGGIN' THAT EYE OF YOURS AT A LASSIE WHEN WE'RE SUPPOSED TO BE SPOTTING A SPY.

SHE NEEDS A LIGHT, CAUTIOUS. GIVE ME YOUR MATCHES.

CATCH, MISS!

OH!

HOOTS, MON! WEREN'T YOU TOLD NEVER TO THROW THINGS TO A LADY?

HE'S NO LADY! MARIUS SPANDAU, PRESUME?

CURSE YOU!

HE LOOKS A DIFFERENT PICTURE WITHOUT THE WAR-PAINT, MARVELL. HOW DID YOU SPOT HIM?

TWO THINGS, CAUTIOUS. THE FIRST —HE WAS TRYING TO BUTTON UP A WOMAN'S COAT THE WRONG WAY. A NATURAL HABIT CONSIDERING HE WAS WEARING A GARMENT WHICH ALWAYS BUTTONS ON THE OPPOSITE SIDE TO A MAN'S.

YOUR MATCHES HELPED TOO. WHEN YOU THROW ANYTHING TO A LADY, SHE AUTOMATICALLY MAKES A "LAP" TO CATCH IT. WHEN I THREW THE MATCHES, THIS CROOK CLOSED HIS KNEES —A TYPICAL MASCULINE GESTURE. I KNEW THEN HE WAS NO LADY AND TOOK A CHANCE ON IT BEING SPANDAU. I WAS RIGHT!

NEXT WEEK — Kim Marvell in THE PASSPORT PLOT

EAGLE EXTRA-FUNNIES

THAT CHAP

JUST JOHNNY

By VALENTINE

EDISON BRAIN — THE BOY INVENTOR

By HICKEY

PEDRO THE PIRATE

By MARTIN

EAGLE FREE-FOR-ALL FUN AND GAMES PAGE

Alec, the office-boy, comes back from lunch to find the office ransacked and Miss Potts, the secretary, sitting tied in her chair.

Alec unties Miss Potts and phones the police. "What's happened?" he cries. Before Miss Potts can explain the police arrive.

Miss Potts tells the police inspector that two men held her up and tied her in the chair. Then they started to ransack the office before they found the week's takings.

The inspector seems to be satisfied – but Alec isn't. He tells the inspector something he's spotted which leads to Miss Potts' arrest. Can you spot what gave Miss Potts away?

WHAT DID ALEC NOTICE?
Alec noticed that the chair legs and the secretary's feet were resting on the papers strewn on the floor, proving that the girl must have been tied up after the office had been ransacked. Later Miss Potts confessed that she had staged the robbery with the crooks.

Richard Murdoch's QUIP CORNER

Hello *Eaglers*! Feeling glum? Then try these gloom-chasers from your old friend – Dickie Murdoch.

What can you keep after giving it to your pal?
Your word.

* * *

SON: (wondering whether to go and play in the park) "What would you do, Dad, if you were in my shoes?"
DAD: "I'd clean them!"

* * *

Why is a bald man like a greyhound? Because he makes a little hair (hare) go a long way.

What is always moving and yet stays in the same place?
The sea.

A tramp reached a toll-bridge where the charge was one penny. He hadn't a penny; no one gave him a penny and yet he paid a penny and crossed the bridge. How?
He had a halfpenny, was given a halfpenny, paid the keeper and crossed.

* * *

Why is hotel cutlery like doctor's medicine? Because it's frequently taken after meals.

* * *

Tommy was amazed to see a dog playing chess with an elderly gentleman. "My word that's a clever dog, sir," he exclaimed.

"Oh, I don't know," replied the old gentleman. "I can usually beat him!"

One Junior Reporter to another: "Our editor's tough."
"Oh, why?"
"He's just dropped ten stories into his waste-paper basket and isn't even scratched!"

* * *

BILL: "A cold bath every day is the thing to make you really athletic."
BERT: "I know, I broke my high jump record the first time I stepped into one."

SERGEANT-MAJOR: "Be careful with that gun, man! You just missed me with that last shot."
RECRUIT: "Did I? I'm very sorry, sir!"

* * *

"Our dog is just like a member of the family," said Johnny, who liked to boast. "Really?" answered his friend. "Which one of you has a tail?"

YOU TOO CAN BE A WIZARD!

Dumbfound your friends with these mysterious experiments and tricks. Keep them by you for that boring rainy day!

THE MAGIC EGG

Lightly roll up a narrow strip of silver paper or any metallic covering of this kind and balance it upon an egg. Ask your friends if they can knock the tinfoil off the egg without touching it, blowing it or jerking the table. When they have failed you merely walk towards the egg, hold out your finger to the foil which will spin round and fall off.

The secret is that, as you walk, you rub your feet lightly on the carpet. Friction generates electricity, your fingers become lightly charged and when it is near the tinfoil the roll is attracted. Many forms of friction cause static electrical effects. It sometimes happens that rubber motor-tyres 'generate' so much electricity on a dry road that the car radio crackles badly. Some tyres are made electrically conductive so that the electricity can leak away to the earth to avoid radio interference.

FLOWERS OF WAX

Here is a simple way of making wax flowers. Light a candle and hold it over a bowl of cold water. Let the drops of melted wax fall into the water. On striking the water the wax spreads out into very attractive patterns. After practice you can more or less get any pattern. Put flowers on wires and add green leaves.

BOTTLE AND BAG

Try this trick! And when you know how to do it, try it on your friends. All you need is a bottle and an ordinary paper bag. The problem is to find out how to lift the bottle without touching the outside of it.

SOLUTIONS.

Bottle and Bag
Push the bag into the bottle, leaving sufficient outside so that you can blow up. Do this, screw up the neck of the bag and you'll be able to lift the bottle easily.

Form Fours
Answer will appear next week.

SPY AND COUNTER SPY

CRIME on a POST CARD

by BERNARD NEWMAN

As you see, this looks just like a very ordinary picture postcard. But agents of the Special Branch were watching the place to which it was addressed, and they examined the card. Very soon they traced the code. Can you?

If you can, send in your solution to EAGLE, Code No. 1, Long Lane, Liverpool 9. First ten correct solutions received on 15th September, win a prize. Solution next week.

Greenock, Sept. 2nd
Having strenuous holiday. Am nicely scorched. Ask Aunt Abigail immediately can Arthur fix another week at Greenock till Wednesday?
Edward.

Mr. George Cassell
617, Rother Road
London S.E. 17

FORM FOURS

Can you divide this draughts board below into four pieces, all the same size and shape and all containing three draughtsmen?

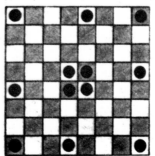

HEY, FELLERS!

IT'S FUN, IT'S FREE, IT'S BY THE SEA
Holiday Playtime

Keep this page for future reference

Here's some super holiday news! This year, we are again having our FREE seaside fun and games – specially arranged for our readers' holidays.

Last summer, lots of you wrote in and told us how much you enjoyed taking part in these HOLIDAY PLAYTIME activities. This seaside entertainment will take place during August, and there will be races, games, fancy-dress parades, mystery hunts and a good chance to win a *wonderful prize*. There are even races for Mum and Dad!

LOOK OUT for the big striped tent and the square marked out on the beach, or grass verge by the sea-front. Flag pennants and EAGLE/ GIRL/SWIFT and ROBIN symbols will welcome you to join in the fun.

CARRY THAT WEEK'S EAGLE – show it – and WALK IN! Once inside, you will be invited to join in the races and other exciting events, and you may walk away with a prize!

HULTON'S HOLIDAY PLAYTIME ORGANISER

HOLIDAY PLAYTIME will be held at these towns

Every Monday, Tuesday, Wednesday, Thursday and Friday during August at
**Bridlington
Broadstairs
Cromer
Douglas (I.O.M.)
Exmouth
Lowestoft
Llandudno
Margate
Minehead
Goodrington Sands**
(Paignton)

Coney Beach
(Porthcawl)
**Skegness
Teignmouth
Walton-on-Naze
Weston-super-Mare
Weymouth**

Every Monday, Wednesday and Friday during the month of August at
Littlehampton

Every Monday, Tuesday, Wednesday, Thursday, Friday and Saturday from 28th July to 30th August at
Bognor Regis

ENJOY YOURSELF

Says Sandy Dan The Holiday Man

At all the resorts mentioned here, Holiday Playtime operates either in the morning or afternoon, according to the tides. Watch the events board near the site for exact details.

TREASURE HUNTS at other seaside resorts

If you are at any of these places, watch for the EAGLE/GIRL/SWIFT/ROBIN cars; they will be driving round the town announcing exciting TREASURE HUNTS. There are many SUPER PRIZES TO BE WON!

Girvan	21st July	Hastings	13th Aug.
Ayr	22nd July	Hove	14th Aug.
Troon	23rd July	Woolacombe	14th Aug.
Saltcoats	24th July	Westward Ho!	14th Aug.
Largs	25th July	Littlehampton	15th Aug.
Morecambe	28th July	Sandown (I.O.W.)	18th Aug.
Seaton Carew	28th July	Paignton	18th Aug.
Filey	29th July	Dawlish Warren	19th Aug.
Fleetwood	29th July	Ryde (I.O.W.)	19th Aug.
Cleveleys	30th July	Shanklin (I.O.W.)	20th Aug.
Withernsea	30th July	Lyme Regis	20th Aug.
Cleethorpes	31st July	Sandbanks (Poole)	21st Aug.
St. Annes	31st July	Ventnor (I.O.W.)	21st Aug.
Southport	1st Aug.	Sandown (I.O.W.)	22nd Aug.
Mablethorpe	1st Aug.	Southsea	22nd Aug
Hunstanton	4th Aug.		
Prestatyn	4th Aug.		
Colwyn Bay	5th Aug.		
Cromer	5th Aug.		
Gorleston	6th Aug.		
Pwllheli	6th Aug.		
Barmouth	7th Aug.		
Felixstowe	7th Aug.		
Jaywick	8th Aug.		
Borth	8th Aug.		
Langland Bay	11th Aug.		
Herne Bay	11th Aug.		
Deal	12th Aug.		
Barry Island	12th Aug.		

Treasure Hunts begin at 3 p.m. except for Fleetwood and Deal, which start at 11.30 a.m., and Herne Bay at 4 o'clock.

WATCH FOR THE TREASURE HUNT CAR

EAGLE CLUB NEWS

COME TO CRICKET!

By arrangement with the M.C.C. and County Cricket Clubs, EAGLE Club Members, on presenting their membership card, can attend the following matches **FREE** after 4.30 p.m. (unless times are otherwise stated).

Kent v. Notts. *at Blackheath*	June 14, 16, 17
Leics. v. Lancs. *at Leicester (Grace Road)*	June 14, 16, 17
Middlesex v. Gloucester *at Lord's*	June 14, 16, 17
Worcs. v. Derbyshire *at Kidderminster*	June 14, 16, 17
Yorkshire v. Surrey *at Sheffield*	June 16; after 2.10 on 17
Northants. v. Somerset *at Rushden*	June 16; after 2.10 on 17
Warwick v. Glamorgan *at Coventry (Courtaulds)*	
Surrey v. Surrey Assoc. of Cricket Clubs *at The Oval (Hobbs's Gate)*	June 18, 19
Glamorgan v. Essex *at Llanelly*	June 18, 19, 20
Hants. v. Somerset *at Bournemouth*	June 18, 19, 20
Notts. v. Lancs. *at Trent Bridge*	after 2.10 on 20
Warwick v. Kent *at Edgbaston*	June 18, 19; June 18, 19, 20
Worcs. v. Leics. *at Worcester*	June 18, 19, 20
Yorkshire v. Gloucester *at Leeds*	June 18, 19, 20

MINOR COUNTY Matches can be seen FREE all day from 16th to 21st June at: Loughborough; Wollaton; Old Trafford; Aylesford; March; Melton Mowbray; Braintree; Whitehaven.

* * * * * * * * * *
Free Steamer Trips

NOW is the time to decide your holidays and steer your course in the right channel, by selecting a resort where you can take advantage of the steamer trips available through the companies mentioned here. Remember, you travel absolutely FREE by showing your Club Card at the time of booking, but you must be accompanied by a fare-paying adult. Write to the coastal lines for information about these trips, and please enclose a stamped and self-addressed envelope for your reply.

Your request should not be sent to EAGLE

DAVID MACBRAYNE LTD.,
44, Robertson Street, Glasgow C.2.

THE LIVERPOOL & NORTH WALES STEAMSHIP CO. LTD.,
40, Chapel Street, Liverpool 3.

P. & A. CAMPBELL LTD.,
4, Dock Chambers, Cardiff.

BIRTHDATES
16th NOV. 1943
20th AUG. 1944
7th JULY, 1945
5th MAR. 1946
18th APR. 1947
23rd OCT. 1948

If you are an EAGLE Club Member, and your birthdate appears in this week's list, you are entitled to a FREE birthday gift! Choose it from the following: EAGLE autograph book, stamp album, model construction kit, stationery box, 300 foreign stamps or propelling pencil. Then state your choice on a post-card, giving name, address, Club Number and date of birth, and post to: BIRTHDATES (24), EAGLE Club, Long Lane, Liverpool 9, to arrive by Thursday, 19th June. Overseas members whose birthdates appear will receive a present automatically.

IF you would like to join the EAGLE Club, then turn to PAGE 15!

Lash Lonergan's Quest

By MOORE RAYMOND

Chapter 1

LASH LONERGAN will now attempt to ride Thunderbolt!" The announcer's voice rang across the Sydney Showground, and a buzz of excitement swept through the crowd of 60,000 people who lined the arena - tier upon tier under the blazing Australian sun.

"Thunderbolt's a killer!"

"Lash Lonergan's not much more than a boy, is he?"

"Just twenty, but he's the greatest rider since Snowy Baker away back in the twenties."

"That stallion has killed three men already."

All eyes were on the slim, wiry young man who was perched on the rails of the mounting yard away over in the corner.

Lash Lonergan looked down on the wicked black stallion and smiled. It was a flashing gay smile that belied the fierce pumping of his heart.

Thunderbolt snorted and strained at the ropes, flattening his ears and showing the whites of his evil eyes. His hind hooves flashed out viciously, thudding on the timber in fury.

"Ready?" As the announcer called across the arena, the great crowd became silent.

Lash tugged his broad-rimmed hat a little tighter. "Thunderbolt," he muttered through gritted teeth, "here comes your boss."

Shouting "Okay!" to the announcer, he snatched the reins, dropped from the rail into the saddle, and felt for the stirrups as the handlers let the horse go.

Away swung the gate, and Thunderbolt plunged into the arena.

"One!" called the timekeeper.

The horse became a mad beast. Head down and back arched like a wildcat, he went buck-buck-bucking across the arena, sending up clouds of dust.

"Two!"

With body tensed yet flexible as a steel spring, Lash stayed in the saddle.

"Three!"

Already the crowd was murmuring its admiration while it wondered how long such skill would last.

"Four!"

Thunderbolt redoubled his frantic efforts, leaping and twisting his body in the air, so that Lash was almost wrenched from the saddle.

"Five!"

Thousands began to cheer. Thousands more stood up to watch such horsemanship.

"Six!"

Thunderbolt squealed with anger. Only Lash heard the danger signal, as the noise was drowned by the roar of the crowd.

"Seven!"

Never before had they seen such a sight as this raging devil-horse hurling himself into the air, contorting himself in fury.

"Eight!"

The cheers were redoubled till the whole arena seemed to tremble with the noise. Jarred and dizzy, with dust choking his throat and gritty in his teeth, Lash was almost thrown time and time again.

"Nine!"

Lash felt a shudder go through the half-crazed horse. Then Thunderbolt squealed again - a horrible, evil sound.

"Ten!"

Now the wildly cheering thousands sent a tornado of sound across the arena. Then, in a second, the noise turned into a great gasp of fear and dismay.

Thunderbolt reared up and hurled himself backwards, intending to crush his rider. But Lash was ready. He kicked away the stirrups, thrust at the pommel, and flung himself free. As Thunderbolt crashed almost on top of him, he rolled away to safety and sprang to his feet.

Though ready to reel with dizziness and shock, Lash pulled himself together and walked calmly towards the competitor's box while the stewards rode in and took charge of the sweating, snorting, limping Thunderbolt.

Jarred and dizzy,
Lash stayed in the saddle . . . . .

The tremendous ovation continued till Lash was inside the barrier. Then came the announcer's voice:

"Ladies and gentlemen, that is the end of the buck-jumping contest. It is also the end of all horsemanship contests this year for the title of Champion of Champions.

"For the first time in the history of these shows, one man has won all four contests. First in the stockwhip contest, first in the cattle-drafting contest, first in the fancy riding contest, and first in the buck-jumping contest . . . *Lash Lonergan!*"

Once more the cheering broke out as Lash came cantering into the arena on his own splendid horse, Monarch. Pure black except for a white "sock" on each foot, the horse pranced as if proud of the young man who rode him with such natural grace.

Lash bowed to the cheering thousands and flashed his bright, boyish smile as he cantered across to the Governor-General's box.

A light touch of the bit on Monarch's mouth reined the horse before the flower-decorated box. As was the custom, the Governor-General rose from his seat and bowed to the Champion of Champions.

As Lash bowed in return, his hand went to the coiled stockwhip that hung at his belt. He jerked it free and flicked wide the plaited thong.

Crack-crack-crack-crack! It was swift and brilliant whipwork of the kind that had earned him the nickname of Lash as well as a reputation for such skill throughout the land.

So, to the accompaniment of tremendous applause, Australia's champion horseman turned and went riding from the arena . . . riding into an adventure more exciting than anything he had ever dreamed about,

"WELL, me flabbergastin' boy, you've been and gone and done it!" cried Rawhide O'Reilly, hitching up his dusty corduroy trousers around his lean hips. "Give us your dook!"

Lash grinned agreement as he shook the hairy hand of the weather-beaten, sun-scorched Irishman.

"Stone the crows and stiffen the lizards!" Rawhide went on. "Jist wait till we git back to Coolabah Creek. There'll be such celebratin' as will set all the kangaroos jumpin' into one another's pockets!"

"But first," replied Lash, "we're going to do some celebrating right here in Sydney. Come and see the sideshows."

They walked down the lane between the noisy, gaudy booths. African Pygmies. The Wall of Death. The Pit of Adders. And so on.

Lash stopped outside a tent that carried this crudely-painted sign: "The Living Boy in Solid Ice. He Speaks. He Eats. He Drinks. The Marvel of the Age. Admission 6d."

"Just the thing for a scorching day like this," smiled Lash. "I think we can spare a zac to see the marvel of the age." He handed the money over to the woman at the entrance.

Inside the almost empty tent they stopped, stared, and laughed at the sight.

On a platform were a number of blocks of gleaming ice built to form a sort of transparent box with one end open. Inside, a boy of 14 or 15 lay on a mat. He wore only a faded flannel shirt and short, tattered trousers.

"Hi, cobbers," greeted the freckle-faced, curly-headed youngster, sticking his head out of the opening. He grinned, showing strong, white teeth.

"We've been had!" cried Rawhide. "We've been diddled out of our zacs!"

Lash bent down and looked the smiling boy straight in the face. The strong, handsome teeth were chattering, and the freckled face was tinged with blue.

The roughrider caught the boy by the shoulders, hauled him out, and stood him on his sturdy feet.

"You're freezing to death in there," said Lash in a curt but kindly tone.

"But it's me job," wailed the boy. "I'll git belted if——"

"What's up?" interrupted a harsh voice. They turned to see a big, brutal-looking man enter the back of the tent. He was followed by two more toughs.

"I couldn't help it, Mr. Scow!" cried the boy in terror. "This cove——"

"Git back in there!" snarled Scow, swinging a heavy boot.

Lash reached out swift hands and caught the foot in mid-air. He gave it a sharp twist. Scow yelled, swung round, and fell on his face.

"Get the kid out of here," ordered Lash to Rawhide. The Irishman grabbed the boy's arm and hauled him towards the rear exit.

A stream of abuse poured from Scow's lips as he scrambled to his feet and lunged at Lash with great fists swinging wildly.

The roughrider stepped lightly aside, and, balancing himself like a ballet dancer, turned on his toes as he swung his open hand in a swift arc. The side of his hand caught Scow just below the ear.

"Ugh!" he grunted, and fell in a semi-conscious heap.

Just as Rawhide and the boy disappeared through the rear exit, Scow's two beefy companions flung themselves at Lash.

"What's the idea?" panted the boy to Rawhide.

Standing at the back of the tent and listening to the bangs, grunts, thumps, and scuffling noises inside, Rawhide chuckled in reply: "It's only me young friend havin' a bit of exercise. It's three to one, I know. But one Lash Lonergan is a multitude of furies in a fight. If he wants me, he'll whistle."

SOON there was silence. Lash emerged from the tent, limping a little, but smiling gaily.

"Zonk?" queried Rawhide.

"Zonk-zonk-zonk!" laughed the roughrider. "They're sorting themselves out, and they'll soon start looking for this young squib. Come on, kid."

He took the boy by the arm and started off. The lad dragged back, declaring that he had to return to Mr. Scow.

"Now listen, Squib," said Lash briskly. "I can see you're being booted and banged about in that sideshow. So come on!"

Before the boy could recover his breath he was sitting between Lash and Rawhide at a table in one of the big showground restaurants. Though dazed by the suddenness of it all, he still had a boy's appetite. Wolfing down the fried steak and onions with sweet potatoes, he told his story between mouthfuls.

An orphan for as far back as he could remember, the boy had been adopted by an uncle who was a circus clown. The uncle had died, the circus was disbanded, and Scow, the assistant ringmaster, went into the sideshow business, taking the boy with him. It was then he got the idea of the Living Boy in Solid Ice.

"No more of that," Lash assured him.

"But, me flabbergastin' lad," began Rawhide. "What——"

"Pull your head in!" snorted Lash with a laugh. "From now on it's going to be Lash, Rawhide and Squib - the Three Dinkum Cobbers."

The Irishman lifted his eyes to heaven and sighed: "Stone the crows and stiffen the lizards! I'll jist have a double responsibility in future."

"Have another helping of passion fruit jelly," said Lash to Squib, "and I'll tell you the story of Lash Lonergan.

"Just like you, I'm an orphan who was adopted by an uncle. My Uncle Peter's got a place out West called Coolabah Creek. He breeds cattle and horses. That's where I was brought up - and I was brought up tough.

"On the day I was seventeen my uncle chucked me out. He said I was a coward."

"Gawn!" cried Squib in disbelief.

Lash grinned and went on: "Uncle's got a chestnut mare called Chuckle. Ever since I can remember he's been terribly proud that he's the only man on Coolabah Creek Station who can ride Chuckle. Every now and again he'd offer ten pounds to anyone on the station who could stay on her back. They all tried – and they all came off."

Squib gulped down a mouthful of jelly and asked: "Did you git thrown, too?"

"Uncle said I was too young to try ridin' Chuckle. But at night I used to go down to the paddock and make friends with her. It took months and months, but in the end she let me get on bareback. Yes, bareback. But of course I never let Uncle know.

"Then, the day I was seventeen, he called me out in front of all the men and said I was old enough to try to ride Chuckle. And I refused."

"What!" cried the amazed boy.

Rawhide cut in: "Lash could have ridden her back to front with his hands in his pockets. But don't you see it would have broken Uncle Peter's heart? It was his great pride that he was the only one who could sit this rumbustious mare."

Lash went on to describe how his uncle said he was ashamed of his own flesh and blood. Finally he ordered him off the station, telling him not to return till he'd proved himself a man.

"Then up steps Rawhide O'Reilly," put in the Irishman, "and I takes the lad's part. Uncle Peter gives me a shrivellin' look and tells me to do a git as well. So before sundown we was jist a couple o' wanderers on the face o' the earth."

Lash laughed and said: "It all turned out for the best. I was determined to make a name for myself – a champion roughrider and stockwhip expert – with the help of the best adviser and friend a man ever had. I mean that hairy Irishman, Rawhide O'Reilly."

"What a heart-rendin', body-bruisin' three years the lad has been through," said Rawhide. "But now he's Champion of Champions!"

"And now," said Lash, with a warm smile for the other two, "we're going back in triumph to Uncle Peter Lonergan. And this time there'll be three of us."

At that very moment, Uncle Peter lay at

the bottom of a ravine 15 miles from the homestead of Coolabah Creek. Over his lifeless body stood half-a-dozen aborigines, shaking spears and boomerangs with grief at the death of one whom they knew as Big White Friend.

As they wailed, they wondered why he should be clutching in his hand a piece of rock that glittered deep purple and ocean blue and fiery red in the rays of the slanting sun.

THE whisper ran through the bush: "Three fella makem longa Coolabah Creek."

In their own secret and mysterious way, the aborigines passed on the message as the three riders ambled along the dusty road that led to the far West.

It was three weeks since they had left Sydney, and they were all looking forward to the end of their long and arduous ride.

Rawhide let the reins trail on the neck of his lean and wiry chestnut, Skinny Liz, as he twanged at his banjo and sang:

"Oh, we ride through the gidyea
And the mulga scrub,
And across the saltbush plain,
And we sing as we go:

With a yo-heave-ho!
We'll soon be home again."

On his left rode Lash, mounted on proud-stepping Monarch. The third of the trio was Squib, who rode Patch, a white pony that Lash had bought for him in Sydney.

"I'll bet the tail o' me shirt to a bushel of emu feathers that your Uncle Peter will make you overseer," declared Rawhide.

Squib grinned: "I reckon he'll git a bit of a surprise when he sees me."

"He'll get a surprise to see all of us," replied Lash. "I haven't written to him to say we're coming home. I thought it would be best if——"

He stopped short. His keen eye had caught the glint of sunlight on the twirling boomerang.

"Duck!" yelled Lash, reaching swiftly for the stockwhip at his belt.

Rawhide and Squib flattened themselves on their horses' necks as the curved, sharp-edged weapon whizzed towards them.

Lash flicked the handle of his whip, and the thong writhed into the air. The horsehair tip struck like a snake at the boomerang.

"Bull's-eye!" The boomerang fell harmlessly at Monarch's feet.

"Into the scrub!" cried Lash. All three turned their horses towards the mulga trees.

"Them blisterin' myalls!" scowled Rawhide, peering ahead into the shimmering summer air.

"Mo-poke!" The plaintive notes came from a nearby patch of sandalwood.

Lash and Rawhide looked at each other sharply. No mopoke bird ever called in broad daylight. It must be Mopoke the man.

"Mo-poke!" called Lash in a melancholy tone.

A moment later there stepped from behind a tree a tall and strong young blackfellow. He wore nothing but a loin-garment of plaited reeds, and he carried a boomerang and a spear.

The black man beckoned. Then he disappeared behind the tree again.

"It's Mopoke all right," said Lash as he urged his horse forward.

"What's he playin' hide-and-seek for?" grinned Squib.

"No savee," said Rawhide. He told the

boy that the aborigine was a good friend of theirs. He was one of a tribe of blacks who lived in a camp on the outskirts of Coolabah Creek station.

"Mo-poke!" came the cry from the bush somewhere ahead.

Riding on, Lash was puzzled by this strange behaviour. Suddenly they came to a clearing. Beside a little waterhole stood Mopoke.

This time the aborigine came forward to meet his friends. His black face wore a grin that displayed flashing white teeth.

Suddenly Mopoke's face became grave, and his voice took on a sad note. As he told his story in a mixture of English and his own native words, Lash learned for the first time of the death of his Uncle Peter.

Dazed by the news, he listened as in a dream to the story of how the owner of Coolabah Creek had been found by some blacks at the bottom of a ravine. The man's skull was broken, and he had obviously been killed instantly by his fall.

When they brought him to the homestead he was still clutching a piece of beautiful opal.

"Then there *is* more opal up there!" cried Rawhide. "I reckon——"

"Quiet!" cried Lash with a fierce intensity that shocked the Irishman into silence.

The aborigine said that Messiter the foreman had taken charge and had arranged the funeral at the nearby settlement called Tarrawarra.

"Dago Messiter!" snorted Rawhide furiously. "Why, he——" The Irishman cut himself short at Lash's swift glance.

As Mopoke went on with his story, he became very excited. He used more and more of his own native words that only Lash could understand. The young roughrider's face clouded with anger and dismay.

Abruptly the aborigine said: "This fella go longa walkabout. Goodbye." He turned and made for the trees.

Lash turned Monarch's head towards home. "There's trouble ahead," he told his companions as they made for the road again. "And the name of that trouble appears to be Dago Messiter."

To be continued next week

WONDERS OF INSECT LIFE

by George Cansdale

THE GOAT MOTH

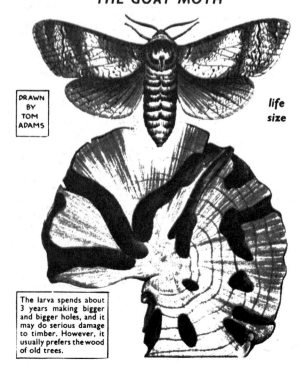

DRAWN BY TOM ADAMS

life size

The larva spends about 3 years making bigger and bigger holes, and it may do serious damage to timber. However, it usually prefers the wood of old trees.

The night-flying Goat Moth gets its name from the unpleasant smell, supposed to be like that of a goat, given off by its larva or caterpillar. The forewings are pale brown and grey; the hindwings darkish grey-brown. It is one of our larger moths, with a possible 3½ inch wing-span.

The female selects a tree, such as poplar, willow or apple, and proceeds to lay several eggs at its base.

When the larva is fully grown, it eats its way out. Then it burrows into the soil and makes itself a strong silk cocoon, with chips of wood and rubbish stuck to it. Soon, it turns into a pupa, or chrysalis, from which it will later emerge as a perfect insect.

The larva hatches from the egg and burrows down through the bark; then it feeds between the bark and the wood, rather like the Bark Beetle. But, as it grows, its appetite grows too, and the flesh-coloured larva turns and works its way into the solid timber. It chews and swallows a considerable quantity of wood but digests only part of it, leaving the galleries full of rubbish behind it.

COCOON PARTLY OPENED WITH PUPA

NORTHBROOK'S BURNING!

Written by
PETER LING
Illustrated by
PETER KAY

Keith shows his true colours, and the smoke clears at last!

Chapter 12

THE FIRE GOES OUT

ALMOST at once, the 'J's discovered where the smoke was coming from; a grey-brown cloud billowed out of the back door of the school kitchens.

"You don't suppose that they've burnt the bread-and-butter pudding again?" said Jacko lightly.

"Not unless they've got a new recipe which includes old rags and . . ." John sniffed again and his face hardened; "*Petrol!*"

With one accord, they sprang towards the kitchen door, and Specs muttered: "If Keith Inglish is mixed up in this one, I'll grab hold of him and *spifflicate* him!"

In the kitchen, an extraordinary scene was going on, and Keith Inglish was certainly mixed up in it – very much so.

Smoke was pouring up from a pile of old rags, smouldering in a corner. On the table, a petrol-tin was overturned, dripping in a puddle on the linoleum. In between, a wrestling-match was going on; a three-cornered match between Keith Inglish, Bradbury, and (to the great surprise of the 'J's) a burly man whom they did not at first recognize. His face was hidden from them, since he was lying at the bottom of the scrimmage, almost invisible under the threshing arms and legs of the two boys.

"*Quick!* We've got to put that fire out, before the whole place goes up like a rocket!" snapped John, heading for the burning rags.

As he stamped on the sparks, Specs brought a bucket of water from the sink and flung it over the last traces of the fire. With a sizzle and a splutter, the smoke turned to a cloud of steam.

"That's that!" panted John, turning his attention to the free-for-all which was still going on. "Now – what's the idea? Break it up, chaps. Who's that at the bottom?"

"He's in the right place this time," grinned Keith, as the fight broke up and the two boys scrambled to their feet. "In fact, he's been at the bottom of the whole thing – the mysterious Firebug himself!"

The burly man sat up, red-faced, furious and breathless.

"Why – you – you little . . . ! Why can't you leave me alone?" panted Mr Harris.

It was the assistant cook, who had al-

Keith picked up his cream bun and planted it firmly in Bradbury's face

ready been caught stealing the silver at the beginning of the term. . .

Some hours later, the 'J's sat on the grass outside the Tuck Shop, treating Inglish and Bradbury to a well-deserved feast of ginger-pop and cream buns.

"I still don't understand exactly," said John. "I mean, I know the police have taken care of Harris, and the whole mess has been cleared up – but just how were you two mixed up in it? Go back to the beginning and explain it all slowly!"

"The beginning?" Bradbury took a long swallow from the ginger-pop bottle. "The beginning was by accident. The fire in the chemi-lab really *was* an accident – faulty wiring, or whatever it was. But it happened when Harris was caught swiping the silver, and it gave him an idea . . . "

"He'd been shown up and lectured and warned by the Head, and he had a grudge against Northbrook School," Inglish chimed in. "I know he ought to have been grateful to be given another chance, but he was a bit crackers, and he wanted revenge; so he decided to burn the place down. It made him feel big and powerful, I suppose!"

"So that was when he started the fire in the Library," Specs frowned. "And you two were there when it happened – as we found out!"

INGLISH and Bradbury looked at each other awkwardly, and at last Bradbury spoke up,

"Inglish was – er – helping me with my homework; you know that." he mumbled. "We saw Harris start the fire – but he saw us too, and he threatened that if we told anyone, he'd – well, he threatened all kinds of things. As Inglish said, he was crackers; and – and – honestly, we were scared stiff!"

John smiled. "Don't look so miserable. Brad – it takes a lot of nerve to admit that you were scared. . ." He changed the subject tactfully: "By the way, I suppose it was Harris I saw climbing out of the Library windows that day?"

Inglish nodded, and replied: "That's right. He got away with it then – and he got away after he started the next fire, in the Great Hall."

"Ah yes!" Specs looked up. "And how did you manage to get in on *that* one?"

"I saw Harris sneaking into the Hall, and I followed him. Like Brad, I was too scared to tell anyone about Harris, but I

had an idea that, if I could keep close to him, I might put the fire out before it did any damage . . . Only he spotted me first. We had a bit of a row and, as I turned away to go, he conked me from behind. Then he left me there . . . After that, I knew he was a desperate man who would even risk murder – I didn't dare tell anybody what had happened."

"Except me," broke in Bradbury. "I'd guessed anyway, of course. We had a talk about it, and Inglish persuaded me that our only hope was to catch Harris red-handed at the scene of the next fire, and keep him there till help came. It was pretty risky. . . "

"I didn't know *how* risky, till he knocked over that petrol-can!" Inglish shuddered. "But, anyway, it worked."

"Congratulations!" said John. "Have another cream-bun . . . Apart from catching the Firebug, I think you deserve congratulations for turning old Brad into a human being – or nearly! Only a few weeks ago, you were grovelling if he so much as raised his little finger; but now *you* seem to be telling *him* what to do."

"He's not such a bad chap, really," said Inglish, carelessly.

Bradbury exclaimed indignantly: "Why, you cheeky young fathead – you wait! I'll jolly well bash some sense into you . . ."

"It's no good, Brad!" Inglish laughed. "Now the Firebug stuff is all over, I'm not scared so easily any more. I'm certainly not scared of *you!*"

And, to prove it, he picked up his cream bun and planted it firmly in the centre of Bradbury's face.

When Bradbury had disappeared to get cleaned up, and the laughter had died down, Specs said: "Just think . . . I actually suspected that you were starting the fires yourself, to get out of taking the end-of-term exams."

"Ugh! Don't remind me . . ." Inglish grimaced, then shrugged his shoulders. "I'm not going to lose my head if I don't come first. But I shall make up for all the work I've missed before *next* term; there's plenty of time – next term is a long way off."

Jacko raised his ginger-pop in a toast. "Thank goodness!" he grinned. "Here's to the holidays!"

Next week, the Three J's set out on a brand new holiday adventure: 'Letters to Northbrook'!

THE CAPTAIN WHO HOISTED NELSON'S SIGNAL

by MACDONALD HASTINGS
EAGLE SPECIAL INVESTIGATOR

Captain B.A.W. Warburton-Lee was the second V.C. of the war. He was killed fighting a destroyer action in the tradition of Sir Francis Drake when he singed the King of Spain's beard, and of Nelson too, because as his ship was hard hit he hoisted Nelson's signal

IF you were asked which was Nelson's favourite signal, I hope you would not reply that it was 'England expects every man to do his duty'. In fact, that wasn't the signal Nelson wanted to hoist at Trafalgar. He wanted to signal the fleet: 'Nelson confides that every man will do his duty', and it was only the officers about him who persuaded him to change his mind.

Nelson's favourite signal, which he flew again and again, was 'Engage the enemy more closely', a rousing call to the British seamen to get in, if they could, to point-blank range, because throughout history the British have always fought their best when they could see the whites of the enemy's eyes.

One hundred and thirty-five years after the battle of Trafalgar, the Captain in command of five destroyers of the Second Flotilla hoisted that signal again as he led his ships in line ahead to ferret out the German naval forces who had occupied the iron-ore port of Narvik, in Norway.

His name was Captain B. A. W. Warburton-Lee. In bitter weather, on the night of 8th April, 1940, he had been called upon to make a decision which was enough to make any man wince with the responsibility of it.

IT was the same sort of decision that Nelson had to make when he decided to blockade Napoleon's navy off Toulon. Indeed, Warburton-Lee, when he learnt that there was a force of German destroyers in Narvik harbour, would have been quite justified in blockading the entrance to the fjord until such time as the enemy tried to escape. That was the classical naval answer. Results would be slow, but sure.

'Slow but sure' didn't suit Warburton-Lee's temperament. On his way in to occupy Narvik harbour, which was believed to be free of the enemy, he stopped at the mouth of the fjord to pick up what information he could from the lighthouse there. The lighthouse-keeper gave him the surprising news that six enemy destroyers and a submarine had entered the harbour. It was a superior force to the five destroyers under Warburton-Lee's command, but not overwhelmingly so. But to engage them in the open sea, and to hunt them out in enclosed coastal waters, were two different propositions.

WARBURTON-LEE was only too well aware that if he could successfully navigate his ships through the fjord, there was the danger that he would be surprised by a torpedo attack from enemy destroyers hidden in the bays and inlets, before he could hit back.

But Warburton-Lee reasoned that, if it was a surprise to *him* to learn that Germans were in occupation of the harbour, it would be a surprise for them to discover the British in the same waters. A little more than an hour after he had heard the news from the lighthouse, he signalled: 'Intend attacking at dawn high water'. The Admiralty replied: 'We shall support whatever decision you take'.

Shortly after midnight, on the morning of the 10th, the British destroyers cleared for action and steamed in line ahead up the narrow, rocky fjord. A snowstorm blanketed visibility down to 400 yards. But by a brilliant feat of navigation, H.M.S. *Hardy*, Warburton-Lee's flotilla leader, led the destroyers to the entrance of the harbour. The surprise was complete. Not a single enemy gun opened fire.

Hardy led the way in. She fired three torpedoes at one German destroyer, four more at the harbour installations, and opened fire at a second destroyer lying at anchor. She withdrew without a scratch. Two other destroyers of the flotilla followed her in, fired their torpedoes, and got out again without damage while the other two covered the withdrawal with a smoke-screen.

By this time the Germans were opening fire in reply. The firing was wild, and the torpedoes were easily avoided. Captain Warburton-Lee estimated that two enemy destroyers had been sunk and two others damaged by gun-fire. That, according to his information, left only two more to be knocked off. Warburton-Lee turned back to make a second attack.

Although the element of surprise had been lost, the second attack was completely successful, the only hit on a British destroyer having done no serious damage. As the British flotilla disengaged again, Warburton-Lee, in the *Hardy*, sighted four more enemy vessels. He reported them as a cruiser and three destroyers. They were, in fact, four destroyers. In other words, they now knew that the total of the enemy was at least eight – two more than they had reckoned on. And, shortly after, they sighted two more enemy destroyers, bringing the total to ten.

Warburton-Lee could not believe that they were enemy ships. He thought they were British cruisers. But when he challenged them, he was answered by a deadly salvo. It was then, in the realization that he was overwhelmed by numbers, that Warburton-Lee hoisted Nelson's signal. A minute or two later, a German shell burst on the bridge, killing Warburton-Lee himself and killing or wounding everyone else. *Hardy* was on fire and, with her helmsman killed, was out of control. She was run ashore with one of her guns still firing. Two other destroyers were badly damaged. But the Germans were so distracted by the sudden attack that three of the ships got to sea in safety.

EVEN then, the brilliant action was not quite over. The retiring British destroyers sighted a ship coming in. She was stopped, her crew taken prisoner, and the ship sent to the bottom. She was a German supply ship bringing ammunition and torpedoes for the enemy destroyers. So ended one of those engagements in which the British navy has always been incomparable. But it still wasn't the end of the story.

Three days later, a second battle was fought. The battleship *Warspite*, supported by nine destroyers, went in to Narvik to finish the job which Warburton-Lee had so brilliantly begun.

It turned out that there were eight more German destroyers in the harbour. Five of them were sunk or run aground as wrecks. The last three crept deep into the plug-hole of the fjord. When our destroyers followed them in and opened fire, there was no reply. The enemy had abandoned ship.

Next week: 'One Man against the Chinese.' The story of Captain Anthony Farrar-Hockley, D.S.O., M.C.

HERE IS THE LATEST NEWS ON THE VENUS SITUATION — SPACE FLEET H.Q. ANNOUNCE THAT THE NEW ROCKET SHIPS OF A LARGER TYPE CANNOT BE READY FOR AT LEAST THREE MONTHS...

A LATE DESPATCH FROM PEKIN REPORTS CONTINUED RIOTING IN CENTRAL CHINA DUE TO THE BREAKDOWN OF RATION SUPPLIES...

.. EMERGENCY MEASURES ARE BEING TAKEN TO FLY FOOD THERE FROM THE WORLD STRATEGIC RESERVE...

...BUT THIS MEANS THAT A CUT WILL HAVE TO BE MADE IN THE EUROPEAN AND NORTH AMERICAN RATION SCALES TO REBUILD THE RESERVE.

SUFFERING CATS! NOT *ANOTHER* CUT.

CONTROL YOURSELF, DEAR. WE'LL JUST HAVE TO BUY MORE OF THOSE WRETCHED 'VITAMINEAT' BLOCKS.

A FLAT IN NEW YORK.

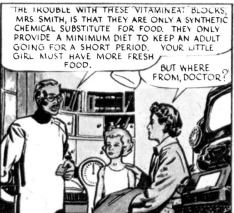

THE TROUBLE WITH THESE 'VITAMINEAT' BLOCKS, MRS. SMITH, IS THAT THEY ARE ONLY A SYNTHETIC CHEMICAL SUBSTITUTE FOR FOOD. THEY ONLY PROVIDE A MINIMUM DIET TO KEEP AN ADULT GOING FOR A SHORT PERIOD. YOUR LITTLE GIRL MUST HAVE MORE FRESH FOOD.

BUT WHERE FROM, DOCTOR?

A DOCTOR'S SURGERY IN BIRMINGHAM

YES, INDEED, WHERE FROM? — I WONDER WHAT COLONEL DARE *DID* FIND ON VENUS?

AREN'T YOU PROUD OF YOUR NEPHEW, ANASTASIA? — IT SAYS HERE THE HOPES OF THE WORLD REST ON ALBERT.

HM. — 'REST' IS WHAT THEY'LL DO WITH *HIM* — HE WAS ALWAYS A GOOD ONE AT RESTING.

ANASTASIA DIGBY'S HOUSE IN WIGAN.

EE — ITS FUNNY TO THINK OF HIM UP THERE ON ONE OF THOSE LITTLE TWINKLING STARS. JUST FANCY!

I CAN FANCY WELL ENOUGH WHAT ALBERT FITZWILLIAM DIGBY IS DOING WHEREVER HE IS — SNORING IN PEACE AND COMFORT I'LL BE BOUND.

PHEW! LETS HAVE A BREATHER HERE, SIR — THIS CLIMBING'S TOUGH WORK.

I THINK WE MIGHT AS WELL, DAN — THE TREENS CAN'T BE VERY NEAR HERE YET!

RIGHT, SIR.

THE OLD BOY'S FEELING HIS AGE AND DIG'S NO GREYHOUND. I WISH I KNEW WHERE THE TREENS WERE.

IT HAS BEEN PARALYSED BY AN EARTH PISTOL

LOOK — A SPACE FLEET JACKET

ITS THE ONE THE FAT HUMAN WAS WEARING.

GOOD — PUT THE ZOM ON THE SCENT.

WE HAVE THEM NOW.

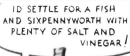

RIGHT NOW I'M THINKING OF A BIG JUICY STEAK, FRIED ONIONS AND POTATOES!

I'D SETTLE FOR A FISH AND SIXPENNYWORTH WITH PLENTY OF SALT AND VINEGAR!

IF YOU MEN OPENED YOUR EYES AND STOPPED DREAMING YOU'D FIND PLENTY TO EAT

LOOK! FRUIT AND NUTS FOR THE TAKING!

BUT IS IT SAFE TO EAT?

PERFECTLY SAFE, ACCORDING TO THE PEABODY POCKET TESTER — A LITTLE THING I DESIGNED WHEN I WAS PICKED FOR THE JOB.

WELL!

THESE ARE GOOD, SIR!

YOU SHOULD TRY THESE, DAN, THEY'RE DELICIOUS.

YUM! YUM!

PERHAPS THERE'S SOMETHING TO BE SAID FOR THIS PLANET AFTER ALL.

SEE THIS! PLUMS AS BIG AS MARROWS. THIS SOIL MUST BE RICH IN VITAMINS.

WELL, WE'VE CERTAINLY FOUND WHAT WE CAME TO FIND. I'VE NOT THE SLIGHTEST DOUBT THAT PROPERLY USED THE SOIL COULD PROVIDE FOOD FOR MILLIONS OF PEOPLE.

AND IT'S PRETTY OBVIOUS THE VENUSIANS DON'T NEED IT ALL. LOOK AT IT GOING TO WASTE IN ALL THAT JUNGLE DOWN THERE.

WE COULD ORGANISE THIS PLANET ALL RIGHT — IF ONLY WE COULD GET BACK.

AND IF IT WASN'T FOR THESE WRETCHED TREENS.

AND SPEAKING OF THE GREEN HORRORS, WHAT'S HAPPENED TO OUR TAME ONE? HE'S GONE BROODY.

I DO NOT UNDERSTAND THESE EARTHMEN, THEY DO THINGS NOT TO THEIR ADVANTAGE AND THEY LAUGH.

WAKE UP, SONDAR! WE'RE DISCUSSING YOUR FRIENDS WHY DO THEY WANT US SO BADLY?

FOR THE EARTH PLAN! TO SEE IF IT IS WORTH TAKING OVER YOUR PLANET.

HASN'T IT OCCURRED TO YOU THAT WE MIGHT HAVE VIEWS ON THAT?

WHY? — IF IT IS IN THE INTEREST OF SCIENCE?

COME ON, CHAPS, LET'S GET CRACKING AGAIN.

THE THREE EARTH CREATURES AND TREEN SONDAR — AS REPORTED, THE FOURTH HUMAN IS DEAD.

POOR OLD DAN. AND IT WAS ALL MY FAULT.

THANKS TO YOU, SIR, HE DIDN'T FEEL ANY PAIN — I WISH I COULD SAY THE SAME FOR US — LOOK!

AN OLD EARTH CUSTOM — LADIES FIRST!

FRANK HAMPSON

Sir Hubert orders the Treens not to harm Professor Peabody.

THERE IS NO NEED TO BE ALARMED *YET*, SIR HUBERT.

THE DISINTEGRON IS NOT A WEAPON — IT IS THE ONLY THING THAT CAN CUT YOU OUT OF YOUR PLASTIC PRISONS.

DO NOT TRY TO ESCAPE AGAIN IT IS CRIMINAL TO DEFEAT THE ENDS OF SCIENCE — BESIDES, IT IS USELESS.

THEY DID NOT TRY TO ESCAPE, O MASTER — THERE WAS AN ACCIDENT TO THE HELICOPTER.

GOOD OLD SONDAR.

THERE ARE NO ACCIDENTS IN A SCIENTIFIC STATE — NOR IS THERE FAILURE — COME.

MEANWHILE, FAR TO THE SOUTH, DAN STRUGGLES UP TOWARDS THE LIGHT FROM THE CAVERNS WHERE THE SUB-VENUSIAN CATARACT HAS SWEPT HIM.

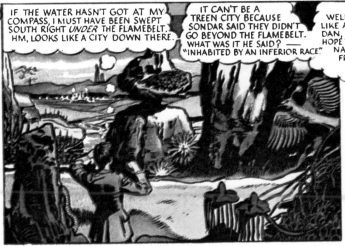

167

The Mekon, Lord of the Treens, summons the three captives to his presence

ENTER, O EARTHMEN

REMEMBER — WE MUST SAY THE OPPOSITE TO WHAT WE THINK

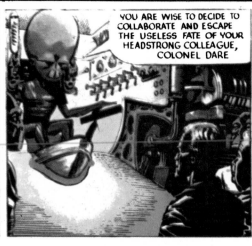

YOU ARE WISE TO DECIDE TO COLLABORATE AND ESCAPE THE USELESS FATE OF YOUR HEADSTRONG COLLEAGUE, COLONEL DARE

WE ARE ABOUT TO ORGANISE THE EARTH — IT IS TIME YOUR RIDICULOUS PLANET WAS REGULARISED AND USED TO FURTHER THE ENDS OF SCIENCE..... COME, I WILL SHOW YOU SOME OF OUR PREPARATIONS

CUTE LITTLE THING, ISN'T HE, DIG ?

WM, ABOUT AS CUTE AS A WAGONFUL OF WEASELS, MISS !

COME OVER HERE, MY FRIENDS

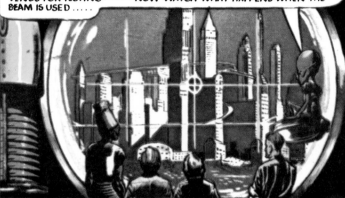

THIS IS A TELEZERO BEAM TRANSMITTER — AT PRESENT IT IS FOCUSSED ON A FULL SIZE REPLICA OF AN EARTH CITY, WHICH WE HAVE BUILT ON VENUS FOR TESTING —— NOW WATCH WHAT HAPPENS WHEN THE BEAM IS USED .....

YOU SEE ? COMPLETE ANNIHILATION ! BY THIS MEANS, AMONG OTHERS, WE SHALL OVERCOME ANY MISGUIDED RESISTANCE AND LATER REDUCE YOUR POPULATION TO SCIENTIFIC LIMITS !

I THINK YOU WILL AGREE THAT THE TELEZERO IS FAR SUPERIOR TO YOUR ATOMIC BOMBS AND OTHER PLAYTHINGS — IT CAN DEVASTATE A LARGE OR SMALL AREA AT WILL — IT CAN BE FOCUSSED WITH PINPOINT ACCURACY AND OPERATED WITH COMPLETE SAFETY FROM SPACE STATIONS THOUSANDS OF MILES FROM THE TARGET — AND THERE IS *NO* DEFENCE AGAINST IT !

WHEREAS, IN THESE SPECIAL SUITS, OUR TREEN SOLDIERS CAN WALK UNHARMED THROUGH THE VERY CENTRE OF AN ATOMIC EXPLOSION

JUST THE THING — HOW CLEVER !

THEY'LL GO WILD ABOUT *HIM* IN WIGAN !

BUT WHERE DO *WE* COME IN ?

WE WISH TO TEST THE EXTREME LIMIT OF HUMAN RESISTANCE — THEN WE SHALL EXTRACT YOUR BRAINS FOR FURTHER STUDY

O, ER, WELL OF COURSE, WE'LL BE GLAD TO HELP IF YOU TELL US MORE OF YOUR PLANS

I CAN'T THINK OF ANYTHING NICER

MEANWHILE IN THE FAR SOUTH DAN STANDS IN THE CENTRAL SQUARE OF THE MYSTERIOUS CITY

I GIVE IT UP—I'VE BEEN TRAMPING ROUND FOR HOURS WITHOUT MEETING A SINGLE SOUL......

AND YET THERE ARE MACHINES WORKING AWAY LIKE MAD IN HALF THESE BUILDINGS —— I WONDER IF I COULD SPOT ANYTHING IF I GOT UP TO THE TOP OF THAT TOWER?

NOBODY AT HOME AS USUAL —— HELLO — CULTIVATED FIELDS OUT THERE AND SOMETHING MOVING — LOOKS LIKE SOME SORT OF HARVESTER — THERE MIGHT BE A CLUE DOWN THERE —— PRESS ON, DAN, MY BOY

AUTOMATIC EH?—WELL, IT MUST TAKE THE STUFF SOMEWHERE —I'LL FOLLOW IT

HM, A SELF-PROPELLED ROAD — I'VE GOT TO GET TO THE BOTTOM OF ALL THIS

HERE'S FOR A HAYRIDE!

LULLED BY THE WARM VENUSIAN SUN DAN FALLS INTO A SLEEP OF UTTER EXHAUSTION

ACROSS HILLS AND VALLEYS, OVER BRIDGES, THROUGH TUNNELS, THE MYSTERIOUS ROAD HUMS QUIETLY ON ITS WAY, BEARING ITS LOAD OF FARM PRODUCE — AND ONE SLEEPING HUMAN BEING.

UNTIL, FINALLY, IT ARRIVES AT ITS DESTINATION

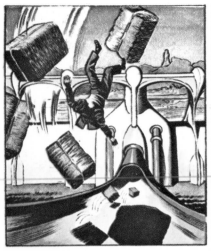

I MAY LOOK LIKE A DOG'S DINNER — BUT IT'S THE FIRST TIME I'VE BEEN TAKEN FOR A COW'S SUPPER!

HEY, MAC — WHAT'S COOKING?

GOT ANY GUM, CHUM?

WHO ARE YOU? WHO TAUGHT YOU THAT?

COME, EARTHMAN — I TAKE YOU TO HIM.

CLIMB ON BEHIND — IF YOU CAN TAKE IT!

HOLD TIGHT, EARTHMAN — DON'T BE AFRAID!

SHE'LL BE COMING ROUND THE MOUNTAIN

SUR LE PONT D'AVIGNON

HANK! PIERRE!

PRESIDENT? LISTEN, SIR, I'M SORRY TO RUSH YOU, BUT EVERY MINUTE COUNTS. AS LEADER OF THIS EXPEDITION, I MUST ASK TO SEE YOUR PRESIDENT AS SOON AS POSSIBLE.

I'VE TWO THINGS TO DO URGENTLY — FIX UP FOOD FOR THE EARTH, AND RESCUE THE PEOPLE FROM MEKONTA.

THREE THINGS, COLONEL — SOMETHING MUST BE DONE TO FOIL THE TREENS' "EARTH PLAN."

YES, DAN — YOU HAVEN'T HEARD ABOUT THAT, HAVE YOU?

I'VE GOT AN INKLING THAT THEY'RE UP TO SOMETHING — WE MUST CERTAINLY GET IN TOUCH WITH EARTH AGAIN — QUICKLY. HOW SOON WILL YOUR ROCKET BE READY?

IN ABOUT TEN DAYS, WE HOPE. SHE'S JUST DOWN THERE — IN THE GLADE WHERE WE CRASHED. COME AND HAVE A LOOK.

I'D HAVE SAID SHE WAS A WRITE-OFF, BUT THESE GUYS SURE KNOW THEIR WAY AROUND WITH A WRENCH!

COLONEL DARE — I HAVE BEEN IN TOUCH WITH THE PRESIDENT AND HE SAYS THAT....... *COLONEL!?*

DAN! WHAT'S ZE MATTER?

Dan awakens in strange surroundings

YOU ARE IN MY HOUSE, YOUNG MAN. I AM VOLSTAR, A THERON OF THE SOUTHERN HEMISPHERE OF VENUS

BUT WHO AM *I*: AND WHAT THE DICKENS AM I SITTING ON? A MAGIC CARPET?

YOU ARE LYING ON A BLANKET OF NATURAL MOSS SUPPORTED BY RAYS WHICH ALLOW IT TO CONFORM TO THE SHAPE OF YOUR BODY. YOU ARE BEING WARMED BY NATURAL SUNLIGHT AND TREATED BY CURATIVE WAVES WHICH HAVE BROUGHT YOUR TEMPERATURE TO NORMAL

.. AND TEMPORARILY BLANKED OUT YOUR MEMORY. THAT WAS TO STOP YOU WORRYING AND ALLOW YOU TO HAVE THE REST YOU NEEDED.

YOU COLLAPSED FROM PROLONGED FATIGUE AND EXPOSURE YOU'VE BEEN THROUGH QUITE A LOT RECENTLY. I'LL SWITCH THE WAVES OFF NOW AND YOU'LL REMEMBER

WHY DID I NEED REST? WHO AM I AND WHAT'S ALL THIS ABOUT?

YES — IT'S COMING BACK NOW — VENUS — TREENS — MEKONTA — DIG — *DIG!* THAT'S IT! I'VE GOT TO RESCUE DIG AND THE OTHERS FROM MEKONTA. OH, I'VE GOT TO GET OUT OF HERE AND *DO* SOMETHING!

DON'T GET EXCITED, COLONEL DARE! COME AND HAVE A LOOK OUTSIDE.

GREAT RACKETTING ROCKETS! WHAT KIND OF A HOUSE IS THIS?

JUST AN ORDINARY THERON HOUSE, COLONEL — IT SEEMS MORE CONVENIENT TO US THAT THEY SHOULD BE ABLE TO FLY — YOU ARE ON YOUR WAY TO SEE OUR PRESIDENT NOW.

WHAT D'YOU MEAN — WE AREN'T MOVING — THERE'S NO SLIPSTREAM.

ON THE CONTRARY, WE'RE DOING A NICE COMFORTABLE NINETEEN THAKOTS OR ROUGHLY SPEAKING 790 MILES AN HOUR — BUT YOU SEE, WE'RE ENCASED IN A BUBBLE OF AIR WHICH TRAVELS WITH US.

AIR BUBBLE

INCREDIBLE, COLONEL? WHY? WHEN YOU STAND ON THE SURFACE OF THE EARTH YOU'RE TRAVELLING AT SPEED BUT THERE'S NO SLIPSTREAM BECAUSE THE AIR'S TRAVELLING WITH YOU — THIS IS THE SAME EFFECT. COME, LET'S JOIN YOUR PALS AND MY SON ON THE CONTROL TERRACE.

HELLO, DANNY BOY — FEELING BETTER?

BANG ON, HANK! SORRY TO PASS OUT ON YOU BUT THE WILTING LILY HAS NOW BEEN RESTORED.

AND NOW TO WORK EH, DAN? — WHAT WE MUST DO ABOUT DEEG AN' ZE OTHERS?.

THAT'S IT, PIERRE — AND IT'S NOT GOING TO BE EASY.

NO, COLONEL — YOU FACE SOME PRETTY STIFF PROBLEMS IN DEALING WITH OUR FRIENDS, THE TREENS — I'M SURE OUR PRESIDENT WILL GIVE YOU ALL THE HELP HE CAN, BUT . . .

JUST WHAT IS THE LOWDOWN ON THE TREENS, VOLSTAR, AND WHERE DO *YOU* PEOPLE FIT IN? I'M IN A BIT OF A MAZE ABOUT THINGS HERE — ARE THERE ANY MORE RACES ON VENUS?

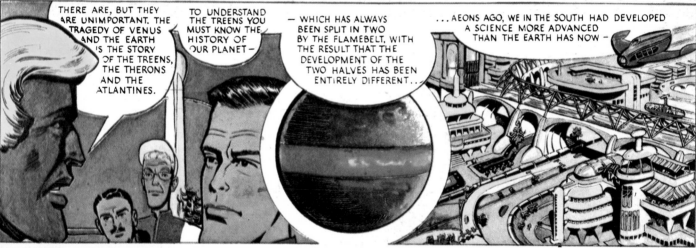

THERE ARE, BUT THEY ARE UNIMPORTANT. THE TRAGEDY OF VENUS AND THE EARTH IS THE STORY OF THE TREENS, THE THERONS AND THE ATLANTINES.

TO UNDERSTAND THE TREENS YOU MUST KNOW THE HISTORY OF OUR PLANET —

— WHICH HAS ALWAYS BEEN SPLIT IN TWO BY THE FLAMEBELT, WITH THE RESULT THAT THE DEVELOPMENT OF THE TWO HALVES HAS BEEN ENTIRELY DIFFERENT . . .

. . . AEONS AGO, WE IN THE SOUTH HAD DEVELOPED A SCIENCE MORE ADVANCED THAN THE EARTH HAS NOW —

. . . BUT IN THE NORTH A SEPARATE CIVILIZATION HAD DEVELOPED . . . BARBAROUS, BRUTAL AND REPTILIAN . . .

...WE BUILT AIRCRAFT WITH REFRIGERATED CABINS TO CROSS THE FLAMEBELT...

...AND EXPLORE THE NORTHERN HEMISPHERE

BUT WHEN WE LANDED, THE TREENS ATTACKED US WITH GIANT REPTILES...

AND FOR A CENTURY THERE WERE FIERCE BATTLES BETWEEN US...

...FINALLY WE TRIUMPHED — WE TAUGHT THEM ALL WE KNEW — BUT THEY CARED ONLY FOR REVENGE — AND POWER. MACHINES BECAME THEIR MASTERS SO WE LEFT THEM TO THEIR OWN DEVICES.

BUT YOU STILL HAVE MACHINES — THIS HOUSE — YOUR FACTORIES AND THE MECHANICAL ROAD...

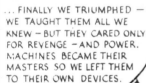

MACHINES HERE WORK FOR US, WE ARE NOT THEIR SLAVES. THEY LEAVE US FREE TO CARE FOR THINGS THAT MATTER...

...OUR CHILDREN, OUR GARDENS, OUR BOOKS, OUR MUSIC...

LET'S GET BACK TO THE TREENS. YOU MAY BE CONTENT TO LEAVE THEM TO THEIR OWN DEVICES. I'M NOT! NOT WHILE THEY HAVE FRIENDS OF MINE IN THEIR POWER!

OUR MACHINES SUPPLY OUR BODILY NEEDS. THEY OBEY OUR WISHES. THEY GIVE US FOOD AND LEISURE.

WHAT'S THIS EARTH PLAN OF THEIRS?

HAVE PATIENCE, COLONEL DARE AND I WILL TELL YOU...

...WE HAD STUDIED THE EARTH FOR CENTURIES FROM CIRCLING SPACE SHIPS WITH REMOTE CONTROLLED TELEVISION EYES. THE TREENS STILL USE THEM TO WATCH YOU. NOW YOU CALL THEM FLYING SAUCERS.

EVENTUALLY WE LANDED HERE — IN A LANDLOCKED VALLEY — NOW THE MEDITERRANEAN SEA, BUT THEN THE CENTRE OF YOUR CIVILIZATION.

...IT WAS A CIVILIZATION OF WHICH YOU ON EARTH KNOW NOTHING NOW. BUT THE LOT OF THE COMMON PEOPLE WAS HARD. — WE WISHED TO HELP YOU...

...WE WERE GREETED IN FRIENDSHIP BY THE HIGH PRIESTS OF THE SUN GOD RULERS OF THE LAND.

...BUT UNKNOWN TO US, THE TREENS HAD FOLLOWED US IN SPACE SHIPS OF THEIR OWN AND HAD LANDED AT ANOTHER CITY, IN THE PLAIN...

...AND SO RESULTED THE GREATEST DISASTER IN YOUR HISTORY...

..LIKE US, THE TREENS, TOO, WERE RECEIVED WITH SIGNS OF FRIENDSHIP BY THE RULERS.

BUT THE TREENS HAD NOT COME FOR FRIENDSHIP..

BUT FOR SLAVES AND SCIENTIFIC SPECIMENS.

THE PEOPLE OF THE CITY RALLIED AND ATTACKED...

MANY ATLANTINES WERE SLAUGHTERED BEFORE THE TREENS MADE OFF...

MESSENGERS WERE SENT TO WARN THE OTHER CITIES IN THE PLAIN.

THE MESSENGER ARRIVED WHILE WE WERE INSTRUCTING THE RULERS.

THE ANGRY ATLANTINES TOOK A CRUEL REVENGE ON US . . .

ONLY ONE OF OUR SPACE SHIPS ESCAPED AS WE ROSE . . .

WE SAW THEM TAMPERING WITH THE OTHERS. WE COULD NOT WARN THEM OF THE TERRIBLE DELICACY OF THE ATOMIC MOTORS WE WERE THEN USING.

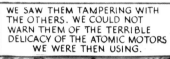

ONE OF THE EARTHMEN PROBABLY SMASHED AT THE MECHANISM WITH AN AXE

. . . THE EXPLOSION SPLIT THE MOUNTAIN RANGE THAT BARRED THE ATLANTIC BETWEEN AFRICA AND EUROPE.

THE ATLANTIC RUSHED IN — A WHOLE CONTINENT WAS SUBMERGED — AND THE MEDITERRANEAN WAS BORN . . .

THAT IS OUR STORY. YOU CANNOT WONDER WE DECIDED NOT TO INTERFERE WITH THE EARTH AGAIN.

THEN THOSE WRETCHED BLUE MEN ARE THE DESCENDANTS OF THE TREEN'S CAPTIVES? — THE LAST ATLANTINES?

YES — THE TREENS HAVE NEVER GIVEN UP PLANNING TO RETURN AND TAKE THE EARTH.

FROM WHAT SONDAR SAID, THEIR PLAN IS NEARLY READY — WE MUST STOP THEM.

YOU'LL BE ABLE TO TALK ABOUT THAT TO OUR PRESIDENT IN A FEW MINUTES, COLONEL DARE.

WE'RE NEARLY THERE — LOOK — THE GUARD SHIP'S COMING UP.

Dan Dare's battle with the Treens was to continue for many months but his eventual victory was marked by the founding of the Venus-Earth food service to save the Earth from starvation.

PROFESSOR **PUFF** and his dog **WUFF**

YES, THIS IS PAPA-GONIA ALL RIGHT. NOW FOR OUR EXPLORATION. CHART & COMPASS SAY THAT WAY...

YES, HERE'S THE RIVER WE MUST CROSS, WUFF — BUT HOW?

AH, GOOD! — WE'LL FORD IT ACROSS THIS HALF-SUBMERGED LOG...

EASY DOES IT, WUFF.. LOOK, I'M A BALLET DANCER..

GOLLY! THAT WASN'T A HALF-SUBMERGED LOG AFTER ALL...

NO, YOU DON'T, MY TOOTHY FRIEND!!

GLUP!

CRUNCH

AND YOU CAN GO ON WEEPING THOSE CROCODILE TEARS...

AHA! OUR FRIENDS THE PAPAGONIANS, I PRESUME...

TAKE US TO YOUR CHIEF AND TELL HIM PROFESSOR PUFF AND HIS DOG WUFF PRESENT THEIR COMPLIMENTS

THE CHIEF SEEMS VERY PLEASED WITH YOU, WUFF...

BIG CHIEF HE SAY HE NEVER TASTE LITTLE WHITE DOG BEFORE.

GLUP!

NO, NO!! — WAIT, WAIT!!

BIG CHIEF WILL LIKE THESE BETTER THAN LITTLE WHITE DOG..

SAY, HERE, BIG CHIEF, 'DELICIOUS SERVED WITH HOT JOINT'...

PHEW! WELL, WUFF, THIS IS THE TIME FOR SOME FAST THINKING...

THINK THINK THINK THINK THINK

FOLLOW THE STARS IN ACTION   Godfrey Evans *(Kent and England wicket-keeper batsman).*   No. 4.

Pictures by Carl Sutton]

HITTING A SIX

GODFREY EVANS started his sporting career as a batsman. For a time he was a successful welterweight boxer. Then he became a wicket-keeper, and such a good one that his early promise as a batsman became forgotten. This season, however, he has been reminding us repeatedly that he is, in fact, a most accomplished batsman, and there have been few better, or more thrilling knocks in the present Test series, than his century against the In-

dians at Lord's. Once he has got his eye in, Godfrey likes to use his feet to get to the ball and hit it hard and often. In the series of six pictures above he gives a loose delivery the treatment it deserves, hitting it for six straight over the bowler's head. Note the follow through.

First Birthday!

EAGLE is one year old

MARCUS MORRIS, *Editor.*

FRANK HAMPSON, *creator and artist of 'Dan Dare'.* 32-year-old Lancashire born. Worked on EAGLE when it was first thought of. Hobby – playing with three-year-old son Peter.

ELLEN VINCENT, *Editorial Assistant.* Worked with advertising firm. Hobby - Music.

CHARLES GREEN, *Editorial Assistant.* Makes model ships and railways. Hobby Amateur dramatics.

ERIC BEMROSE, *head of the firm who print EAGLE.* Hobbies - Photography and Radio.

"TELL them how the thing started," suggested someone.

"What *thing?*" asked the Editor coldly.

"EAGLE, of course – tell them how it began."

"And all that's happened since – up till now," put in someone else.

"Not all, I hope," commented the staff cynic. "There are some things best forgotten."

"Like the time you put in a wrong instalment of a strip, for example?" suggested my neighbour callously. "Though I will say this for you – nobody noticed, which just goes to show."

We were all together in the Editor's room at what we are pleased to call an Editorial Conference. That simply means that the editorial staff were scattered around the room in positions of varying inelegance, perched on the arms of chairs and the edges of tables – and arguing about what special features to put in the birthday issue.

Various suggestions had been put forward. An editorial suggester usually starts off full of enthusiasm and ends up rather lamely – withered by the glare of half a dozen pairs of critical eyes.

But this suggestion seemed to hit the nail on the head – at least the Editor thought so, and his decision is always final.

"Yes, I think that's a good idea," he said, "and we could put in photographs of you all – if the paper will stand it."

So that's how this story came to be written. We weren't at all sure whether you (our readers) would *want* to know how EAGLE started – still less what we all looked like. But we decided to risk it.

"Of course, it really all started in the bath – the idea of EAGLE I mean," went on the Editor. "But we'd better miss that part out – and how Hampson and I worked on the idea at home for nine months and then touted it round London, getting turned down by one publisher after another. Better start from when Hulton Press took it up, and decided to publish. Now who's going to write the story?"

The Editor looked round the room. We shuffled uneasily in our chairs.

"Better make it a combined effort," he said, in a determined voice. "All put down your impressions – and then we'll sort them out."

IT was towards the end of 1949 when EAGLE really got going six months before the first issue came out. While the Editor and the staff contacted artists and writers, sorted out material, planned features and then scrapped them, and gradually battered the paper into shape, others carried out complicated research into what boys liked most to read, how much pocket money they got, and what they spent it on.

Others planned the advertising campaigns to launch the paper. Others again planned schemes for giving the paper publicity among those who were (we hoped) going to read it.

Some suggestions were more hare-brained than others. The Editor, one bright spark suggested, should parachute into Hyde Park dressed up as an eagle. Then someone thought of letting off 200,000 balloons in various parts of the country – until the thought of the time and puff required to blow up that many balloons put it out of court.

At last we decided on the *Hunt the Eagle* plan. Cars with giant effigies of golden eagles on them were engaged to tour the country. Inside the cars, loudspeakers announced "EAGLE is coming". Gift vouchers were hidden everywhere – the finder could claim a free copy at the nearest newsagent. And that nearly started a riot! We heard of one gang who gathered a handful of vouchers, collected their free copies from the shops, and then sold them at the street corner.

So the first number went off – and, back in the office, we held our breaths.

Then came the avalanche. Orders poured in from newsagents all over the country. EAGLE was selling like hot cakes.

But we needed more than a good start. We needed paper too. And of paper there seemed to be less and less every week – at a higher and

EAGLE *gets around – in fact, all over the world. Some of our keenest readers are the children of Tombstone, Arizona.*

Many thousands of letters reach us week by week. Here is the Editor and his secretary looking through some of them.

higher price. We had to take two bitter decisions. We must limit the size to sixteen pages, and that meant putting lots of ideas in cold storage. And EAGLE would have to go up to 4d. But our readers went on buying it in spite of that, in ever increasing numbers.

Meanwhile the rapid success of EAGLE Club almost overwhelmed us. Over 60,000 joined in the first week – and sixty thousand is a lot of letters to have about the place. An emergency staff worked all hours to get out the badges and membership cards – and each week the numbers increased.

That's how we began meeting some of our readers – at the trips and parties and prize-winning expeditions we arranged for Club members. That was the best part of all – meeting our readers.

The MUG's Badge took on too – though some people didn't understand the name at first. "A

An EAGLE reader takes a tumble while winter sporting in North Italy. The rest of the party tell him what he did wrong.

EAGLE *readers inspect the latest Minic toys. A visit to this London toy factory was one of the outings organized recently by EAGLE Club.*

special badge for those who are especially helpful to others – that's the idea," we explained. "We call them MUGS because that's what the spivs call people who help others. So we'll turn the tables on the spivs by being proud of the title."

Some got the wrong idea about how to win a MUG's badge. They thought the only way was to rescue someone from drowning. "Bill spends all his time by the canal waiting for someone to fall in," one father wrote. We hurriedly explained some of the thousand other ways of earning a MUG's badge. And now the idea seems to have caught on.

Then there are the letters – hundreds of them every week – from readers, giving their views and criticisms and preferences. They are very frank and very helpful, and we keep a careful record of them all. We built up a staff of experts to answer the questions we received. "Please explain shortly Einstein's theory of relativity," one boy wrote. "Can you get me two tickets for the Cup-final?" asked another. (We couldn't!)

Then we started a *Hobbies Advice Bureau* and a *Pen Pals Scheme* – and that brought in thousands more letters.

How does it all work? And who does the work? As well as our Editorial staff, we have our staff of full-time artists – some of whom you see here. Then we have many other artists and writers and ideas men working for us.

Here's how it usually goes. The script-writer sends in his script for a strip-cartoon – *Riders of the Range*, for example (in this case Charles Chilton). This goes off to the artist who draws it in rough pencil form, back it comes for editorial

ROSEMARY GARLAND, *Editorial Assistant.* writes children's books. Expert on lighthouses. Hobby Painting pictures.

JAMES HEMMING, *Editorial Consultant.* Author of five books. Went round the world lecturing in 1949. Hobby - Tennis.

CHAD VARAH, *Editorial Consultant.* Reports on all manuscripts. Escaped after arrest by Nazis in 1934. Hobby Photography.

RUARI McLEAN, *Editorial Consultant,* expert typographer. Ex-submarine Officer. Hobby Driving an Austin 7.

PHYLLIS WASEY, *Secretary.* Has been with EAGLE since the first issue came out. Hobbies - Swimming and Cycling.

JOHN RYAN, *artist and creator of 'Harris Tweed'*. Teaches art at big Public School. Hobby – Collecting Roman coins.

ASHWELL WOOD, *Centre-spread artist*. Trained engineer, one-time draughtsman in aircraft company. Hobby – Cricket.

JACK DANIEL, *'Riders of the Range' artist*. Was a newspaper cartoonist. Ex-Desert Rat. Hobbies – Sculpture and Squash.

NORMAN WILLIAMS, *'Great Adventurer' artist*. Trained in Sheffield. Was a newspaper strip-cartoonist. Hobby – Stamp Collecting.

STROM GOULD. *'P.C. 49' artist*. Has 'panned' for gold, caught sharks and snakes. Hobby – Collecting New Guinea carvings.

HAROLD JOHNS, *Assistant artist on 'Dan Dare'*. Born in Devon, trained at Southport School of Art. Hobby – Photography.

approval; back to the artist to do the finished artwork. Then when the balloons are lettered, the page is ready – some time in advance, we hope, of press day. Similarly the great number of stories sent in to us are vetted by one of our Readers, approved or rejected – and if approved, sent to an artist to be illustrated.

At last all the material is ready and up it goes to Liverpool by train in a special sealed satchel. A week later we get back a pasted-up "dummy" of the issue for our corrections and alterations. And so the issue goes to press, and the copies roll off the machine, 12,000 an hour, 200 a minute, 3⅓ a second. Our centre-spread this week shows how it is done.

And meanwhile our EAGLE Club staff are busy arranging the holidays and outings, and despatching the Club badges, the MUG's badges, the articles of one kind or another that EAGLE Club produce.

It's a busy life and it never stops.

How about the future? Well, we've got plenty of ideas and plans – but it would rather spoil things to tell you about them now. Our aim is "Bigger and Better" – and we hope to make use of many of the ideas you have sent in to us.

Meanwhile, thank you for all your letters, encouraging and congratulating us. Although its our birthday, not yours, we still want to wish you – and ourselves – "Many happy returns" of EAGLE birthdays.

Here are Miss Peabody, Sir Hubert and Digby posing in EAGLE studio for artist Frank Hampson in a dramatic scene from DAN DARE.

JOHN RUSSELL, *Club Staff*. In charge of outside activities. Served in the Navy. Hobbies – Squash and Swimming.

DAN DARE, *Colonel*, Chief Pilot of International Inter-planet Space Fleet. Hobby – Jet Cricket.

When EAGLE was first started, we sent out cars bearing these huge golden eagles to all the most important towns in the country, to announce "EAGLE is coming".

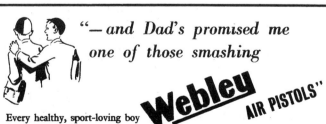

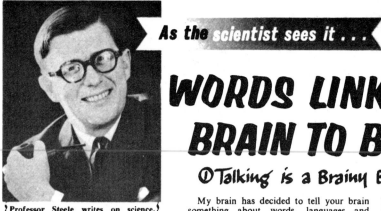

As the *scientist sees it* . . .

WORDS LINK BRAIN TO BRAIN

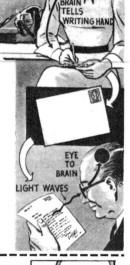

HOW MESSAGES PASS FROM BRAIN TO BRAIN

BRAIN TELLS MOUTH WHAT TO SAY — EAR TELLS BRAIN

SOUND WAVES

BRAIN TELLS WRITING HAND

EYE TO BRAIN

LIGHT WAVES

Professor Steele writes on science, exclusively for EAGLE, every week.

① Talking is a Brainy Business

My brain has decided to tell your brain something about words, languages and messages. So I begin to write, knowing that the printer will copy what I put down. Then you will get this week's EAGLE from your newsagent and, when you read my words, your brain will understand what is going on in mine.

Last week, I told you about your brain, and how much more powerful it is than the brains of other animals. But it doesn't, by itself, save you or me from being as ignorant as monkeys. What matters is that human brains can pass messages to one another, so that they can share what they know. If you had to start from scratch, teaching yourself geography by travel, and science by doing experiments, you wouldn't get very far!

We know much more about atoms, rockets, radio, the human brain, and so on, than our grandfathers did. They knew much more about building bridges and railways and ships than the Romans did; and the Romans knew much more about making roads and houses than the Ancient Britons did. The reason why men get 'cleverer' all the time is that words carry messages between old brains and young brains, and old books serve as an enormous 'memory' for all the things that men have ever done.

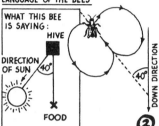

LANGUAGE OF THE BEES

WHAT THIS BEE IS SAYING:

HIVE

DIRECTION OF SUN 40°

DOWN DIRECTION

40°

FOOD

② Can animals talk?

Animals can make noises. Sometimes a bird utters a warning cry, and the other birds take flight. Lions roar and dogs bark. Even at the bottom of the sea, one can hear grunts and croaks from the sea-creatures.

Animals have languages of their own. For example, a worker bee which has found a food supply, returns to the hive and does a little dance on the upright wall of the honeycomb. By this dance, she shows the other workers in what direction the food lies. The nearer the food, the faster she dances. So she 'tells' the others all they need to know to find the food. It is unlikely that the worker bee 'makes up her mind' to pass this message. It is much more probable that she does the dance because instinct makes her.

A parrot can imitate your voice, and very funny it can be, too. But the words mean nothing to the parrot. If he says "Good morning" and "Good evening" at the right times of day, it is only because he remembers when humans say them.

You may have come across a 'talking horse' which taps out messages with his hoof. You might ask such a horse to tell you what number

√49 ?

THE TALKING HORSE

multiplied by itself makes 49, and he would deliver seven taps. This seems marvellous. But, in fact, the horse cannot even understand the question. He is just alert to the humans around him. He can sense when they want him to tap and when they want him to stop. Unknowingly, you are telling the horse the answer!

PALATE — NASAL CAVITY

LIPS 'I'

TEETH TONGUE

DIAGRAMS OF MOUTH, SHOWING TONGUE & LIPS' POSITION FOR TWO VOWELS

'A'

EPIGLOTTIS LARYNX WINDPIPE

③ How you talk

Learning to talk was probably the most difficult thing you ever did. You have a kind of musical instrument in your throat – the larynx – which you can 'play' by puffing air through it. It makes a sound like an organ. You then have to use your mouth, your tongue, your lips and your nose, all at the same time, to make words. You also have to learn the words and what they mean.

Say carefully to yourself the words 'hay, he, high, hoe, who', and feel how your lips and tongue move. You may be surprised at the number of complicated things that you do whenever you talk.

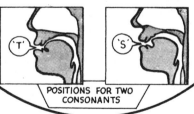

'T' 'S'

POSITIONS FOR TWO CONSONANTS

ALPHABET – WRITING: ROMAN, 5th CENT.

SCALAELIAIP DISCURRUN

SUMERIAN PICTURE WRITING INSCRIBED ON CLAY, 5,000 YEARS AGO

④ Writing Old and New

The simplest kind of 'writing' is what a hunter does when he cuts notches in his gun to record his kill. More than a hundred years ago, the Houses of Parliament burned down when fire broke out in a great store of notched sticks used for Government money records.

Another very old kind of 'writing' is picture-writing. Stories can be told by drawing a row of little pictures. Chinese writing began as picture-writing, and strip-

HOW SMALL LETTERS GROW FROM CAPITALS

WHEN PENS WERE INVENTED, WRITING A A Λ d u a a a SPEEDED UP: THE SHAPES BEGAN TO ALTER.

PRESENT DAY a a a FORMS

ONE KIND OF 'SHORTHAND'

The production model of this Xeronic computer output printer, made by Rank Precision Industries Ltd., will print 3,000 lines a minute, 128 letters on a line, and its own forms to contain the information.

cartoons are an up-to-date version of a very old idea.

Little by little, picture-writing gave way to alphabet-writing, where each mark or letter did not stand for one thing, but for a sound. That is the kind of writing I am using now. Shorthand is quicker; the marks stand for sounds, but they are easier to write.

Ways of writing have changed a lot, too. From chiselling in stone and scratching in clay, we have moved on to ink and paper and printing machines. Modern computers turn out 'answers' so quickly, that machines have had to be invented using a kind of electrical photography, which can print 3,000 lines a minute, 128 letters on a line – a wonderful achievement.

③ Codes and special languages

If you think about it, you will see that there are all sorts of 'codes' that messages can be put into for different purposes. I don't just mean things like the Morse Code for spelling out messages in dots and dashes, or secret codes and ciphers. Some of the others are shown here. A blind man can read with his fingers because, in Braille, letters are replaced by sets of little pimples raised on the paper. In deaf and dumb language, they are turned into finger signs.

Other 'codes' designed to be simple and quick are the red light on the roads and railways, the SOS signal and the distress call 'Mayday'. Computers are not usually designed to 'read' ordinary letters and figures, so their 'orders' are often fed into them in the form of a code of carefully arranged patterns of holes punched in a stack of cards or a reel of paper-tape. The computer 'senses' where the holes are, and reads the code. Not just the code, but the 'machine language' in which the orders are given, has to be carefully thought out by the man using the machines. The best computers nowadays can understand instructions based on simple English; the others have to be addressed more or less as you would talk to a dog – with very simple orders.

COMPUTER-
LANGUAGE
ON PUNCHED
PAPER–TAPE

…MAYDAY…

DISTRESS–SIGNAL LANGUAGE

ENHRC   JCMPA PCQLL

SLYAB   UDOER NJQRT

CIPHER LANGUAGE

RAILWAY
LANGUAGE

$$x_0 \pi (ai + ki) \propto \int_{t=0}^{t=T} \frac{po}{x^2} \, dx - e^{-\frac{dPo}{x_0 T^2}} \log(1-x)$$

MATHEMATICIANS' LANGUAGE

A B C X Y Z

SIX LETTERS OF BRAILLE LANGUAGE

E   G   L   E

DEAF-AND-DUMB LANGUAGE

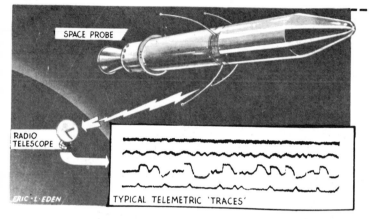

SPACE PROBE

RADIO
TELESCOPE

ERIC·L·EDEN

TYPICAL TELEMETRIC 'TRACES'

⑥ Telemetry: Messages from Space

Now men are throwing unmanned space vehicles, carrying complicated scientific instruments, far away from the Earth, and new 'languages' have been worked out so that scientists can know what is going on out there. The 'bleep-bleeps', buzzes and whistles that come over the radio contain a great deal of information about atomic rays, temperatures, meteorites and magnetism in speed, but you have to have the right equipment to be able to pick out messages, and you have to know the code to make sense of it. Each scientific instrument in the space probe or satellite may send out, on the radio, a certain musical note which is high or low, depending on whether it is 'reading' high or low at that moment. Each instrument may have a different part of the musical scale for itself, so that they can all transmit together; on the other hand, they may send out their signals in turn.

So, you see, for the hunter notching up his score, the story-teller, the short-hand-reporter, the airline pilot, and the space rockets, men's brains have found suitable languages, ways of writing or codes.

Professor Steele

EAGLE ROUNDABOUT

A visit to 10 Downing Street

The unpretentious front door that is known all over the world

Left, above: No 10 Downing Street as it is today; left: as it will appear after extensive alterations have been completed.

THE Prime Minister's home at No. 10 Downing Street is due for a face-lift. Built in the seventeenth century, it is beginning to show marked signs of old age, and architect Raymond Erith has been called in to improve the building at an estimated cost of nearly half a million pounds – without destroying its character. He has borne in mind that it has to serve three purposes: a family home for the Prime Minister, a place where important people can be entertained, and an office which is the nerve centre of the government, manned 24 hours a day, for seven days a week.

I went along with a group of reporters to take a last look at the old house before the builders move in to disturb the ghosts of Walpole, Pitt, Gladstone, Disraeli and the other famous men who have lived and worked there. We were shown the historic State rooms (which will not be altered in appearance), including the famous Conference Room, with its terrace over the garden, where so many statesmen have strolled to take a breath of air between talks. But perhaps the most impressive room we saw was also the smallest – the Prime Minister's private study, with its big desk covered in blue leather, and his personal black and green telephone. What exciting stories that telephone could tell!

AS we looked around, it was easy to see why rebuilding was necessary. Everywhere, floors sloped, door lintels were crooked, and big cracks had appeared in some of the walls. New foundations were necessary, and a complete new staircase. The reception-room floor was so frail, that only 200 people at a time could safely be allowed on it. One piece of damage will remain, however; the hole in the drawing-room wall, made by a bomb splinter, which Winston Churchill had preserved as a memento with a glass cover.

Other memories of the war linger in the basement, where the Prime Minister used to entertain the King to dinner during air raids. It had its

The Prime Minister's study

own blast-proof shelter, and I saw there a pile of old tin hats that looked as if they had not been disturbed since the blitz.

The reconstruction work will take about two years; meantime, the Prime Minister will live in Admiralty House. On his return, he will find many changes for the better, but the familiar façade – with its famous black front door – will still be there, unchanged; so will the policeman who guards it, and the ever-hopeful crowds who wait and watch outside, hoping to catch a glimpse of history in the making.

The truth about Cowboys

by Grierson Dickson

(2) Six Shooter and Round-up

Illustration by Jack Nicolle

BULLETS, of course, are always measured by decimals of one inch. The size most people know about is the .22 bullet – the sort used on fairgrounds. The .22 can do quite a lot of damage; it travels a long way at a high velocity and can be fatal if it penetrates a vital organ such as the brain or the heart. But if it hits the stomach or a lung it might pass right through your victim's body without immediately disabling him.

That would not have suited a cowboy. In a gun-fight he wanted to disable his opponent with the vital first shot So he preferred a heavy bullet which hits with sufficient shock to knock a man off his feet even if he is wearing a bullet-proof vest. The smallest bullet which will do this is a .380 (which is the calibre of the Webley & Scott automatics used by Scotland Yard).

There was, of course, an upward limit to the size of bullet most suitable for a cowboy. A heavy bullet has to be fired from a heavy weapon, and cowboys did not want a gun that was too big and clumsy to be used with one hand on horseback.

So in the great days of the old Wild West the almost universal weapon was a long .45 Colt or Smith & Wesson. This type of gun, the six-chambered, solid frame, single action revolver, was first made by Samuel Colt as far back as 1835.

The Colt six-shooter did not immediately become popular. Those were the days of the old hunters: picturesque chaps in their coonskin caps and moccasins and fringed buckskin tunics. Few of them had horses, which were of little use in forest country. A pistol is essentially a horseman's weapon: these old hunters naturally preferred a rifle, because they needed an accurate long-range weapon. But their long muzzle-loading rifles were not much use in fighting against the Indians, who, armed only with bow-and-arrows, tomahawk, and scalping-knife, literally made rings round them. Galloping round and round the palefaces, the redskins would twist one foot into their pony's mane, hang head downwards on the side away from their enemy, and shoot their deadly arrows under the pony's belly.

It was the Texas plainsmen, living their lives on horseback, who realised the value of the revolver, and were virtually the only customers Colt had when he manufactured his first model. The time came when a Texas Ranger, galloping as fast as the Indian, could literally kill six startled braves with one hand in a few seconds.

I referred to Colt's invention as a single-action revolver.

Later, the double-action revolver was introduced, in which pressure on the trigger first cocked the hammer and then released it.

It was not until about 1890 that Smith & Wesson, the gunsmiths, invented the self-ejector. The frame of this type of revolver was in two parts, hinged beneath the barrel which could thus be bent downwards. This action was called "breaking" the gun. It exposed the ends of the chambers and at the same time automatically pushed out all the spent cartridges at once. So a lot of valuable time was saved in reloading.

From the 'fifties to the 'eighties of last century every cowboy, gambler, sheriff, and a good many Indians, carried a solid frame Colt. It abolished the advantages possessed by bigger and stronger men over weaker opponents. All that mattered was to be able to draw quickly and shoot straight. The revolver was called with truth, in grim American slang, "the old equaliser".

In the 'nineties, however, there was no longer a universal weapon. Some men still carried the old solid frame guns, awkward to reload, but throwing a heavy bullet with deadly accuracy. Others had self-ejectors, quickly loaded but less accurate and rather unsafe with heavy bullets. And before the century ended the familiar automatic pistols favoured by modern gangsters were coming into use.

Automatics became popular among some of the few remaining Western "bad men". They are lighter than revolvers, loaded in a second or two, can fire three times as fast as a revolver, and being flat can be more easily carried in the pocket of a store suit. Their speed would have pleased the cowboy.

The sneering gambler with an automatic could have emptied a magazine of ten bullets into his cowboy opponent before the cowboy had fired three times. And the gambler could have snapped a fresh magazine up the butt of his pistol while the cowboy was pulling out his ejector rod to clear the first chamber.

So it is a good thing that at that very time the advance of civilisation was making it unnecessary for every man in the West to carry a gun.

THERE were no fences on the prairies in the old days, and cattle belonging to many different ranches roamed about freely. When at last they were driven to the stockyards to be slaughtered and sold as beef, it was only the brand burnt into their hides that decided which ranches should be credited with their value.

Horses were rounded up in the summer and steers in the autumn, but neither was quite so important as the round-up of calves (or "rodeos") in the spring. Calves which missed being driven in and branded at the round-up eventually left their mothers and then nobody knew to which ranch they belonged.

Each ranch in a district would send to the round-up an outfit roughly proportionate to the size of the ranch. An outfit might consist of five or six cowboys, each man taking as many as eight or ten horses. There would also be a chuck-wagon carrying food, tents and other equipment, and that very important person - the cook!

It was not often that men from different ranches had an opportunity to get together. So the round-up was a social occasion. There would be horse races, trick riding displays, contests to see who could 'rope, throw and tie' a steer single-handed in the shortest time, or who could stay longest mounted on the bare back of some old longhorn.

In the evenings there would be games of cards, little groups round a camp fire listening to the tall stories of some leg-pulling old-timer, and isolated figures among the tents and silent wagons chewing a 'cud' of tobacco as they oiled their leather equipment or limbered up their ropes ready for the stern work ahead.

And perhaps someone would get out his concertina and start up one of the plaintive old cowboy songs that are still so popular on the radio.

On the night before the round-up began, everyone would turn in early to get a good rest. With the dawn the camp would come to life. After a substantial breakfast, each outfit would ride out to its appointed area, split up, and begin the task of driving scattered groups of cattle back to the main camp.

What made the work a little easier was the tendency of the cattle to herd together. Groups of dozens would merge to form herds numbering hundreds, and at last, after days of hard riding, there would be perhaps several thousand animals collected into some convenient valley, amid clouds of dust and a mad medley of noises from lowing cows and yelling men.

Then there was time for a good meal and a rest for the sweating cowboys, under wagons, out of the scorching rays of the sun. This was necessary to give the herd time to mill around and sort itself out, lost calves bawling pathetically until they were found by their mothers, who never made a mistake. For the whole object of the round-up was to identify the calves by branding them with the same marks that appeared on the hides of their mothers.

When the herd had quietened down, all the cows that had calves running beside them were cut out from the main herd by cowboys who rode fearlessly into the packed mass of long-horned beasts.

By that time the fires were burning brightly, and the ends of the rows of branding irons were cherry-red. A group of mounted cowboys roped and threw the calves, and dragged them up to the fire. Another group noted the mother's brand and selected the right iron to mark her offspring.

And nearby stood an important person called the 'tally man', sharpening a stub of pencil with an enormous clasp knife. He was likely to be a sick or injured cowboy, or some old-timer whose cow punching days were over.

Branding was simple in the early days because the only instrument needed was a 'running iron', which was no more than a steel rod, red hot at one end, with which the design of the brand was drawn on the animal's hide as with a huge pencil. Then, as so often happens, the activities of a few dishonest men made things difficult for everybody.

These crooks were called 'brand blotters' and were not the same as the ordinary cattle thieves, or rustlers. The brand blotter worked more cunningly, using a running iron to alter the brands on any cattle he found bearing marks similar to his own. When we remember how simple were some of the designs of the early brands, and how easy it is to alter a 'V to a diamond, or a '3' to an '8', we can understand why, in time, the use of a running iron was made illegal in some States.

In addition to the brand burned into its hide, a steer might have a pattern of notches cut into its ears, with sometimes a 'vent mark' as proof of legal sale when it bore more than one brand. Thousands of these marks were registered and recorded in the State Brand Book, and the cowboys needed good sight as well as a good memory to distinguish them.

In the fall of the year came the 'beef round-up' which was simpler and involved no branding. Steers ready for slaughter were cut out into a separate herd called the 'beef cut', and driven to the stockyards or to the nearest railhead.

Broncos were much more difficult to round up than steers. The cowboy's horse might be no swifter than the broncos it had to chase and was hampered by the weight of its rider. And horse herds had an irritating habit of suddenly doubling back on their tracks just when the cowboys thought they had got them running in the right direction.

It took about a fortnight for the wounds from brands and ear cuts to heal, after which they were soon forgotten. Then the calves resumed their natural roaming life until they were fat enough to be slaughtered, but the colts were destined to lose their freedom and spend their lives as the servants of man.

The end

Next time:
Bronco Busting and Pony Express.

The Indians literally rode rings round them

SCHOOL FOR SPIES

Another real-life Spy story by

BERNARD NEWMAN

HOW do you become a spy? Quite a lot of boys seem interested in this question, to judge by the letters I receive. One lad of 9 asked if I could recommend a good spy school, and if it had its own junior or prep. school!

Naturally, the War Office does *not* advertise for its agents: "Spies wanted, all sorts and sizes. Apply —"

Nor would it be of much use if you yourself were to advertise: "Boy, aged 14, offers services as spy. Knows French up to the pen of the gardener's aunt. Very good with a catapult. Can ride a bicycle. Has studied Dick Barton. What offers?" I can give you the answer at once – none!

However, I can tell you of two or three methods of entering the ranks of the secret agents.

You are called up for your military service in war-time, let us say. You speak German very well: not just matriculation standard – you have lived in Germany for some years. Your company officer soon notices that.

Then one day your unit captures some prisoners. Your officer says, "Look, I want some information out of these fellows, quickly – can't wait for the Intelligence Corps. You get busy on them."

So, when an Intelligence Officer comes along, he finds that *you* have carried out the preliminary interrogation very efficiently. He makes a mental note.

Then, later, he gets you transferred to his staff. At first you question prisoners, or read captured German documents. But one day your officer says: "There is a big batch of prisoners coming into the cage. These Fritzes don't talk very freely. Now, here's a German uniform – get into it. Now I'll brief you —"

He gives you a name and number. You belong to a unit just north of those to which the prisoners belong. You learn the name of its officers, and similar details. You are herded into the cage as if you were a German prisoner yourself. And men who refuse to talk to a British officer *will* perhaps talk to one of themselves.

Next comes a precarious job. You crawl out in front of our lines lie hidden near a German post, and listen to the conversation of German sentries. You can pick up all kinds of details – the morale and casualties in their unit, for example. Or you may get nothing – and all the time lie under the fire of your own guns!

One day a senior officer sends for you. "The reports on you are very good", he says. "Your German is first-class, and your nerve is sound. Are you willing to have a go behind the lines?"

He will not press you – only volunteers are of any real use in espionage.

But if you agree, a suitable background will be arranged, and before long you will be dropped or infiltrated behind the German lines, a fully-fledged spy.

Or maybe you are a business man who often goes abroad – a commercial traveller, for example.

Some astute man in Military Intelligence gets to know about you. First he makes some careful enquiries, to prove that you are thoroughly British, have a flair for intrigue, and control of yourself. Then he will approach you – apparently quite casually.

"Keep Your Eyes Open!"

"You're going to Cologne next week, aren't you? Well, look, we think that the 21st Division has been replaced by the 60th. Could you just keep your eyes open?"

That's a fairly easy job, and you do it. On your next journey the officer suggests something else.

After a long trial on petty tasks, you may be asked to do something bigger. You have the advantage of a good ready-made cover. You continue to do your job as a commercial traveller, and do your spying in your spare time, so to speak.

A third method: you are a naval, army, or air force officer, thoroughly trained, especially on the technical side. Your German is also very good, and you are a natural actor. If you are willing to volunteer for secret service work, you are sent to a spy school. That is not the military title of the establishment, but describes it very well.

If a war is on, the course is short. In peace time it is very thorough. When you pass out, you will not only be a trained spy yourself - you will be qualified to take charge of a group of sub-agents.

You will learn a good deal about codes and secret inks – I shall write more about these in future articles.

You will be able to drive any make of British or *foreign* car - and ride a horse as well. You will have made several parachute jumps, and in emergency could take charge of an aircraft.

Your languages have been given special attention, and you know a lot about dialects. The thrillers seldom mention this point, but it is important. A foreign spy who knew only "Oxford" English, for example, might be completely foxed if he overheard a conversation in really broad Lancashire!

You are taught to act as an ordinary man, and to look ordinary. If you belong to the R.A.F. and favour "handle-bar" moustaches, off they come!

You learn a lot about radio - and about detonators for sabotage purposes. You become an accomplished burglar, and can pick an ordinary lock with ease.

Naturally, you must keep in first-class physical condition, and your nerve is constantly tested.

At one German spy-school the doctor would take the recruit out into the park surrounding the isolated building. Suddenly three or four men would run across the turf: a machine gun would open fire, and the men would fall and lie still. The recruit might be horrified - perhaps this was his first sight of sudden death. Immediately the doctor would pounce upon him to test his pulse and heart. Then the "dead" men would get up and walk away - the episode was just a test of the spy-recruit's nerve.

At another school the would-be spy was dressed in a pneumatic suit, which was inflated. Then he sat on a mechanical contrivance which whirled his chair round and round. Suddenly his seat collapsed, and he was flung wide.

Jump from a Train

The pneumatic suit prevented him from suffering injury. He went through this test day after day - until he did it without the special protective suit. It proved to be first-class training for *jumping from a moving car or train.*

All the while you are having lectures on your own technical subject, whether it be guns or aircraft. As a relief, you learn quite a lot about disguise.

In the thriller the spy is a "master of disguise". He comes into a room disguised as a Chinaman: the police are after him: a few rapid passes with greasepaint, some business with wigs and whiskers, and he goes out through the window disguised as a Russian, singing the Volga boat song and kicking the snow off his boots!

If you think that you could get away with wigs, whiskers and greasepaint, just try them! I promise that you won't get very far! The local small boys will notice you even before the police do.

The best disguise of all is a *character.* You are taught to *live* it, not to put it on. A background is worked out for you, and all your passports and other papers are beautifully forged. If your name is to be Hans Schmidt, then you will use the name for weeks, so that you will get used to it. You know all about this Hans - where he was born, details of his father, mother and friends. You know all about his work, too - and you will be prepared to do it, whatever it is! Thus, by a mass of details, you build up the *character* of Hans Schmidt, and it is your best protection.

You may need some little changes in your appearance, in case you run into some old acquaintance. If your hair is dyed, it will make a big difference to your appearance: and you are taught to *keep* it dyed to the same shade. For an emergency, even a detail like altering the parting of your hair can have its effect.

You can appear to be about two inches shorter by practising a slouch. To pass an opponent who might recognise you, the shape of your face can be temporarily altered by stuffing slices of apple or potato under your cheeks.

Injecting Molten Wax

If your "character" demands more permanent alterations, there are many possibilities. There are solutions to darken your skin, and others to bleach it. You can alter the shape of your nose by injecting molten wax under the skin, and then moulding it into shape. For goodness sake don't try this, for it is very, very painful. If you *do* try it, don't blame me when it hurts – as it will!

You can imagine that after months or years of this training you know a thing or two! You must study the politics of the country where you are going to work, and any local customs and peculiarities.

Idioms and slip-shod habits in speech are important - one foreign spy couldn't understand when some people talked about drinking "minerals" - he thought that the word meant things like coal and iron, while the people were actually talking about lemonade and ginger beer!

In war-time, as I said, training is naturally much shorter. Often a spy is trained for one particular job - say, reporting on the lay-out of factories in a munitions town. He must know the language, of course: he will be taught how to use a radio transmitter, and how to use some codes for his messages. These "short term" spies are seldom very successful.

Immediately after the first World War I went to a German spy school in Antwerp, and more recently to one in Hamburg. Both were very interesting. The Antwerp school specialised in naval spies. In one room were models of battleships, cruisers, destroyers, and so on - and the spy-recruits had to identify them by their outlines or silhouettes. I saw some of the students' examination papers, and I must say that they weren't very good. One man mistook a mine-layer for a cruiser!

I know that it must be very disappointing for you to learn that a spy has to go to school. Not very glamorous, I agree!

However, parts of the spy course are more interesting than compound fractions and isosceles triangles. Another time, for example, I shall tell you about some of the codes which spies are taught to use.

*Another
true spy story
by Bernard Newman
soon*

Sebastian Snow —
Master of the Mighty Amazon!

Travel down the river of death with one of the youngest and bravest explorers of modern times!

THERE could hardly be a better name for an explorer than Sebastian Snow. You can imagine a man with this name standing on a great icy glacier, and shouting the name like a challenge, making the mountains ring with the words! Sebastian Snow! But you need not imagine too much. There IS a person called Sebastian Snow, and although he is only in his twenties he has already lived through incredible adventures – any one of which would last most of us a lifetime.

Sebastian always wanted to be an explorer, but this was easier said than done. True, he did know General Norton, who accompanied an expedition to Everest in the nineteen-twenties, and he never tired of the General's account of the great battle with this mightiest of mountains, and of the countries and peoples on the far side of the earth. That was the way to live, thought Sebastian! And he did his best to get on various small expeditions, but he was always turned down as being too young.

He had to earn a living of course, and went into the City of London to learn about insurance. But he never took kindly to office work. All the time he was dreaming of jungles, deserts, mountains and rivers. It was no good. No matter how hard he tried to put these things from his mind, they surged back at a moment's notice.

And so, haunted by his dream – he did something about it. He heard of a school friend who was off to Arctic Lapland, to study the little Lapps who wander with their reindeer across the wastes of Northern Sweden. "I'M going with you!" exclaimed Sebastian. "All right!" said his friend. And off they went.

The journey was a great success. Sebastian had started! Within a year or so, he had travelled alone, first across India and then into Central Asia where he reached Kabul, capital of Afghanistan on the borders of Russia, and then to the peaks of the Andes, the great mountains of South America. It was in these solitudes, marked by the ruins of ancient Inca cities, that Sebastian first thought of the amazing venture that has made his name famous. He decided that he would try to go all the way down the Amazon, that mighty river whose source is in the Andes near the Pacific and which runs for 3,500 miles to Para where it flows into the Atlantic!

Everything was done to dissuade him. "It's suicide!" they said. "He should be stopped!" And the natives of Peru drew their fingers across their throats and pointed out that even if the river did not drown him, the snakes would get him, or the savages with their bows and arrows. A few volunteers came forward, but when they heard the nature of the job they quickly faded away. But Sebastian's mind was made up. If no one would go with him, he would make the trip alone!

The task he had set himself was a staggering one. He had to make his way from the source of the Amazon, through the Andes, following the bank where the stream was too narrow, to where he could get a balsa raft or maybe a canoe from the wild Indians. The first eleven hundred

Launching the balsa raft

miles was the worst! He had to descend from 16,000 feet to the jungle, through rapids, gorges, whirlpools, and over waterfalls. And after this through country inhabited by murderous tribes. Once he got to the jungle city of Iquitos he knew he would be all right, as the last two thousand miles was just straight downriver to the Atlantic, and he could get a launch.

He said his goodbyes, and set off for the source of the Amazon, high in the Andes. But as it turned out, to begin with, he was not entirely alone. A young Peruvian called Pacchioni accompanied him. They rode horses, and had a packhorse for the stores.

They reached the source and started on their way. They soon ran into blinding snow showers. Inside two hours there was disaster. Sebastian tried to get the packhorse up a difficult slope, and it crashed down a hillside, rolling over and over, scattering stores everywhere, and lying as if dead at the bottom. It looked as if they weren't going to get very far! But at the bottom Pacchioni gave the horse a kick, and to their amazement it got to its feet. They coaxed it back up the hill, and went on.

Before long, however, they were forced to sell their horses to Indians in order to buy food. They continued on foot, each with sixty pounds of baggage carried in rucksacks.

After a hundred miles, they got hold of some more animals. Mules this time, and very troublesome! Soon they entered the *verrugas* belt. This is the name for a dreadful disease, caused by cactus sandflies. Much to Sebastian's horror they came upon a man suffering from this disease. He was covered in bleeding sores and had been left by the roadside to die. Sebastian Snow tended this man, and bound up his wounds. And a year later this very man got to the city of Lima, fully cured and full of praise for his deliverer, the great 'Don Sebastiano'!

Worse followed next day. A yellow viper slid from the bushes and bit Pacchioni. He became very feverish, but recovered just in time to nurse Sebastian, who was also attacked by fever. Every night, despite the huge fires they built, they were plagued by mosquitos and bitten hundreds of times. Both Sebastian and his guide felt very ill and when they saw puma tracks near their camp, they felt even worse.

After three weeks they had covered 200 miles. By now Pacchioni was very ill indeed. Obviously he could not continue. Sebastian gave him money and food, and after he had rested Pacchioni went back the way they had come. Sebastian went on alone, until he collapsed downriver at Tayabamba. By now the flood season had arrived. Sebastian would have to wait a while until he could start work on his raft. Anyway he was ill, and unable to go on for a time. He was nursed by natives who took pity on him, and then by a great stroke of fortune was befriended by a man called Don Gustavo, who owned a large ranch.

Sebastian waited six months. Then, his strength regained, his raft made ready, he launched out on to the Amazon, now 250 feet wide at its upper reaches and running at tremendous speed between high canyon walls. Once more he found a companion, a young Indian boy, who most of the time was frightened to death! And no wonder. Once they were off it was like being on a roller coaster. The raft tore along on the face of the torrent, bucking and heaving, rushing round blind corners and spinning like a top in whirlpools. And then, at a point where things seemed a little easier, the raft skidded round a bend and raced down hill at the greatest speed yet - straight for a terrific drop. To rush over the waterfall would mean certain death. With a great threshing of paddles they tried to steer the raft to the bank. They managed to make some headway, but all the time the raft sped like a bullet to the waterfall. With a last prodigious effort they swung the raft against the bank and leapt on shore.

An escape from death? Yes, but another setback too! Sebastian had to go inland underneath the falls, build another raft and start all over again. At this time he met his last companion in this great undertaking, a young man called Cara-millo. His skill proved invaluable, and his courage outstanding. Almost at once the two men became the closest of friends.

Another raft was built. Once more the frail timbers were launched upon the mighty flood. Away they went, skimming through the gorges, always in great peril, until the most dreaded moment of all arrived. This was the voyage through the vast Pongo de Manseriche (The Gateway of Parrots in the Indian tongue), an enormous black canyon with towering walls a thousand feet high, and in the middle a huge whirlpool which had killed many travellers in the past. The walls shut out the sun. It was very dark, and they could hear nothing but the awful roar of the waters. Presently they felt themselves on the fringe of the whirlpool. They paddled madly to escape, but of no avail. In spite of frantic efforts, they were sucked into the heart of the whirlpool. At one time they thought they were pulling away, but all the time the pool held them and slowly but surely attracted them to their death. And when the raft began to go round in circles, faster and faster until the great canyon was spinning around them, Sebastian felt sure that this was the end of the trip.

AND then a miracle! Across the rocking waters came a sudden stiff breeze. A strong puff of wind across their path made a cross-current in the water. In a flash the raft had shot from the centre to the edge of the whirlpool. Now then! They paddled for dear life, and suddenly they were free, born forward once more on the racing river.

Soon they would reach Iquitos. Away they went, speeding through the land of the headhunters of Jivaro. The savages were astounded to see a raft coming from the south. None of them could remember a raft coming from *that* direction! Instead of attacking the raft's occupants, they actually gave them an escort of war canoes until they reached a police post.

And this is the end of the story. A day or so later the raft, riding easily now on the ever-widening river, swept into the jungle city of Iquitos. Sebastian paid off Caramillo and boarded the downriver launch for Para. A fortnight later he saw the Atlantic.

Sebastian Snow had won through. For ten months he had battled, bit by bit, from the source to the mouth of this great river. The difficulties had seemed insuperable, the obstacles supreme, but in the end his grit and courage and his faith in himself won the day – hands down. Young Sebastian Snow had mastered the mighty Amazon!

For next week's adventure see page 11.

EAGLE'S new true-life story!

THEY SHOWED THE WAY

THE CONQUEST OF EVEREST

Between the years 1921 and 1952, eleven expeditions set out to climb to the top of the world's highest peak — the 29,002 feet of Mount Everest, in the Himalayas. All of them failed. Now, in the autumn of 1952, Colonel John Hunt has been appointed to lead another expedition .

Told by PETER SIMPSON
Drawn by PAT WILLIAMS

Hunt retails his plan for the attempt on Everest to the Joint Committee of the Alpine Club and Royal Geographical Society . . .

MOST EARLIER ATTEMPTS HAVE BEEN MADE FROM THE NORTH, THROUGH TIBET — I INTEND TO TRY FROM THE SOUTH, THROUGH NEPAL!

I CALCULATE THAT THE WEATHER WILL BE SUITABLE ONLY FOR A FEW DAYS IN MID-MAY NEXT YEAR — SO WE MUST HURRY!

DON'T FORGET, HUNT — THERE'S A SWISS EXPEDITION ON EVEREST NOW — IF THEY SUCCEED, WE'LL HAVE TO THINK AGAIN.

In spite of the Swiss challenge, Colonel Hunt begins his search for the special equipment needed .

There is still no news of the Swiss attempt, and Hunt is given until 10th December to confirm orders for equipment. Hoping for the best, he goes ahead selecting men and, on 15th November, those who are to make up the Everest team meet for the first time . . .

LEFT TO RIGHT IN THIS GROUP ARE WARD, NOYCE, BOURDILLON, WYLIE, BAND AND EVANS.

TWO NEW ZEALANDERS WILL JOIN US IN INDIA — LOWE AND HILLARY.

Next, the equipment is put to test in Switzerland . .

MINUS TWENTY DEGREES CENTIGRADE — EVEREST WEATHER!

NEARLY THE TENTH OF DECEMBER, AND THERE IS STILL NO NEWS OF THE SWISS ON EVEREST

Two days later . . .

TELEGRAM FOR COLONEL HUNT!

THIS IS IT! NOW WE SHALL KNOW IF THE SWISS ATTEMPT ON EVEREST HAS SUCCEEDED.

THEY SHOWED THE WAY

THE CONQUEST OF EVEREST

In the autumn of 1952, Colonel John Hunt is appointed to lead an expedition to climb Mount Everest the following May. He, and other members of the expedition, have been testing equipment in the Alps when, on 8th December, John Hunt receives news of the rival Swiss attempt on Mount Everest . . .

Told by PETER SIMPSON
Drawn by PAT WILLIAMS

DESPITE GREAT BRAVERY, THE SWISS COULDN'T GET BEYOND 20,000 FEET.

SO LOOK OUT, EVEREST — HERE WE COME!

The day of departure approaches, but then . . .

I'M AFRAID THERE'LL BE NO SEA-VOYAGE TO INDIA FOR YOU, HUNT—THIS MEANS AN OPERATION!

DON'T SAY THIS MEANS THAT I CAN'T TACKLE EVEREST!

On 12th February, the main party sails from Tilbury on the first stage of their journey to Nepal, in Northern India.

SEA-LEVEL — AND TO THINK EVEREST IS 29,002 FEET ABOVE THIS!

Then, at the end of February . . .

THANKS TO YOU ALL, I'LL STILL BE IN TIME IF I FLY OUT TO INDIA!

Eventually, on 8th March, the whole party assembles at Katmandu, capital of Nepal, and here Hunt meets the two New Zealand mountaineers

I'M ED HILLARY, AND THIS IS GEORGE LOWE.

AND THERE'S TENSING—LEADER OF THE SHERPA PORTERS.

On 10th March, the King of Nepal sees off the first contingent . . .

COLONEL HUNT, PLEASE LEAVE ONE OF THESE NEPALI FLAGS ON THE SUMMIT OF EVEREST!

Then follow sixteen days' march through the foothills of the Himalayan Mountains . . . .

. . . until, at last, they reach First Base Camp, at Thyangboche, over 12,000 feet up. From now on, Hunt and his companions are faced by the real mountains!

MY GOODNESS, LOOK AT EVEREST! TO THINK WE'VE GOT TO CLIMB UP THERE!

THEY SHOWED THE WAY

THE CONQUEST OF EVEREST

Led by Colonel John Hunt, the 1953 Commonwealth expedition to climb Mt. Everest – 29,002 ft. – is under way. Camps 5, 6 and 7 have been established on formidable Lhotse face. Then Wilfred Noyce and Sherpa Annulu set up camp on South Col, and all is ready for the main assault on the peak.

Told by PETER SIMPSON
Drawn by PAT WILLIAMS

The camp on the South Col is built up beside the broken and scattered remnants of one left by the unsuccessful Swiss Expedition in 1952 . . .

Far below, at Base Camp, Evans and Bourdillon, the first assault party, and John Hunt, set out on their climb up to the South Col.

At such heights, a man's physique is tested to the uttermost. On 25th May, though the weather is fine, the tired climbers have to rest at the windswept South Col camp. On 26th May, the first assault team prepares to tackle the summit . . .

GOSH, LOOK HOW FAR WE'VE COME!

However, there is a hold-up . . .

I'LL HAVE TO REPLACE THE VALVE ON MY OXYGEN MASK.

The valve repaired, they set off up the South Ridge on the last haul towards the summit . . .

THIS IS SLOW GOING, AND WE'VE LOST VALUABLE TIME.

When they can go no further, Hunt and his Sherpa establish a dump of stores. Bourdillon and Evans leave their companions behind and go on into the unknown . . .

Then follow many anxious hours waiting on the South Col, until they return . . .

THEY'RE BACK – SAFE!

BUT NO VICTORY SIGNS!

WE JUST HADN'T ENOUGH TIME AND OXYGEN TO GET THERE AND BACK.

THEN IT'S UP TO THE SECOND ASSAULT PARTY, NOW-HILLARY AND TENZING!

THEY SHOWED THE WAY

THE CONQUEST OF EVEREST

Led by Col. John Hunt, the 1953 Commonwealth expedition to climb Mt. Everest, towering up to 29,002 ft., is under way. From the camp on the South Col – 26,000 ft. up – Bourdillon and Evans attempt to reach the summit. Following many anxious hours, they return and break the news of their failure to Colonel Hunt . . .

Told by PETER SIMPSON
Drawn by PAT WILLIAMS

WE HADN'T ENOUGH OXYGEN TO GET BEYOND THE SOUTH SUMMIT

NEVER MIND — YOU GOT UP TO 28,700 FT.!

That day, the second assault team to tackle the summit, Hillary and Tenzing, reach the South Col . . .

WE LEFT STORES HIGHER UP

MAYBE WE'D BETTER CAMP THERE TOMORROW.

Next day, the weather is too bad to move. The following day, Hillary and Tenzing, in company with Lowe, Gregory and Sherpa Ang Niyima, move up, collect the stores dumped by John Hunt, and establish a tiny camp nearly 2,000 ft. above the South Col. Then the support team leaves, and the two climbers are entirely alone . . .

Hillary and Tenzing settle down for the night. Their tent just fits into a sloping ledge in the mountainside.

DON'T FALL OUT OF BED—YOU'LL DROP ABOUT 10,000 FT.!

Dawn on 28th May, 1953 . . .

COME ON, TENZING— IT'S A FINE DAY TO CLIMB TO THE TOP OF EVEREST!

They start for the Southern Summit.

Eventually, at 9 a.m., they reach their first goal!

SO FAR, SO GOOD — BUT LOOK WHAT LIES AHEAD...!

THE SUMMIT RIDGE !

Carefully, Hillary and Tenzing make their way to where no men have ever stood before . . .

Then they sight their greatest test – 40 ft. of sheer rock, and not a chance of a foothold!

OH, NO — DON'T SAY WE'VE GOT TO CLIMB THAT !

THEY SHOWED THE WAY

THE CONQUEST OF EVEREST

Adapted from THE ASCENT OF EVEREST by Sir John Hunt, published by Hodder & Stoughton

Edmund Hillary and Sherpa Tenzing, of the Commonwealth Everest Expedition, are on the last lap of their climb to the mountain's summit (29,002 ft.), when they encounter 40 ft. of sheer rock, smooth and almost holdless . . .

Told by **PETER SIMPSON**
Drawn by **PAT WILLIAMS**

But, even at this height, skill and strength are equal to the problem. A crack between the rock and the snow-cornice gives Hillary an idea

PRAY GOD THIS CORNICE STAYS ATTACHED TO THE ROCK, OR IT'S ALL UP WITH ME!

Edmund Hillary struggles up the funnel-like crack: and hauls on the rope as Tenzing follows. Finally, the two men succeed in surmounting the obstacle.

NOTHING SHALL STOP US NOW!

And so at 11.30 a.m. on 27th May, 1953, Hillary of New Zealand and Tenzing of Nepal place the United Nations, British, Nepalese and Indian flags on the summit. For the first time, man has conquered Mount Everest!

Hillary leaves a crucifix, and Tenzing offers a number of gifts, in thanks for the success of their formidable mission.

Back at Advance Base Camp, they are jubilantly greeted by Colonel Hunt and the others.

While the Expedition are making their way back from the Himalayas, the news of their achievements speeds round the world, inspiring the hearts of all who admire courage and the spirit of adventure. Nowhere is there more rejoicing than in London, where the news comes as herald to another triumphant event . . .

CORONATION TOMORROW

EVEREST CLIMBED!

Queen Elizabeth II later knights Colonel Hunt and Hillary, and decorates Sherpa Tenzing

CONGRATULATIONS, SIR JOHN.

IN THE HONOUR DONE ME, YOUR MAJESTY RECOGNIZES EVERY MEMBER OF THE EVEREST EXPEDITION!

THE END

Index